LISA LOUTZENHEISER

Passages
of **Pride**

Kurt Chandler

Passages *of* Pride

Lesbian and Gay Youth

Come of Age

T I M E S Ⓣ B O O K S

R A N D O M H O U S E

All rights reserved under International and Pan-American Copyright
Conventions. Published in the United States by Times Books, a division of
Random House, Inc., New York, and simultaneously in Canada by
Random House of Canada Limited, Toronto.

Library of Congress Cataloging-in-Publication Data
Chandler, Kurt.
    Passages of pride : lesbian and gay youth come of age / Kurt
Chandler.
        p.   cm.
    Includes index.
    ISBN 0-8129-2380-4
    1. Gay youth—United States—Psychology—Juvenile literature.
2. Gay youth—United States—Social conditions—Juvenile literature.
3. Lesbian youth—United States—Psychology—Juvenile literature.
4. Lesbian youth—United States—Social conditions—Juvenile
literature.   5. Coming out (Sexual orientation)—United States—
Juvenile literature.   I. Title.
HQ76.26.C43   1995
305.2'35'08664—dc20   95-6931

Book design by M. Kristen Bearse

Manufactured in the United States of America on acid-free paper

2   3   4   5   6   7   8   9

First Edition

For Cathy, Benjamin, and Emma,
my life force

Preface

Let me begin with a word about how this book originated. *Passages of Pride* grew out of a year-long newspaper project, published as a special section of the *Minneapolis Star Tribune* in December 1992. I was more or less invited to participate, tapped by my friend and colleague Rita Reed, a lesbian photographer who had been working for years with gay youth. Rita was strongly committed to lending a sympathetic ear—and eye—to this silent and invisible population. Her work was the genesis of the newspaper project. And her inspiration was carried over to this book.

When I first began the project, though, I had two reservations: First, I didn't believe any teenager on earth would be willing to speak candidly and openly about growing up gay or lesbian. Second, I wasn't sure that I, a straight man, could win the trust of those teens. As a journalist, I had written with some measure of authority and compassion about people from all sorts of groups of which I was not a member. And as a parent, I naturally was inclined to empathize with youth in trouble. Yet I wasn't completely certain that gay and lesbian youth would not harbor suspicions of me.

I was proven wrong on both counts. Through the course of my research and reporting, my own sexual orientation was never a factor in gaining the confidence—and in many cases the friendship—of lesbian and gay teens. Never did they question my sincerity or suggest that my heterosexuality somehow disqualified me from writing their life stories.

I was doubly surprised to discover how many teens were willing to speak on the record when asked about their most private thoughts and feelings. They wanted to help, they told me again and again. They wanted their stories to be heard—by families, friends, teachers, ministers, and, most notably, by future generations of sexual minorities. In the face of prejudice and scorn, their frankness and honesty is nothing less than courageous.

Sadly, not all of them were willing or able to be identified. For a variety of reasons, many teens still find it necessary to hide their sexual orientation. While the book's six "main characters" agreed to be identified explicitly, others could not take that chance and asked that their names be changed. Accordingly, scattered throughout the book are pseudonyms. All the names in Chapter 10 except Gary and Karen are pseudonyms, and all the names in Chapter 22 are fictitious, though their statements and stories are very real. In several other chapters, the first names Glen, Richard, Tom, Jordan, Kelly, Michael, Andy, Jonathon, Warren, Martha, Melissa, Gretchen, and Annie are also pseudonyms.

The locus of *Passages of Pride* is Minnesota—specifically, Minneapolis and St. Paul, my home and workplace during most of this writing. Dozens of experts, activists, and teenagers from around the nation were interviewed. Yet the majority of the teens included in this book live in the Twin Cities.

Without a doubt, they could be from anywhere—any state, any town in the country. Their stories are universal, and their voices are resonating across America, louder and in greater numbers than ever.

It is regrettable that their stories were not told earlier, years ago, decades ago. Attention to their plight has been scant. When the newspaper articles were first published, the *Star Tribune* received hundreds of letters and phone calls from readers expressing gratitude for the acknowledgment of the struggles that gay and lesbian youth face. Included were these typical responses:

"I wish I had read something like this seventeen years ago in senior high. I grew up the child of parents afraid to know me because of the

negative messages they received. Gay and lesbian youth are isolated. My hope is, reporting like this will help."

"This gives teenagers hope. I'm a fifty-five-year-old Roman Catholic priest who is gay and is out. If only something like this had been around when I was growing up."

"I work in the public schools, and this prompted me to let our school social worker know I'm gay, so that if there are kids in school feeling alone or want to talk to someone gay, they can talk to me."

"As the parents of two gay young adults—a gay son and a lesbian daughter—it's been a very challenging issue for our family. The more understanding people have, the better."

"I had a friend who was a lesbian who committed suicide when she was eighteen. I think that if there had been more understanding and information—and less fear and hatred—it could have been avoided."

"I am a forty-six-year-old man who came out at thirty-seven. I wish someone had done the same for me when I was sixteen. It would have eliminated years and years of feeling bad about myself."

A question is asked frequently by those who live the secret life of a gay or lesbian teenager, a question posed rhetorically, almost in jest, yet remarkable for its underlying seriousness: Is there life after "coming out"?

A close look at what that life is can be found in the following pages.

Acknowledgments

These pages would not have been possible without the help of many friends, acquaintances, colleagues, and accomplices. I am especially and forever indebted to:

Rita Reed, friend and guide, for taking me along.

Lou Kilzer, for opening the door.

Ron Meador, for his encouragement and clear-sighted journalism.

Leo Treadway, for his patience and wisdom.

Michael Kaplan, Tina Garrett, and all the rest at District 202 Teen Center, a true lifeline, for their unhesitating trust.

Dr. Gary Remafedi, John Yoakam, Taylor Wilcox, and Charles Tamble at the University of Minnesota's Youth and AIDS Projects, for their vast resources and expertise.

Al Bertke, Jane and Niles Schulz, David and Ruth Waterbury, and others with P-FLAG (Parents, Families, and Friends of Lesbians and Gays), for introducing me to their proud sons and daughters.

Janet Williams for finding the time to listen after transcribing hours of taped interviews.

Jane Dystel, my agent, for her direction and ardent support.

Mitchell Ivers, my editor at Random House, for his vision and dedication.

And lastly, I am deeply grateful to all the courageous women and men who shared their stories with me and with the world.

Contents

Prologue:

Outreach

Taylor Wilcox and Ben Dykes stand side by side at a blackboard in a public high school in Minnesota, chalk in hand, big welcome smiles on their faces. They're unfazed by the whispers and the grimaces of the students in the room, most of them sitting as far to the back as they can. Taylor, a lesbian AIDS educator, and Ben, a gay college student, are outreach workers. And their assignment is to break down a few myths and stereotypes of gays and lesbians, using themselves as guinea pigs.

They know the drill. They're well rehearsed. They've taken their show on the road to schools around the upper Midwest, addressing principals, teachers, counselors, and nurses. But on this day, they're trying to change the minds of a few self-conscious freshmen who probably have never knowingly met anyone gay.

Ben and Taylor kick it off with a little shock treatment, an R-rated name game. They ask the students to come up with a list of labels and descriptions of homosexuals. Toss sensitivity out the window, Taylor urges. "Just shout out anything you can think of. Give us another word you've heard for someone who's gay."

The words begin to bubble out, punctuated by a snicker here and a giggle there.

Ben records the words on the blackboard, making a list of labels that he has heard too many times before: "Fags and fairies, fruits and fudge packers. Homos and queens, Bruce and Lance. Limp-wristed sissies, sick perverts."

The list goes on: "Gays lisp, don't like sports, work as hairdressers, waiters, dancers and actors . . . wear long hair and makeup, molest little children, recruit teenage boys . . . eat quiche, want to be women, don't believe in God, have lots and lots of sex. . . ."

The students bite their nails or stare at the floor as the "dirty words" are uttered. It's clear that the drill has dredged up a discomfort, or maybe a personal familiarity with the labels.

Taylor runs through the name game for lesbians. The words on the list are just as demeaning, and just as universal: *Dyke, butch, lezzy, lezbo, carpet muncher,* she scribbles, trying to keep up with what she hears.

"Lesbians are truck drivers, ride motorcycles, wear Birkenstock sandals, have a lot of cats . . . tattoos, leather, short-cropped hair, no makeup . . . fat or muscular, hate men but want to be like men . . . teach gym class and eat tofu, became lesbians because they were sexually abused when they were girls. . . ."

The chalkboard is filled with every slur and epithet imaginable of a homosexual.

"If you put all these words together," Taylor tells the students, "these are people that nobody knows. They're non-persons, they're myths, stereotypes. They just don't exist."

But society allows these stereotypes, she says, and in many ways reinforces them. The names are used everywhere, by everyone—families and peers, teachers and talk-show hosts.

You could make a similar lists for any other minority, says Ben, from blacks to Hispanics to Jews. The words are a "language of oppression." They have negative consequences for homosexuals. Out of fear and guilt, gays and lesbians are forced to hide their sexual identity, he says. That breeds isolation, and causes problems that some adolescents carry into adulthood.

Having made their point, Taylor and Ben invite questions from the students. "Anything and everything," Ben says. "All you wanted to know about being gay or lesbians." But no one asks. Too embarrassed? Or indifferent? Afraid of appearing a little too curious and mistaken as gay?

Finally, one girl breaks the ice and asks Ben what his parents said when they found out he was gay. Another asks Taylor if lesbians can have kids. Do gays dress up in women's clothes? Do they shave their legs? In a lesbian couple, does one person play the man and the other person play the woman? Has Ben or Taylor ever gotten beat up?

"When," someone asks Ben, "did you become gay?"

Ben pauses. He knew he was somehow different by age five or six, he says, though he didn't have a name for it. He began thinking he liked boys instead of girls in his early teens.

"Did you *want* to be gay?" asks a boy from the back.

Ben answers with his own questions: "Why would anyone choose, consciously choose, to be part of a group that has all these labels attached to it?" he says, pointing to the blackboard. "Why would someone want to be hated?"

Part I

Awareness

*T*heir journey begins early.

For as long as they can remember, from five, six, seven years old, they have felt "different," say gay and lesbian youth, nothing that they could fix a label to at such an early age, yet something that set them apart and deepened as they grew into their teenage years.

By early adolescence, say gay teens, they were aware of an affection for people of the same gender. Sometimes it came as an attraction or sexual fantasy, a crush on a teacher, a lingering glance in the locker room. Whatever it was, they kept it to themselves.

Most teenagers are socialized to believe that they eventually will pair off with partners of the opposite sex. So when the attractions of some teens begin to lean instead toward other young men or other young women, they begin to think that something's wrong, that they're sick or evil or immoral.

Adolescence is tough enough. But to suddenly put a word to their life-long "difference," a word used so contemptuously in society—lesbian or gay—can be a wounding experience for teens. On top of all their fear and confusion, they become vulnerable targets of harassment, prejudice, and hatred.

Derek I:

The Science of Living in the Closet

No matter what he did, Derek Johnson could not make himself feel sexually attracted to women. It was pointless even to try.

In 1985, during his first year of junior high school, Derek met Donna, a sweet young woman with light brown curly hair that swung around her shoulders when she walked. They soon began exchanging notes in class. Other students were pairing off with partners of the opposite sex, so it was only "natural," thought Derek, that he and Donna should do the same.

"This was somebody I was close to," he recalls, "and therefore that meant I should be attracted to her."

But Derek was more intrigued by another classmate, a dark-haired student named John. Although the two never spoke, Derek couldn't keep his eyes off John. He was captivated by John's deep green eyes and his slender physique. But whenever any affection or fantasies toward John crossed Derek's mind, he would quickly substitute Donna in John's place.

A year later, Derek came across a stack of pornographic magazines while snooping through an older relative's bedroom. The magazines were filled with photographs of naked women. "I was sitting there, trying to focus, looking at the pictures and trying to get some kind of stimulation or arousal," Derek says. "But nothing happened."

In the back of one of the periodicals, he noticed an advertisement for a gay men's magazine. Guiltily, he ripped out the ad and dropped the subscription form in the mail. Weeks later, his order arrived, sealed in a brown paper envelope and addressed to him.

"Immediately, I noticed my interest level was much higher than with the straight magazines."

Even in grade school, Derek's affectional "pull" was not toward the opposite sex. His friendships with girls were never sensual. There were none of the prepubescent games of "doctor," or the "I'll show you mine if you show me yours" explorations typical of young boys and girls. Instead, Derek's "experimentations," as he calls them, were with other boys. Throughout his childhood, from age five on, Derek would sneak off with a friend into someone's basement or the woods along the back alley, where they would take off their pants and play with each other, usually fondling each other's genitals. It became habitual.

"At that time, I didn't quite have a name for it," says Derek. "It was something that I liked doing, that felt good, that I wanted to do as often as I could. The other kids always recognized it as being something bad and dirty. And all I wanted to know was, When can we do it again?"

By the time he was fourteen, he began to put two and two together. Something clicked. Although he only had a murky sense of what it meant to be "gay," the label seemed to fit him.

"I was just thinking it through, analyzing the situation to death, asking myself, What does this mean? And I realized I might be gay," Derek says. "Once identifying that, I came to the conclusion that these were the cards I was dealt. I knew people didn't approve of it, so I decided to keep it to myself rather than open myself up to ridicule."

Though he felt sure he knew himself, he revealed nothing about his sexual identity to his mother or father. Until the day he was caught.

Derek grew up in St. Paul, in a large African-American family. He was the baby of the family, the last of six children—four boys and two girls—raised by Donald and Vernita Johnson. Theirs was a "blended" family; each parent had two children from a previous marriage.

A month before Derek was born, the Johnsons moved into a three-bedroom rambler in a multiracial, solidly working-class neighborhood. Derek was never short on companions. Every holiday, his relatives would gather at the Johnson home for dinner. His mother would often baby-sit for her toddler grandchildren, and there always seemed to be a cousin or two pedaling a trike up and down the sidewalk, Derek recalls.

Kids were plentiful in the neighborhood, too. "Everyone's backyard was your backyard," Derek says. Towering shade trees formed a natural awning over the city streets, while along the alleys, thick woods and dense undergrowth provided easy hiding spots for Derek and his buddies.

Derek's father worked in the administrative office of an automobile dealership. Born and raised in Charlotte, North Carolina, Donald Johnson was never prone to discuss much about his life, Derek says. "He kept everything in, whether he was happy or sad. There never were any outbursts or anything. But he was like a bomb waiting to go off. As a result my mom sort of tiptoed around him, and made sure the kids were in line."

It fell to his mother to be the disciplinarian of the household. "She was good-intentioned," Derek says, "opinionated, feisty in a sweet kind of way." But step out of line and her feistiness would quickly turn to wrath. She could be relentlessly demanding of her children, Derek says. "Our existence basically was to please Mother. The worst thing that could happen was to disappoint her."

The Johnsons were Roman Catholics, one of only a few African-American families in their parish. Derek remembers his father sitting in his easy chair reading the Bible after work.

"Even though we went to church every Sunday and said prayers before dinner, I wouldn't say we were an overly religious family," Derek says. Nor were the Johnsons a politically active family. While Donald and Vernita tended to vote as liberal Democrats, they were never crusaders for civil rights. Instead, Derek says, his parents professed an inherent suspicion of most white people. "Stick to your own kind" was the attitude they conveyed to their children.

Once, on a driving trip to Vernita's hometown of Dallas, Texas, the Johnsons were turned away at an A&W restaurant, after being told that the fast-food diner didn't serve "coloreds," Derek recalls. Thus began a lifelong boycott of the restaurant chain by the Johnson family.

Derek's early years of grade school were uncharitable times. He was fitted with glasses at the early age of five to correct a "lazy eye," and then, when that approach failed, was required to wear a white adhesive patch over his left eye periodically in first and second grades. "I remember being teased even by my closest friends for wearing the patch, being called 'pirate,'" he says.

Derek describes himself as an average student, "a well-mannered kid, very quiet, very shy. I just kind of existed. Teachers never really had any expectations of me." But in third grade, to his dismay, his teacher decided he was more than just shy. His parents were informed that he was "slow," possibly mildly retarded. And Derek was placed in special-education classes.

Looking back, he believes he was misunderstood by his teachers, that his lack of motivation and interest in school was misinterpreted as "retardation." Later, in tenth grade, he pulled himself out of the special-ed classes and resumed a conventional curriculum. "Against the advice of my advisers, I decided to declare myself normal," Derek says.

But at age eight, this special placement was just one more link in a chain of circumstances that made him feel "different" as a child. He was hopelessly bashful. He wore glasses, and then an eye patch. He was one of only a handful of black kids at his church. And then suddenly he was singled out at school as being "retarded."

"I kind of felt like the oddball," says Derek. "I was always the last one to be picked for sports. Even at family gatherings, I can remember having to sit and watch everybody else play football."

But even more unordinary was his perennial attraction to boys. "In every grade, there was at least one boy that I had a certain fondness for," he says. "And later on, I guess I recognized this as crushes. I wanted to spend as much time as I could with them."

His sexual experimentations with the neighbor boys kept up until the summer before seventh grade. Usually, they would fondle and kiss. Sometimes they would role-play: "You be the boy this time, and I'll be the girl." Derek never felt contrite about what he was doing. Just a little confused.

"It was always this thing that no one talked about," he says. "But I knew that acting on these feelings wasn't being untrue to myself and wasn't hurting anybody."

Although he had heard the word *gay* at school and at home, it was always steeped in negative connotations. *Fag* was a common schoolyard slur.

"I can remember my grandmother talking about a friend of the family who was transsexual," he says. "And my mother's reaction to comments on TV never were in a positive light." His father's term for a gay man was someone who was "being funny." "Immediately, I could read between the lines on that one."

The insinuations framed Derek's perception of how gays are viewed by society and exemplified the social stigma that marks homosexuality. Yet he felt no identification to his parents' derogatory descriptions. "They still seemed to be talking about something that I didn't identify with," he says.

He saw no association at all between his sexual feelings toward other boys and the notion of being "gay"—until he was fourteen. Then it hit him like a thunderbolt. His secret experimentations and an infatuation he had had over a boy in his chorus class formed a nexus of self-realization.

"All of a sudden, these two things fit together and I realized what was going on," Derek says. "It was a surprise to finally put a label onto my feelings. At some particular point—after all the experimenting—I had come to terms with my feelings without labeling them. So when I had finally attached a label to it, I realized, Oh, this was something potentially dangerous, and I should keep it to myself."

Derek's mother, thinking she could steer her youngest son clear of the bad influences she'd heard about at the nearby junior high school, enrolled Derek in a school far removed from the inner city, St. Paul's Highland Park Junior High. Because the Johnson home was beyond the range of bus service, Derek's father drove him to school every morning on his way to work.

The new school was a lonely place for Derek. He was the only student of color in most of his classes. The only kid he knew from his neighborhood had nicknamed him "Cyclops" because of his "lazy" right eye.

At Highland Park, hardly a word about homosexuality was uttered by Derek's teachers, except for the harsh accusation that it was homosexuals who got AIDS. Early in the year, at the beginning of a swimming lesson, a gym teacher delivered a stern warning to his class: "If you find anyone looking at you, let me know and I'll get him out of here." Another teacher condemned gays and lesbians as "perverts who have no purpose or place in a civilized society," Derek recalls. Though they were unaware of it, these role models—teachers and coaches that he respected and looked to for guidance and approval—were negating a fundamental piece of Derek's personality.

The dubious messages made him even more introverted, and pushed him deeper into the closet. Not for an instant did he consider disclosing his sexual orientation. "It was clear to me that there wasn't much approval from society of homosexuality," he says.

Yet his same-sex attractions wouldn't be denied. When a fire caused damage in the junior high school, Derek and his classmates were required to use the locker room at the adjoining high school to suit up for gym class.

"I remember seeing high school guys who were much more developed than we were in seventh grade," Derek says, "and that reinforced in my mind that I was definitely more attracted to males than females."

Try as he might, he couldn't dismiss his feelings. "I remember telling myself, This entire day I'm not gonna look at any boys, and trying to suppress those feelings." He knew he had to be cautious; a lingering glance in the shower or the wrong word to a classmate could have devastating results. More important, he could never tell his parents. "My being gay was inconsistent with wanting approval from my parents, from my mother mainly," he says.

But how could he ignore such an essential part of who he was?

Home alone one day after school, after finishing his homework and straightening up his room before his parents came home, Derek turned on the television. Flipping to a local newscast, he suddenly couldn't believe what he heard. "Next, a report on gay youth," announced the anchorman. Derek was astonished. Veiled in shadows and silhouetted to hide their identities, a group of gay and lesbian teenagers were actually describing their lives, telling how unfair it was to have to live in fear of being labeled a homosexual. Derek sat mesmerized by the TV screen. They were describing *his* life.

"This was the first realization to me that there were other gay people out there," says Derek. As the report concluded, one teen mentioned a support group for gay youth that met every week in Minneapolis. But no names or telephone numbers were given.

Derek rushed to the phone book to look up the number of the TV station. He needed more information. He wanted to find this youth group. And as he dialed the phone, he knew in the back of his mind that contacting a gay organization was an admission—fully and finally—that he was gay.

A switchboard operator came on the line.

"Ah, I'd like the phone number of the youth group from the report that was just shown," Derek said.

"And what youth group would that be?" she asked.

Derek quickly hung up the phone. He couldn't say the word *gay*. It was too incriminating, too revealing.

But the next day, he called the station again. This time, he could say it: He wanted information about the support group for *gay* teens that had been featured on an earlier broadcast. He was promptly given the phone number of the St. Paul-Reformation Lutheran Church, sponsor of the gay-positive Wingspan Ministry.

A couple of days later, he placed a call to the church. Again, he felt anxious and inhibited—wary of who might be on the other end of the line. A woman answered. She told Derek that the facilitator of the support group, Leo Treadway, a Wingspan Ministry associate, was out of town for two weeks. Derek was relieved; he could put off the encounter a little longer.

But he didn't allow himself to be deterred. Two weeks later, he was back on the phone with the church, asking to speak to Treadway.

"I'm calling about the youth group," Derek said, quietly but steadily.

"Which one?" asked Treadway, and again, Derek was obligated to say the word *gay.*

Treadway gladly filled him in, giving Derek a full introduction to Lesbian and Gay Youth Together, telling him when and where the group met, who typically attended, and what topics were usually discussed. He even told Derek which bus to catch to get to the meetings.

Derek thanked Treadway for the information and hung up, resolved to check it out. He had been given a key, it seemed, to an exclusive club, a pass into a foreign community—and permission to take his first step out of the shadow of obscurity that he believed was so necessary to protect himself.

It took two months for Derek to muster the courage to attend the support group, which he came to know by its acronym, LGYT. He was curious yet mistrustful, a little afraid of whom he might meet and what he might be asked. Would he need to declare his homosexuality? Would he have to talk about sex? Would his parents be notified?

"I didn't know what to expect," Derek says. "I wanted to meet other people like me, other kids my age who were going through the same thing as I was." And, in the back of his mind, he was hoping to maybe find a boyfriend.

The year was 1987. Derek was fourteen, soon to turn fifteen. Although the Twin Cities border each other, his parents had never permitted him to travel the short distance from St. Paul to Minneapolis alone. He was nervous. As he prepared for his first visit to LGYT, he devised a bogus alibi to cover his whereabouts. "My mother knew where I was every minute of the day." So he told her he was going to a movie. In fact, he had made a point of seeing a movie earlier in the week, just in case his mother questioned him about what he had seen.

His plan was set. Derek had estimated the time it would take to ride the bus to Minneapolis and had invented excuses that he might give should anyone happen to see him on his way. He dabbed a little after-shave lotion on his face, some Aqua Velva he had found in the medicine chest in the basement bathroom, and started out for the bus stop, walking in the *opposite* direction to assure that he wasn't being watched by his parents or any neighbors. After three blocks, he turned and ran to catch the number 21 bus into Minneapolis.

Derek arrived early at his destination. Standing outside the doors of the building were three or four other teens, talking and laughing. Derek stayed silent. After a few long minutes, Treadway arrived to unlock the doors and, recognizing Derek from a brief description he had given over the phone, introduced himself. An avuncular gay man in his fifties, with a full beard and stubby ponytail, Treadway led Derek and the others up a stairway and into a large, bright room. Gradually, a group of about fifteen teens took their places in chairs arranged in a circle.

Derek was tense. Across the room, roosting on the top of a table, was a young man in a leather jacket and cowboy boots, wearing eyeliner, makeup, and lipstick. "Seeing this guy was a little overwhelming, to say the least," Derek recalls. "He immediately played into all the stereotypes I'd heard about."

Treadway announced that there would be a demonstration that afternoon on massage, which alarmed Derek even more. "My first reaction was to just leave," he says. "I tend to be kind of a nervous person anyway."

But he stayed, sticking close to Treadway for the duration and saying very little. "I was very uncomfortable. I kind of had this feeling of terror," he says. "I remember thinking it was more formal than I had thought it would be."

Before he left the meeting, he was handed an LGYT "Welcome

Pack," which included a resource guide listing churches, bookstores, bars, restaurants, support groups, and newspapers within the gay community; a series of comic books about gay and lesbian teens called "Tales of the Closet"; and an information pamphlet on HIV and AIDS. "I think there were even some condoms in there, too." He smuggled the contraband into his house under his jacket and hid it in his room under the mattress.

The next day, Derek stayed home from school with a nervous, upset stomach. He had mixed feelings about his first support-group meeting. "I was let down. I'd thought I'd at least have found somebody to talk to. I told myself that I would never go back again."

But three weeks later, he did. Again, he used the same alibi—he said he was going to a movie—and made sure the show time coincided with his departure from home.

"I went back because, like it or not, it was all the access I had to the gay community," Derek says. "And if I didn't meet somebody the first time, maybe I would the second time."

Derek attended LGYT off and on over the next several weeks, encouraged by the sense of camaraderie and piqued by the frank discussions on sexuality. Sometimes, the conversations stunned him. Teens his age talked freely about things he had always kept to himself—condoms and safe sex and masturbation. "I had never talked about that before. And I remember thinking, Wow, there are other people who do this."

Slowly, Derek began to open up to this new circle of friends, and eventually, he became an LGYT regular. "I went to school from Monday to Friday and this is what I did on the weekend," he says. "I lived for Sundays. Here, I had finally met others like myself. I had finally started developing some sense of pride about myself. . . . Going to group was admitting to myself that I was gay. Yet it didn't mean that at times I didn't wish that I wasn't. I knew, for basic survival, that it wasn't a good idea to let anyone in school or my parents know."

One Sunday evening, Derek missed the bus to St. Paul. A young man from group, Glen, offered to give him a ride home. On the way, they drove through downtown Minneapolis, and Glen pointed out the gay bars—the Gay 90s, the Saloon—the gay bookstores, and the site of a gay bathhouse that had been closed down. They talked about their childhoods, about growing up gay, about hiding their sexual orientation all their lives. Glen had moved to Minneapolis from a small rural town on his own, no small feat in Derek's eyes. Though he was only three years older than Derek, he was going to school and had a job, his own apartment, and his own car. As the two grew into friends, Glen became a role model to Derek.

In his resource guide, Derek discovered a list of books about gay youth. He could relate to one book in particular, *The Best Little Boy in the World,* by John Reid. "It's basically this guy narrating the story of when he was a kid, and basically coming out," says Derek. Every week on his Sunday excursions into Minneapolis, he picked up copies of the local gay newspapers, folding them into issues of a mainstream newspaper or magazine so he could sneak them past his parents.

"I made a science out of living in the closet."

When Derek was sixteen, he caught the bus into Minneapolis one day after school, armed with the address of an adult bookstore downtown. His friend Glen had lent him his membership card to the Broadway Books and Video store so he could rent a video. Panicky, he walked around the block before entering the store, "praying that no one I knew would see me walk in there." Once inside, he quickly located the display rack of gay videotapes. A jacket cover caught his attention right away: *The Look,* starring porn star Jeff Stryker. But rather than renting the movie and having to bother to bring it back, Derek decided to buy it—for $70. He had been working part-time at a day-care center in St. Paul after school, and had been saving some money.

On an evening when his parents had gone out, Derek locked all the doors to the house and slipped the videotape into the VCR in his parents' bedroom, drawing the window shades three quarters of the way down so he could see the headlights of his parents' car if they arrived home unexpectedly.

The movie was arousing to Derek. Men having sex with men was a turn-on. It was worth the $70, he thought.

After carefully resetting the VCR counter to its original count, Derek returned the tape to its hiding place in his bedroom—a cardboard box under his bed, pushed up against the wall and out of sight behind his shoes and a pile of dirty clothes. Inside the box was Derek's "booty"—a stack of gay newspapers, books, magazines, condoms, his resource list, and his videotape. Unless someone was looking for it, the box was safe from view.

He thought he had been careful. He thought he had taken every precaution necessary to disguise his true identity from his parents. He thought no one suspected anything.

But a secret cardboard box is only a secret until it's found.

2

Amy I:

The Only One in the World

It was Valentine's Day, 1992, and Amy Grahn was chasing down basketballs in a Minnesota high school gymnasium. She was the manager of the Minnetonka Skippers girls' varsity team, a thankless job that left her feeling trivial and helplessly envious of her peers. Amy had played forward on the team early in the season. But she turned in her jersey when her court time dwindled to nearly nothing. She just didn't feel a part of the team anymore, on or off the court. More than once, her teammates had neglected to invite her to the victory party after a big win. So now she was finishing out the season from the sidelines. Amy stood and watched while the Skippers perfected their free throws and tested their fast breaks, shouting words of encouragement to the players and handing out towels as they came off the floor.

Amy already had her sights set on the upcoming track season. Maybe she'd try out for shot put or discus, she thought. She was muscular enough, broad in the shoulders, big-boned and tall, almost five-foot-ten. To keep in shape, she lifted weights at home and at the Y. The payoff was beginning to show in her upper arms.

Dressed plainly in a pink button-down shirt, tan Dockers, and black hiking boots, Amy looked as if she had raided her father's closet that morning. The clothes gave her a boyish quality, accented by her square jaw and thick, dark eyebrows. Her movement was sure-footed and solid, athletic, never dainty. Three tiny gold-hooped earrings adorned her right ear; another was in her left.

Before game time, Amy spied a classmate sitting in the bleachers. She clambered up to the girl, two steps at a time, to trade gossip:

what couples had broken up, who was taking whom to the Valentine's Day dance. . . . Amy didn't tell her friend, but she had a crush on the Skippers' center, the captain of the team, a six-foot-two-inch Nordic goddess. As Amy spun the rumor mill, she eyed the team captain with fascination and a little bit of lust as she took her last layup.

The buzzer signaled the tip-off and Amy took her place beside the coaches, stashing her gym bag behind the bench. Tucked inside the bag was a paperback copy of *Rubyfruit Jungle,* Rita Mae Brown's modern classic about a young lesbian coming of age. Amy carried the novel with her wherever she went, like a preacher toting a Bible. She recognized some of herself in Molly Bolt, the book's main character.

Off to the side of the gym, the mother of a classmate of Amy's studied Amy from a distance. A quizzical smile spread across the mother's face, and she whispered something to her daughter.

"That's a girl," the daughter answered, a little annoyed. She nodded in Amy's direction. "You mean the one down there in the pink top? She's a *girl.*"

The mother lifted her eyebrows.

The whispers, double takes, and innuendo began years earlier for Amy Grahn. It was the summer between seventh and eighth grades, a summer of disenchantment—and a turning point in Amy's life. She was giving up her tomboy country girlhood for something much more complicated. Adolescence was upon her, an awkward and dizzying time when her life seemed to be driven by hormones and peer pressure.

But an even stronger inclination had struck. Guided by impulse and intuition, Amy was pulled in another direction, and away from her peers. Without really knowing why, she suddenly changed her appearance. She stopped wearing makeup, stopped tweezing her eyebrows, stopped blow-drying and curling her hair. Her new look felt more natural, more *Amy.* "I just want to be myself," she explained.

When school resumed in the fall, her friends were suspicious. Amy looked unhewn, unfeminine—and unlike any of the other blossoming young women in junior high. She didn't fit in anymore. Her classmates snickered at her new style. And without explanation, friends she had known nearly all her life stopped calling.

Amy couldn't figure it out. She tried to ignore the teasing, but the words cut deep. The behind-the-back remarks turned to outright ridicule. Her classmates called her hateful names, and taunted her for acting "butch." They laughed as she passed in the hallway, and mocked her for dressing "like a boy," for walking "like a boy." One day in her English class, a boy passed a piece of notebook paper to Amy. "Do you have a penis too?" read the note. Amy turned purple and promptly handed the note over to her mother when she got home. The boy was suspended from school for three days. But Amy felt little consolation. Her classmates now scorned her completely, incensed that she would dare to complain.

She was devastated. What's their *problem*? she asked herself. What did I ever do to them? She had no answers, only confusion. And hurt. The rejection, sudden and complete, made her unbearably lonely. Lost in her predicament, she was too numb to ask for help.

My parents wouldn't understand, she thought. They might even think it's my fault. Although her parents were patient people and listened when she went to them with problems, she couldn't trust them, she decided. So she buried her hurt deep inside and pretended that everything was perfectly fine. Her parents were oblivious of Amy's stoic mask. She never hinted that she was hurting. But she didn't fool everyone. Detecting that something was troubling Amy, a school counselor took her aside one day and gave her the phone number of the West Suburban Teen Clinic near the school.

Amy made the call and scheduled an appointment with a therapist, Pam Cook. Pam was a likable woman in her late thirties. At the first session, she met with Amy and her mother. They talked about their family, Amy's life at home and at school, and the abandonment by her friends. The issue of sexuality never came up. Even in future sessions, Amy and Pam seemed to dance around the topic, inching up to questions about Amy's love life, then backing away from any admissions that might be embarrassing—and revealing. The underlying motive for the cruel taunting and teasing was left unattended.

Despair clung to Amy, unabated, despite the therapy. "I was so unsure of my feelings," she said. "I felt like a complete outsider."

It would take the better part of a year before she would understand the source of her struggle and finally come to know who she was.

Amy's parents, Sue and Jim Grahn, met in Braham, Minnesota, north of St. Paul, a community of fewer than a thousand residents. Jim, two years older than Sue, lived in the nearby town of Grafton and attended the same high school. They started dating in Sue's sophomore year.

Jim's father owned a local grocery store, where Jim worked after school, butchering meat and stocking shelves. Studious and hardworking, Jim was the oldest of five children, the only boy in the family. In high school, he was captain of the basketball and football teams, and graduated valedictorian of his class. At the University of Minnesota, he studied aeronautical engineering before switching his major to education. After graduating, he took a job teaching math and physics in a small-town high school near Minneapolis.

Sue was the younger of two adopted daughters. Her adoptive father owned the Braham Woolen Mill. Not the type to disappoint her parents or fall into trouble, Sue had a rebellious stripe to her, nonetheless, and was prone to question people's opinions and judgments. After high school, she followed Jim into the Twin Cities, where she attended "beauty school" for a year.

Sue and Jim were married in 1968. Sue converted from Lutheran to Catholic to match Jim's faith just after their wedding. The couple's first child, a son named Chris, was born a year after they married. Next came Amy, five years later, followed by another girl, Alison, two years after that.

When the kids were young, Sue Grahn was diagnosed with Crohn's disease, a chronic inflammation of the intestinal tract. While incurable, Crohn's disease is controllable through medication, diet, and surgery. The illness forced Sue into the hospital for extended stays, sometimes for months at a time. While she was away, the children were sent to live temporarily with family and friends: Alison to the home of Sue's parents, Amy to Jim's parents, and Chris to the neighbors before and after school.

Despite the disruptions, Amy has fond memories of her childhood. "I think my childhood overall was pretty good," she says. "I didn't have too many concerns in life. I was just a kid."

Yet throughout her childhood, Amy, like many lesbians and gays, grew up thinking she was somehow different. Not necessarily bad or strange, just different, something the experts call "gender atypical."

"I used to do a lot of not-feminine things," she recalls. "I never played with dolls. My mom made me a Cabbage Patch doll once and I played with it just to make her feel good." Instead of Barbie and Ken, it was cops and robbers and cowboys and Indians. Her early memories are of Huck Finn and Tom Sawyer adventures in the woods around her home with a neighbor boy, Billy, her best friend. They built tree forts together and once made a raft that sank in a nearby pond when they launched it.

"I knew I was different in the fact that I liked to do things that boys liked to do," says Amy. "But I didn't even know what the word *gay* meant." Amy remembers first hearing the word *lesbian* from a girl who rode her school bus in junior high. "We used to sit in the front seat and joke about going to *lesbian* school, whatever that was."

Her first serious crush was on one of her best girlfriends. Amy was twelve, her friend Jessica a year younger. "I just thought that she was cute. I didn't make anything of it," says Amy. Yet she remembers slow-dancing with Jessica in her bedroom, the door shut, the lights off, and the blinds drawn, holding her tight around the waist. Amy didn't know what to make of her feelings at the time. Her emotions were jumbled. She was at once giddy and aroused, but too young to grasp it all. Jessica eventually drifted away, part of the crowd that spurned Amy.

By junior high, Amy's attractions had become even more confusing. She was never turned on by a boy, but she knew that she was *supposed* to be. Her older brother, Chris, had cruised through adolescence, with few restrictions set by his parents. But the girls were bound to a firm rule: no dating until they turned sixteen and had been confirmed by the Catholic Church. Yet Amy didn't really care to go out. She didn't *want* to date. Being a teenager was too weird, she reasoned. She just didn't understand who she was anymore. Or how to act. To make matters worse, she had no one to confide in.

"I guess my friends ditched me because I was learning to be myself instead of who they wanted me to be," she says, looking back. "I felt like I didn't fit in just because of the things I did. I didn't wear skirts. I always wore jeans and tennis shoes. I didn't wear makeup, because I never felt it was me. And all my friends did. That was the big thing."

She was totally alone, deserted by everyone who mattered and afraid to admit it to anyone else. Instead of reaching out for help, she stopped speaking altogether. Her friends, her family, her teachers— she shut everybody out. "Something made me not want to trust *anybody,*" she explains. Except for her weekly sessions with her therapist, she was completely detached.

Her depression grew worse. One night, from an extension phone in the basement of her home, Amy called her therapist and told her she was going to kill herself. She had hidden a rope in the garage. "I got to thinking, Why even be here if you're not going to have any friends?" Amy remembers. "I just didn't want to live. So I thought, I'll put this rope around my neck and that'll be it."

Pam Cook immediately called Amy's mother. "Amy has a plan to kill herself," the therapist warned her. "And it's *tonight.*" Sue and Jim Grahn were dumbstruck. They rushed Amy to a Minneapolis hospital, admitting her to the crisis unit of the psychiatric ward. The following day, she underwent a battery of psychological tests and evaluations and was assigned to various psychotherapy treatments. She stayed for two weeks. And again, in group therapy and one-on-one sessions with psychologists, there was never any mention of sexuality.

Amy was stabilized and sent home. But two short days after her release, the self-destructive behavior returned: Amy began carving into her left arm with a razor blade—a cross and an *L* and *S,* for "Life Sucks."

"I was pretty depressed," she says. "I didn't think that anything was getting any better. I was kind of hopeless, and couldn't see any light at the end of the tunnel."

Again, she was hospitalized, and this time put on the anti-depressant Prozac. But this time her parents knew her hospitalization would be only a short-term fix. While they couldn't completely sort it out, they knew something profoundly complex was affecting their daughter. After a couple of weeks, they transferred her from the hospital's psych ward to Delta Place, an alternative school for students with emotional and behavioral problems.

Amy stayed for eleven months. A van picked her up at home every morning and returned her in the afternoon. It was just like going to school. At first she hated it. She felt disgraced, marked as some sort of defect. But slowly she opened up to her peers, and friendships developed. She attended classes in the mornings and therapy sessions in the afternoons. She would often take long walks with her classmates or play softball with the counselors. Wednesdays were reserved for "girls' group." In the summer, she and twenty other students went camping for a week in the Boundary Waters Canoe Area Wilderness, a national park on the Minnesota-Canada border. Delta Place became a good place to heal. Amy built a camaraderie with other students. She felt comfortable, unthreatened. Gradually, her depression lifted. Her self-confidence swelled. She began to feel hopeful again.

While she was a student at Delta Place, Amy continued her therapy at the West Suburban Teen Clinic as part of her treatment. One week, in her hour-long session, she was seized by a spell of reticence and barely able to get a word out of her mouth. She just couldn't express herself. So, as an exercise for the following week, Pam Cook asked her to draw up a list of issues that she would want to tackle. She arrived at the next session, assignment in hand. A single word topped her list: *sexuality.*

"Sexuality," Pam repeated. "Now, exactly what do you mean by that?" she probed. And with no apology or excuse, Amy launched into her account of growing up "different" as a girl, and her current same-sex attractions and affections. The words came tumbling out: "I think I might be a lesbian." It had been a gradual awakening, and at fifteen, Amy wasn't even sure what being a lesbian meant. But she was sure of who she was.

Amy was instantly relieved, freed from a tremendous burden. But her comfort was still deficient. She begged Pam not to tell her parents and to keep her admission a secret of their own. "I didn't want my parents to be part of my life," she says. "I don't know why—I just didn't."

Amy still felt terribly isolated, and saw herself as some sort of a freak, a misfit. If she *was* a lesbian, she was the only one she knew.

"I thought I was the only one in the world."

Amy graduated from Delta Place just before Christmastime and transferred to Minnetonka High School for the spring semester, her first enrollment in a public high school. But to protect herself from the ridicule she had painfully endured in junior high, she remained "in the closet." She didn't dare tell her classmates or her parents that she was gay. It was too much of a risk. "I guess I was just kind of scared of what they would think," she says. "I always thought my dad would disown me."

Her parents had suspicions. Amy was approaching her sixteenth birthday and had never had a date. Why not? wondered her mother. What was the matter? Sue Grahn decided to put a question to her directly: "Amy, are you dealing with your sexual identity?" she asked one day after school. "*Yes,*" Amy answered impatiently, and wriggled out of the conversation. Eventually she would tell them, she thought. On her own time.

But without Amy's knowledge, Sue Grahn had called on some of Amy's classmates and friends in the neighborhood, pressing them for details about Amy's social life. Who did she hang out with these days? Did she have any boyfriends? Did she like boys, *period*? Piecing together things that she learned, Sue began to see another dimension of her daughter, one that became clearer the more she looked, like a Polaroid photograph coming into focus right before her eyes. Only now she saw characteristics of Amy that she never before had noticed.

Again, Sue pleaded with Amy to open up, to talk about her feelings—her sexuality. Amy was convinced that admitting she was gay would only lead to further banishment—this time by her family. It was easier to just hide it, she thought. Yet she was tired of the guilt and confusion, tired of concealing a big part of who she was, tired of feeling alone. Finally, in a conversation around the dining room table one evening, she admitted to her parents that, yes, she thought she was a lesbian.

To her surprise, her parents told her they had suspected as much. Even when she was young, they said, it was something in the back of their minds. As she grew older, the signs had become hard to miss. They began to figure it out for themselves.

"If I look at Amy from the time she was a small child, to me it was real evident," recalls Sue Grahn. "There was never anything really feminine about her. . . . She was not what I imagined a little girl to be." It wasn't just her tomboy amusements or her aversion to baby dolls and dresses, says Sue, but something else in her personality, something in the way she related to people, girls and boys, kids as well as adults.

Sue and Jim assured Amy that they loved her and would always love her. But privately, they were shaken. Now that they knew, what would be in store for Amy? they wondered. They weren't prepared for this. Both had been raised as Christians in small rural towns. They had little understanding of homosexuality and, up until then, little reason to even think about it. Sue in particular was thrown off balance by the realization: Her daughter was attracted to women.

"Even though in my heart I knew that's the way it was, that she was lesbian, I felt guilty," Sue says, looking back. "I felt other people weren't going to love her because of what she was. I was really concerned about how my family would feel about her. Amy was always the favorite of my parents. She was the first granddaughter to be born in our family. And I worried about my father being disappointed.

"We didn't want our daughter to be a lesbian," Sue admits. "It wasn't our picture of the perfect family. . . . It was hard to even say the word *lesbian*."

Their acceptance of Amy's sexual orientation would be a vast river to cross.

3

Dan I:

A Deer in Headlights

Dan Birkholz stood in his living room and stared out the window at a gray winter day in 1992. Nothing stirred. A misty haze erased the horizon behind the row of split-levels and ramblers on 225th Lane in his rural subdivision.

Dan's life was without horizons, too, lately. Unlike most high school students, he wasn't thinking much about the future, about getting his driver's license or buying a car or finding a summer job or going to college. Stuck in a lugubrious funk, he thought instead about escape, flight, refuge. He had just one goal in mind—to get out of this backwoods town and move to the city.

"I was ready for the city a long time ago," he complained.

Dan lived with his family in a sleepy bedroom community an hour north of Minneapolis—well beyond the border of acceptance for a gay teenager. His high school classmates had little use for people like him. His friends were put off by his cynical moods. And his parents just didn't understand.

Home alone on a school holiday, Dan was restless. One minute he was on his feet, pacing like a caged animal, dashing to the kitchen for a handful of pretzels and a can of Coke or pouncing at the promising ring of the telephone. The next minute he was slumped on the sofa, nervously gnawing at his lower lip and sweeping his wiry hair behind his ears. All morning long he brandished the TV remote, surfing from *The Brady Bunch* to *Geraldo* to a rock video of Madonna to a Nordic Flex infomercial of sweat-drenched bodybuilders in skin-tight briefs.

Dan was glib about his homosexuality. He wanted nothing more than to be "out of the closet." He first told his parents that he thought he might be gay when he was fifteen, asking for help, to no avail. Gradually and selectively, he spread the word to one or two friends, a couple of teachers, a counselor, and an assistant principal. But it hardly mattered. No one had any advice to give, and no one came out to him in kind. As far as he could tell, he was the only gay teenager in his school.

On his day off, Dan roamed the house dressed in jeans and his favorite shirt—a black T-shirt designed by a friend. Stenciled across his chest in bold white letters were the words UNITY THROUGH DIVERSITY. The slogan was lifted from a biology textbook, but Dan had adopted it as his personal battle cry for gay rights. Trouble was, no one was listening.

Dan's parents moved from Minneapolis to the suburb of Coon Rapids when he was three. It was the first step by his father in a progressive march to the country "to live in the woods," as Dan puts it.

The elder of two sons, Dan was a careful, introspective boy. "I wouldn't run around town or climb trees or anything," he says. "I saw very little point in it. I would sit quietly in the house and read, although I did have a real penchant for volcanoes." He has a happy memory of playing in the backyard sandbox, burying the garden hose under a mountain of sand, then turning on the water and watching his toy cars and houses wash away as the volcano erupted.

Dan's mother was a stay-at-home mom throughout his boyhood. JoAnn Birkholz went back to school to become a licensed practical nurse when Dan was in his teens. His father, Jerry Birkholz, worked as a lineman for a utility company. He was more likely to express himself through anger than affection or conversation, says Dan. Seldom would he take the time to play with his sons. "He didn't know *how* to play," says Dan. Dan's mother, meanwhile, in an attempt to compensate, became the family's social organizer. "My mom's big quest was to make everything normal." She signed her sons up for Cub Scouts, dragged them to church as often as she could, and helped plan family dinners at their grandparents' home on Sundays and holidays.

Dan's childhood was riddled with conflict and contradictions. He remembers frequent fits of disagreement in his home when he was growing up. His family seemed to sink frequently into the depths of emotional dysfunction, with all lines of communication between his mother and father shutting down for days at a time.

Yet both parents did their best to raise their boys on the liberal sensibilities of the baby-boom generation, Dan says, teaching them to honor a person's individuality. Dan and his brother were taught that women and minorities should be afforded the same rights and privileges as anyone else. Racism and sexism were not tolerated in the Birkholz home.

Dan enjoyed school. He turned in his assignments always on time, scored A's when the subjects grabbed his interest, and often was tagged teacher's pet. But school became a battle zone early on. His bashful, bookish personality—and a pronounced overbite—made him easy prey for the classroom bullies. "In about third or fourth grade, kids started noticing my differences and really started teasing me," he recalls. Dan fought back. Push would come to shove and shove would lead to blows as he learned to defend himself in the hallways between classes and on the playground during recess.

Shunned by the popular cliques, Dan found companionship with other grade-school "outcasts," students who were snubbed because of their own differences—kids too fat or too short or too brainy or too shy to be accepted by their peers. Dan struck up a friendship with two boys and a girl who lived in his neighborhood. Their playtime was imaginative, fantastical. The "gang of four," as Dan remembers them, would build snow forts in the winter and hunt for garter snakes and skinks in the summer. The role-playing game Dungeons and Dragons became a daily obsession. As they grew older, they would hang out at a miniature-golf course near Dan's home, spending their weekly allowances at the video arcade.

In his sixth and final year at Hamilton Elementary in Coon Rapids, Dan was surrounded by a new batch of friends, much to his surprise.

As one of the older students who soon would graduate into junior high, he had become popular by attrition. "Everybody just liked me," Dan says, still unsure what he had done to deserve the attention. "I guess I managed to ingratiate myself to the right people." He was on top of the world.

But as his last year in grade school came to a close, Dan's brightened personality was darkened by a singular act of spitefulness. On the day before Memorial Day, he and a couple of friends were on their way to a bowling alley to play video games. As they walked along the road, a car pulled up alongside them from out of nowhere, slowed to a stop, then quickly sped up, spitting gravel and dirt into Dan's face. Two high school teenagers cackled inside the car, and one of them jeeringly flipped Dan and his friends the finger as they drove off. Dan returned the gesture.

When Dan and his friends got to the bowling alley, the teenager was suddenly in Dan's face. "Why don't you step outside," he said to Dan, blocking his path and calling him names. "I'm gonna make you wish you were never born."

Dan dodged the boy and hurried to a phone booth to call home. There was no answer. Panicking, he dialed his grandmother's house. No answer there, either. As Dan listened helplessly to the unanswered ring, the boy slammed down the telephone hook from behind and gave Dan a mighty shove, bashing his head into the side of the phone booth.

Dan turned, and as he watched the boy run away, he realized he could only see out of one eye. "I looked at myself in a mirror and the left side of my face was covered with blood." His head had caught the edge of a decorative iron grate on the phone booth, causing a deep gash in his forehead and loosening two of his front teeth.

Eleven stitches were needed to close Dan's wound, and emergency dental work was performed to wire his teeth in place. "I couldn't even say *Mom*," remembers Dan. "My front gums were so swollen I couldn't pronounce *m*."

Dan's injuries healed quickly, leaving only a faint scar over his temple. But the attack left an indelible mark on his psyche. "It kind of ripped away every illusion a twelve-year-old has," he says. "It was like somebody literally tore a hole in my soul."

Like the swift shove from behind, the incident knocked loose a childhood innocence that had shielded him from adversity, and propelled him headlong into adolescence, a frightening and threatening place that Dan would dread.

Junior high put a fast end to Dan's newfound popularity in school. His best friend moved to Colorado; his other buddies drifted away. Once again, he was alone—and a prime target for harassment. "It was the year from hell," he remembers. "I wore the wrong clothes, I wore the wrong kind of jeans, I had an overbite and acne. It was awful." As a small consolation, his mother bought him a pair of designer Levi's, a pair of Reeboks, and a Swatch watch to help him fit in. But the clothes didn't help, and the ridicule continued, eroding Dan's self-esteem "the way water wears down stone," as he puts it.

As if the constant harassment wasn't irritating enough, Dan's adolescence was coming into bloom. His sexual identity was stirring, sending him a stream of mixed signals. While boys and girls in his class began to pair off, Dan remained uninterested in the rituals of pubescent dating.

"It didn't make any sense to me," he says. "When some of the guys would look at a girl and say, 'Oooo, isn't she pretty,' I thought, Oh, I guess so." He ignored the lewd locker-room jokes—the crass "tits and ass" remarks—and kept to himself. "By seventh grade, I was out of it. All that dating stuff I just kind of missed, because nobody really talked to me."

Yet he could see pieces of his own puzzle coming together. He remembered a day when he was much younger, secretly paging through copies of a *Playboy* magazine with a friend. The lurid photographs of the nude women were curious—and definitely not stimulating. But he also remembered another day, a defining moment even earlier in his childhood. He was in the second grade, shopping with his mother at a bookstore, when they passed a display of calendars, some that featured photographs of women or men in bathing suits. Now, *this* moved him—not the voluptuous women in bikinis, but the *men*. "I liked the guys better," he says. "I was feeling tingly."

The epiphany came when he was thirteen. Dan's father had brought home a stack of bodybuilding magazines after taking up weight lifting. Flipping through the pictures, Dan was mesmerized by the muscle-bound "hunks." He couldn't take his eyes off them, they excited him so. He also remembers having a serious crush on an older boy at school, a football player with perfect characteristics, in Dan's eyes—"big, blond and butch," the three *b*'s.

"I put it all together," he says. "I knew I was attracted to men. But it was no big deal. It wasn't bad or anything. It was just no big deal. I made the discovery and then shut it off. . . . By then I had learned very well how to distance myself from myself, where I could sit back and *think* everything."

In the midst of this self-awakening, Dan and his family moved farther into the country. His parents rented a house in St. Francis, a one-time bustling mill town along Minnesota's Rum River that had become a quiet and distant third-tier suburb of the Twin Cities. It was a temporary residence. A new home was being built for the family on a wooded two-acre lot seven miles north.

Dan was the new kid at St. Francis Middle School, and again, classmates began digging into him because of his "differences." But along with the well-worn profanities and put-downs he had grown accustomed to, a new word of contempt was introduced: *faggot.* Dan had heard the slur before, but never directed at him. Now, all at once, it seemed to be his nickname. *Faggot! You're a faggot. You're a fag.* He wasn't completely sure what it meant. "But I knew that *fag* was synonymous for bad," Dan says. "It was another word for 'different.' "

His parents were no help. "Just try to ignore it," his mother said, and advised him to stay out of fights. His father was even less sympathetic. "This is life," he told Dan. "Get used to it."

Halfway through his school year, Dan's family moved into their new home in the tiny town of Zimmerman. It was a culture shock for Dan. Although he remained in the same school in St. Francis, the move to Zimmerman represented one more degree of isolation. There he was without a friend in sight and, worse, outside the telephone calling area of the metropolitan area. He couldn't even dial up his small coterie of school friends without making a long-distance call.

"The big thing for me was the phone," says Dan. "It was like going three years in high school without the phone, basically." He was utterly dejected.

Dan escaped from his loneliness by reading, diving into Mark Twain, adventure stories by Edgar Rice Burroughs, science-fiction novels by Ray Bradbury. He retreated into his role-playing games and became a steady listener of a Minneapolis radio station that played "synth pop" and "techno alternative"—music that he identified as sophisticated and urban. He became self-absorbed in his isolation—removed from his family and bored with school. And, all the while, his teenage hormones had been rapidly catching up to the realization that he liked men better than women. Intellectually, he could accept his same-sex attractions. Physically and emotionally, he wasn't sure what to make of it.

In his health class during his freshman year at St. Francis High School, his teacher handed out a worksheet one day on sexuality. "There was a paragraph telling you that homosexuality is when people prefer to have sex with people of their own sex. End of story," remembers Dan. "That was the extent of it in my high school. It was too ridiculous. I read it and I thought, A lot of good this does me."

At the suggestion of a friend, Dan joined the speech team during his freshman year. Although he never had acted before, standing before an audience and transforming himself into someone else was exhilarating. It was a chance to dream. He joined the school theater group and drama club later in the year. "It was fun, because I had this latent acting ability that I had never tapped into," he says. "It was very satisfying to be able to step outside of myself for a while."

On an overnight trip for a speech tournament, Dan shared a room with a teammate, Richard. Dan and Richard had become fairly good friends, and Dan found himself attracted to Richard, charmed by his big brown eyes.

After the tournament, the boys went back to their room for the night. Dan left the room briefly to go to the bathroom, and when he returned, the lights were out and Richard was in Dan's bed, waiting. The two boys began "fooling around" under the covers, Dan recalls, kissing, groping, and rolling on top of each other. After ten or fifteen minutes, Richard suddenly pulled away, guilt-ridden and humiliated by what they had been doing.

"I'll never be able to look at you the same way again," he angrily told Dan.

Dan was startled. "What do you mean?" he asked. "I don't think what we did was wrong. We've both just been doing what we've been wanting to do for a long time."

But Richard was consumed by shame. He never spoke to Dan at school again. Years later, Richard and Dan went to a gay bar together with mutual friends, though neither of them made mention of their sexual encounter that night in high school.

"Here we were in this bum-fuck little town, and he's too embarrassed to fess up to something we had known for a while," Dan says regretfully. "There were a lot of things that we could've done together. We had a lot of similarities. But he wasn't ready. He wasn't mature enough to face the fact that this was the way his chromosomes were. I don't know why, he just wasn't."

The experience was an eye-opener for Dan. As brief as it was, it provoked his curiosity about sex with another male. In the summer of his fifteenth year, Dan found a newspaper advertisement for a "fantasy" telephone service. Dan soon was hooked. He rang up dozens of long-distance phone calls, masturbating while he listened to erotic two-minute recordings or talking anonymously to men from all across the country. Phone sex became an outlet for his frustrations and a way of affirming his own sexual attractions. "I wanted to make some kind of connection. It didn't matter how," he says. "I needed to reassure myself that there were people who wanted to have sex with other guys—and I wasn't some twisted pervert living in the middle of nowhere who was going to be condemned to hell."

The calls also symbolized a kick at the walls of his closet. He did little to conceal the calls from his parents. So when the first monthly phone bill arrived after he began making the calls, it included hundreds of dollars in charges to 900 numbers around the country. His calls, Dan says, purposely provided his parents with "smoking gun" evidence of his homosexuality and quickly drew attention to his plea for help.

"They were mad that I had charged all these calls, and they were concerned," he says. "My mom especially wanted to know why."

So Dan tried to explain: "I think I might be gay," he told them, "but I'm not really sure. I want to find out."

"Well, what do you want us to do?" asked his mother.

"I need a book," he said. "I'd just like to read something."

"Fine, we can do something about that," said his father.

"And that's all I really wanted," says Dan, looking back. "But that's all he *didn't* do. He completely ignored it." Weeks later, when Dan asked his father about his promise of finding a book on homosexuality, his father told him he hadn't gotten around to it and the subject was dropped. The long-distance phone calls, too, were ignored. "If you didn't talk about it long enough, it didn't happen," was the typical reaction by his parents, Dan explains.

Near the end of summer, just before starting his sophomore year in high school, Dan picked up a weekly Twin Cities newspaper. Scanning the classifieds, he came upon an ad for a "Man-2-Man" massage. Home alone one day, he called the telephone number listed in the ad and set up an appointment to meet a man named Tom. Tom offered to drive to Zimmerman. So, over the phone, Dan directed him to a secluded road in his subdivision. "Stop where the pavement ends," Dan told him.

A couple of nights later, Dan pulled the broken screen from his bedroom window and slipped out of the house while his parents slept. He hurried to the prearranged rendezvous spot, and there, in the dark of night, he met Tom for the first time, man-to-man. In the back of Tom's van, the two had sex.

"He gave me a little shoulder rub and the next thing I knew his hands were all over me," Dan remembers. "It wasn't a bad thing. I didn't necessarily know it would turn into sex. But I kind of knew what I was doing."

Dan continued the liaisons with Tom throughout the summer and into the following school year, having sex—usually masturbation and oral sex—with Tom in his van or his Minneapolis apartment. Dan would leave his room just before midnight and return by dawn; his parents never knew he was gone. Or sometimes on weekends, he would tell his mother he was taking a long walk and disappear for hours with Tom. Twice, Tom took him to a stretch along the Mississippi River in St. Paul known as Bare Ass Beach, a wooded flats that for years had been claimed by gay men as a private cruising spot. But Dan was uncomfortable with the place. He remembers men wandering silently along the sandy trails along the river in the dark, searching for a companion, and then disappearing into the underbrush to have sex. It was too ritualistic and secretive, Dan says, and seemed dangerous. Two summers later, his misgivings were borne out when a gay man was shot to death and another seriously wounded in the woods near the beach.

Even though Tom was older, almost twice Dan's age, Dan felt unthreatened by him. Dan admits that Tom was a "troll" in every sense of the word—an older, closeted gay man seeking sex with a man much younger. But Dan says he was not intimidated by the discrepancy in their ages. "He kind of had me in a corner in that he knew I didn't have access to anything I wanted," says Dan. "But everything was consensual."

The encounters with Tom were "a mix of coercion and plain old hormones," Dan acknowledges. But he knew no other way, he adds defensively. He had no gay peers in school and no contact with the gay community in the city. In his isolation, he was left to his own devices, Dan says. Tom became a convenient way into the city and an available, albeit exploitative, link for Dan as he established his homosexual identity.

"He wasn't exactly a friend," Dan says of his relationship with Tom. "He wasn't exactly a lover. He wasn't exactly a role model. He wasn't exactly *anything.* What I got out of it was sex, and someone who made me feel nice for once. Sex was a totally different way to feel good. It was a very easy way to get away from the pain. I was young. He brought me down to the city, where I wanted to be. And I was very young."

By his junior year in high school, Dan's life had become an emotional roller coaster. At home, his sexual orientation was ignored. He told his parents of a weekend support group in Minneapolis for gay youth that he had read about, but they were quick with excuses to keep him from joining. "That's an hour's drive to get to Minneapolis," his father told him. "I drive into the city every day. I don't want to do it on the weekends, too."

In school, the harassment wore on, shaming him, turning him numb inside. Gym class was especially intimidating. In the locker room, Dan would remove his glasses to avoid being accused of staring at the naked bodies of other boys.

"I knew if my eyes lingered too long on somebody I was dead, because I knew they'd never let me live it down," he says. "I looked at the floor, I looked at the lockers, I looked at the ceiling tiles. I tried to be as nonchalant about it as I could. But it was very humiliating, what I was putting myself through."

Students, usually "the jocks and burnouts," says Dan, confronted him at every turn—teasing him for the way he dressed or the way he talked or the way he walked. He couldn't walk down the hallway without being laughed at. During the Persian Gulf War, Dan wore a black armband as a sign of protest. Immediately, he was labeled a "commie pinko" and a "traitor." Dan decided to try out for the track team. With his long legs he might make a good sprinter, he thought. But his enemies wasted no time in hounding him off the team. On the first day of tryouts, they mockingly warned the other teammates to stay away from "the faggot" in the shower. No one came to Dan's defense, not even the coaches. He quit after the first practice.

"I decided to do a little project for myself," says Dan. "I wanted to learn how often the word *fag* was directed against me." So he began counting the number of times his classmates used the epithet. "It turned out it was used at least once a day and as bad as twenty-four times a day. And there were only seven hours in a school day. It was constant. It was everywhere."

He tried to ignore the labels. He tried to defuse his tormentors with humor. "But no matter what I did, no matter what I said, it was never fast enough or good enough. They wouldn't stop."

One day, he broke down. During his first hour of school, he stumbled into the office of a special-education teacher he had befriended, one of the few adults he had come out to in the school. Crying, he told her he couldn't take the teasing anymore—the jokes, the slights, the slurs. Students would follow him around school or suddenly appear at his locker, heckling him, ripping posters from inside his locker, taunting him as he tried to turn the other cheek, tripping him as he tried to walk away.

"It kept on and it kept on and it kept on and it kept *on*. It was insane. They wouldn't stop," he says. "It just finally caught up with me. I was like a deer in headlights."

The teacher listened sympathetically as Dan poured out his troubles. But she had no solution to his sad dilemma.

SIDEBAR:

The Rude Awakening

For gay and lesbian youth, coming of age is a quandary, an unbidden puzzle of wonder and confusion. The pieces are dropped at their feet, a collection of inexplicable thoughts and feelings, with no formula to follow or examples to guide them on their way to adulthood. They're left to sort through the jumble on their own, to search for fragments of truth and meaning, to piece together their improbable lives with no direction from family or friends or peers.

To skeptics, gay and lesbian youth simply don't exist. To the doubters, they're only "experimenting" with homosexual behavior, temporarily sidetracked from their "normal" journey to heterosexuality.

But witness the stories of the teens who have been there and you'll hear of an involuntary kinship, of a shared sense of worry and dread that discounts the claim that their path was chosen. You'll hear of the anguish they have faced as they've come to acknowledge their homosexuality. Instead of times of excitement and camaraderie—so routine in the lives of heterosexual teenagers—gay teens tell of the loneliness and dishonor that coming of age brings.

You don't have to spend much time with gay and lesbian teens to know that they're wounded. As their stories are told, painful lessons of personal sacrifice emerge. Despised for their differences and condemned for their "practices," gay youth become social outcasts, separated from peers and parents by an impenetrable wall of shame and secrecy, banished to an isolation that eats away at their self-esteem and shakes their identity to the core.

It's rare to find young gays or lesbians who haven't felt some measure of shame and self-loathing in their lives. "None of them feel that they're okay," says Virginia Uribe, founder of Project 10, a program for gay and lesbian youth in Los Angeles public schools. "They all think that they're somehow morally tarnished. That's what society has done to them."

Sometimes, the self-hatred precedes their full understanding of being homosexual. From early on, they've heard the pejorative labels—"sissy," "faggot," "fruit," "dyke," "lezzy." And, whether they're directed at them or not, they know that each label is a word of reproach.

"It's perceived as a dirty word, a naughty word, so even from grade school time, kids know that it's bad, whatever it is, whatever it means," says Mitzi Henderson, president of the Federation of Parents, Families and Friends of Lesbians and Gays (P-FLAG), a national advocacy group. "And when they discover what it means, and that they indeed might *be* gay, it is very threatening. There's a tremendous amount of fear and guilt, a perception that this is somehow bad and that they are flawed."

With the suspicion that they might be gay comes a profound apprehension, a fear of the repulsion that they surely expect to face, for even before they know the meanings of the labels, they've been taught to believe that homosexuality is one of the most disgraceful conditions known. And as their sexual identity becomes evident—to themselves and to others—their fears often are borne out, demonstrated in rejection, harassment, and ostracism.

"I can't think of a single other problem that an adolescent would have to elicit a reaction like that," says Dr. Gary Remafedi, a pediatrician and executive director of the Youth and AIDS Projects at the University of Minnesota. "Being gay is probably the worst thing in the world that can possibly happen as a teen."

A Trial by Fire

Common to lesbian and gay adolescents is a sense that they were somehow "different" as children. Some teens describe it as a feeling of being introverted—set apart from the popular school cliques, growing up as loners. Others remember it as gender nonconformity—growing up as tomboys or sissies. Still others measure it in terms of emotional and physical attractions toward persons of the same sex—a crush on a classmate or a gym teacher.

"I think probably the best way to describe it is as 'the absence of fit with the proposed heterosexual future,'" says psychologist John Gonsiorek, who served as president of the American Psychological Association's Gay and Lesbian Division from 1992 to 1993. "There is this heterosexual future held out as the outcome for all kids. For some kids it resonates and for some kids it doesn't."

Those kids for whom it *doesn't* resonate quickly learn that their "difference" is not well regarded. As they grow into teenagers, they are taught that not conforming to traditional gender roles or having attractions to people of the same sex is wrong.

Their world is turned upside down: Opposite-sex interactions with peers remind them of what they *don't* feel but should, according to heterosexual conventions, while same-sex interactions remind them of what they *do* feel but shouldn't. So they suppress their sexual identities and withdraw, becoming self-imposed exiles, separating themselves from peer groups—which perpetuates the sense of difference and traps them in a web of seclusion.

What could be worse for a tenderhearted teenager than being different, except maybe being "queer"? As they grasp for an identity and yearn for acceptance, their lives become paradoxical. If they acknowledge their homosexuality, they feel guilty and ashamed about who they are and what they're feeling. While they long for the same experiences afforded to their heterosexual peers, they know if they dare disclose their secret they'll be cursed as misfits and outcasts, perverts and sinners. Adding to the injury, the damning will be done by the people they look to the most for trust and love—parents, teachers, coaches, ministers.

"With the majority of the young people, there's a tremendous stress from the knowledge that all of a sudden they're a member of this hated group," says Joyce Hunter, co-founder of the Harvey Milk School, an alternative school for sexual minorities at the Hetrick-Martin Institute in New York City. "Their first instinct is to not tell anybody. And so they begin a process of hiding. This distorts the whole developmental process, because they can't have honest relationships, they can't discuss sexuality with their friends and be honest about who they are. . . . Their ability to play a role becomes primary. So you don't know who they are."

Learning How to Hide

The predicament of gay and lesbian youth goes to the heart of their very existence. Society presumes that everyone will follow heterosexual customs and that teenagers will be attracted to people of the opposite sex, date people of the opposite sex, and go on to marry people of the opposite sex.

Gay and lesbian adolescents experience this as a falsehood.

"Heterosexuals go into adolescence feeling that they are heterosexual, and they stay heterosexual," says Dr. Richard Isay, professor of psychiatry at Cornell Medical College and past chairman of the Committee on Gay, Lesbian and Bisexual Issues at the American Psychiatric Association. "Gay kids go into adolescence feeling something is wrong with them and *wishing* they were heterosexual."

As all teenagers come of age, they master a number of developmental tasks. Among them: growing away from their parents and toward their peers through personal interaction, establishing role models, and building love relationships.

But for gay and lesbian adolescents, many of the components needed to sustain a healthy development are either lacking or distorted. It's hard for them to make friends who also are gay or lesbian, as most gay and lesbian teens are disinclined to identify their sexual orientation. Role models are scarce. And sexual relationships with peers of the same sex are socially impermissible. So while their heterosexual peers are learning how to date, gay and lesbian youth are learning how to hide.

On top of all the other issues that a teenager faces, gay and lesbian teens face a set of problems unique to their sexual orientation, says Project 10's Uribe. "Number one is isolation, alienation, loneliness. Number two is a feeling that they are morally defective or inferior. They're also unable to communicate with parents about the issue or with other adults in a safe and supportive way. And in that respect, they are different from any other group of teenagers."

Going It Alone

Unlike other minority groups, lesbian and gay teens are unaccompanied in their journey through adolescence, without models to copy or traditions to follow. "It's unusual compared to other minority statuses," says psychologist Gonsiorek, "because if you're an ethnic or racial minority, you have parents and grandparents who can help you negotiate your disparaged status. But there is no generational support system in this minority status."

Sexual-minority teenagers are without the support of society in general. Though more and more schools are recognizing the need for services for gay and lesbian students, most educators are reluctant to broach the topic of homosexuality. Families as well are usually unacquainted with gay and lesbian issues, while media often only reinforce stereotypes and misconceptions. As a result, gay and lesbian teens receive either no information or poor information.

"Gay and lesbian kids do not have the support of the major institutions of society, like the family and the school," says Uribe. "That is a very frightening thing. You're not able to talk to your parents about it, because you fear their rejection. You're not able to go to church or to

Sunday school or to synagogue or wherever you go to talk to some-body, because you're going to possibly face rejection there too. And it's very hard to talk to an adult at school, because you're going to face rejection *there*. So you're really isolated."

The disapproval felt by homosexuals is unlike that felt by any other minority. According to a New York State survey conducted for the Governor's Task Force on Bias-Related Violence, junior and senior high school students were most disapproving of gays, more so than of any other minority group, including those with special racial, ethnic, or religious affiliations. The report pointed out that remarks about homosexuals were often "openly vicious."

In a study conducted at Ohio Dominican College in Columbus, gays ranked near the bottom in various social statuses, second only to "communists," as the most discriminated and reviled minority among a group of six: women, Jews, blacks, recovering alcoholics, gays, and communists.[1] When asked whether each minority should be afforded certain civil rights—including free speech, housing, employment, education, and holding political office—those who were polled ranked gays second to last across the board, and last when asked whether gays should be allowed the right to be parents.

"If you're part of an ethnic group, you have other people to relate to—your own family, your own group. You have some culture," Uribe points out. "But if you're gay or lesbian, you don't have anyone to relate to as a kid. . . . There is no other group like that. It's truly an unusual minority."

Everyone is raised as a member of several social subgroups, identified within the context of family, gender, race, ethnicity, religion, generation, profession, and so on. Accordingly, a person can have numerous social identities. She may be a Latino, a doctor, a Roman Catholic, a mother, and the eldest in a family of origin of six. While gay and lesbian teens have membership in other subgroups, they may deny or conceal their identity as a sexual minority when confronted with the threat of alienation from these other subgroups, particularly from family and peers. So for them, establishing social identity is incomplete and deceptive. Not only are they ill informed about a gay or lesbian identity, but they're reluctant to divulge the identity.

"In adolescence, young homosexually oriented persons are faced with the growing awareness that they may be among the most despised,"[2] said the late Damien Martin, co-founder of the Hetrick-Martin Institute, a community-based agency for gay and lesbian youth in New York City. "As this realization becomes more pressing, they are faced with three possible choices: They can hide, they can attempt to change the stigma; or they can accept it."

The majority choose to hide their sexual orientation by turning to "the closet," a term derived from the skeleton-in-the-closet metaphor. Maintaining a secret identity forces a teen to live a life that is based on deceit, distorting almost all relationships the adolescent tries to develop while plunging him further into the depths of isolation. "This maintenance of a facade becomes all-pervasive," said Martin.

Because of the stigma affixed to homosexuality—and the long-standing myth that gay and lesbian adults are child molesters who recruit adolescents into a "homosexual lifestyle" against their will—adults who typically might serve as role models are reluctant to associate with youth. Many gay and lesbian adults—teachers, clergy, doctors, athletes—themselves are compelled to remain "closeted," out of fear of discrimination. The absence of role models denies adolescents the opportunity to view gays and lesbians in a positive light, to understand that the prejudices of society are false, and to know that they are not destined to lead shamed, degenerated lives.

A 1993 report by the Massachusetts Governor's Commission on Gay and Lesbian Youth, the first commission of its kind in the United States, draws this conclusion: "Gay and lesbian youth exist in a society that in attitude and behavior discriminates against them. Society at large creates a mythology about gays and lesbians, and virtually denies the existence of gay and lesbian youth. Parents, family, peers, and teachers are generally ignorant of what it means to be gay or lesbian. Gay and lesbian youth have little chance of talking with a knowledgeable or understanding person concerning his or her gay or lesbian identity."[3]

The Price They Pay

Like most other youth, gay and lesbian teens are raised with a cultural prejudice toward homosexuality, a fear and aversion known as homophobia. As gay teens mature, they gain a deeper understanding of how their notion of childhood "differentness" relates to their homosexual identity. But at the same time, they begin to heed society's negative responses to their differentness, incorporating anti-gay attitudes into their self-image. They feel bad about who they are, evil, inferior, or sick because they're lesbian or gay. This "internalized homophobia" is more pronounced during adolescence than at any other time. So, along with the rejection that they face from peers and loved ones, gay youth turn against themselves.

"It causes them to feel inhibited," says psychiatrist Isay. "It causes them to withdraw. It causes them to feel that they may not be able to experience any passion. It may evoke overt symptoms of depression."

The fear and disdain leveled at gays—by society, by peers, and by themselves—can hinder the social development of gay youth and sometimes lead to a postponement of certain developmental skills. Consequently, some gay and lesbian teens play a sort of social catch-up as the "coming out" process advances. They might delay dating until late in their adolescence or early adulthood, for example.

"The social development of gay and lesbian youth is so poor," says Uribe, of Project 10. "That's the area where our young gay and lesbian children really suffer, where they really depart from heterosexual society. Socializing in a healthy environment is very difficult for them. . . . You might have a person who is developing very well in some ways, but there is a part that is severely wounded—the social part. And that's why the teenage period is such a terrible time."

Sometimes the self-hatred and society's general disregard can push teens to the breaking point. Some drop out of school or turn to drugs or alcohol to mask their isolation. Some, in the worst cases, turn self-destructive.

"Poor socialization is one of the most difficult things for gay and lesbian students," adds Uribe. "They become very withdrawn, they become very lonely. And sometimes they act out. Sometimes they act out very badly, in ways that are antisocial. Sometimes they get involved in drugs and alcohol and they try to numb the pain that way. Sometimes girls will get pregnant because, in a way, it's kind of hiding the fact that they're lesbian by having a baby. Sometimes they run away. Sometimes they try to kill themselves. They'll do all kinds of things."

A colloquium sponsored by the Child Welfare League of America in 1991 drew together a group of academicians, advocates, practitioners, and representatives of social services organizations from across the country to report on the plight of gay youth. "Because of negative societal portrayals, many gay and lesbian youths live a life of isolation, alienation, depression, and fear," concluded the colloquium. "As a result, they are beset by recurring crises disproportionate to their numbers in the child welfare system."

In its report, "Serving Gay and Lesbian Youths: The Role of the Child Welfare Agencies," the League included a checklist of the potential hazards of growing up gay. Among the risks: physical and sexual abuse; poor mental health; family disruption; homelessness; violence and oppression; sexual exploitation; pregnancy; employment discrimination; sexually transmitted diseases and HIV infection; drug and alcohol abuse; suicide.

As they struggle alone to come to terms with their sexuality, the prospect of a life of disdain is a rude awakening for these teens. Out of shame and fear, they shun what little support there is and retreat into a world of secrecy.

Troy I:

Am I Weird? Am I Sick? Am I Crazy?

Troy Herman can pinpoint his very first homosexual impulse. It came literally in a flash of light.

He was in second grade, a new transfer student at Jefferson Elementary School in Charles City, Iowa, in 1981. It was his first day of school and he was getting ready for recess when he noticed one of his classmates, a boy, standing alone in the back of the room near a wall of windows. Most of the other students had already filed out, and someone had switched off the overhead lights. Except for the autumn sun shining in, the classroom was dim. The boy leaned on the windowsill to look outside, and suddenly he was immersed head to toe in a beam of golden sunlight.

Troy remembers being transfixed. The boy seemed to have the face of an angel and the purest blond hair he had ever seen. He's beautiful, Troy thought, his eyes wide with wonder.

He followed the boy out to the playground, then stopped. Now wait a minute, he said to himself. My sister should like boys. I never see two boys together. Am I weird? Am I sick? Am I crazy?

Although his same-sex attraction didn't make sense to him at such an early age, it was a marker event. He knew instinctively from that point on that he was unlike the other boys. While he never saw his uniqueness as something wrong, it would label him throughout his childhood as a target for ridicule.

▲ ▼ ▲

Troy Herman was born in Charles City, a blue-collar community in the northeast corner of Iowa made up mostly of factory workers and retired farmers. With a population of about eight thousand, it's a town big enough to support a singles newspaper and recycling center, but small enough so that you can still buy a glass of beer for under a dollar.

Bisected by the Cedar River, Charles City is an hour west of Interstate 35. Visitors driving into town from the south on state highway 218 are greeted by a giant billboard: WELCOME TO CHARLES CITY, IOWA, HOME OF THE WORLD'S FIRST TRACTOR, a tribute to the heyday of White Farm, a farm implement manufacturer. A grain elevator and the Floyd County courthouse anchor Main Street to the north and south, with a half-dozen stop lights and just as many bars in between.

Troy's parents divorced when he was five. His mother, Jane Herman, had five children from two unsuccessful marriages by the time she was twenty-five. She remarried again in 1977 and, with her third husband, took her children to Denver to start fresh. Her new husband, Allen Herman, had two daughters of his own living in Colorado and owned a small chain of gas stations in Denver. When he died of cancer two years later, Jane moved her children once again—this time back to Iowa, to be closer to her brothers and sisters. The Hermans settled in Mason City for nearly two years before returning to their hometown of Charles City in 1981.

Troy, whose father was Jane Herman's second husband, was the youngest child. He followed a half-brother and two half-sisters and a birth sister in the family order. Jane Herman did her best to support her family on the Social Security benefits she received following the death of her third husband. But she was a restless and unsatisfied soul, and every six months or so, she packed up the household belongings, loaded her children into her Oldsmobile station wagon, and started over again, in a new house or apartment in some other Charles City neighborhood.

"There were a couple of times when we lived in the same place twice," recalls Troy. By sixth grade, he had attended all three elementary schools in town, two of them more than once. Time and time again, he was forced to say goodbye to neighborhood kids whom he had just begun to get to know. Because of his family's perpetual state of transition, his siblings became his closest friends, especially his sister Linda, Troy's elder by just thirteen months. The two were inseparable in their early years. He remembers exchanging clothes and swapping toys with her. "She'd play with my Tonka trucks; I'd play with her Barbie dolls," he says.

In school, too, Troy hung out with girls. Whenever he would enroll in a new grade school, he would look to the girls for companionship. They were easier to talk to, easier to buddy up to than the boys, who never seemed to like him. "I just felt more comfortable with them," he says. "Guys thought that was very sick." More than once Troy himself was mistaken for a girl, his soft face framed by reddish-brown bangs, his cheeks full and dimpled when he smiled. "I acted very girlish," Troy says. He remembers sitting at his desk with his legs crossed and his hands delicately folded. It was natural to him, something he didn't try to hide.

Troy paid a price for his "girlish" behavior. None of the boys in his classes would have anything to do with him. They called him a sissy and derided him for playing with girls. To dodge the insults, Troy retreated, spending most of his after-school hours at home with his family instead of at the playground with his classmates.

In third grade, Troy's younger cousin, Jackie, told him she had a friend she wanted him to meet, a boy named Jordan. They walked over to Jordan's home, two short blocks from Troy's. As they stepped into the driveway, they were greeted with a rain of rocks. Jackie promptly abandoned her cousin and joined forces with Jordan, and the introduction escalated into a war of rocks and stones hurled back and forth by the youngsters—sidewalk competition between Jordan and Troy over Jackie's friendship.

A truce was called, and over the course of the year the two boys became the best of friends. Jordan, short and skinny, with sandy blond hair, was one year younger than Troy and attended the same elementary school. The two ate lunch together, played together during recess, and began hanging out together after school. Jordan had much in common with Troy. He too was the youngest child in a large family—two boys and six girls. Their fathers had been teenage buddies. And, like Troy and Jordan, their sisters were friends, too.

"I remember thinking it was better to have another boy to play with who liked to do all the things that I liked to do," Troy says. "It was one step better than playing with my sister Linda."

Troy and Jordan soon discovered they shared a common secret—they both were infatuated with boys. They would compare their affections for boys they knew at their school and tease each other about their latest crushes. Both admired one boy in particular, a second-grader named Kelly. Kelly was exceptionally good-looking. Troy remembers thinking he was the type of boy who surely would grow up to be strikingly handsome. Troy and Jordan vied unabashedly for his attention, pushing and elbowing to sit by his side during lunch, and showing off during recess. It was Jordan who won out, finally capturing Kelly's interest. He invited Kelly over to his home, where they would roll and tumble together on an old mattress down in the basement, out of sight of any adults, kissing and hugging under blankets and sheets, sometimes without their clothes.

Troy was jealous, and tried to foil the new camaraderie.

"You know that he's a *boy,* don't you?" Troy told Kelly, hoping that he'd somehow disgrace Jordan and undermine the friendship.

"Yeah? So?" Kelly said, unswayed.

Kelly seemed to enjoy fooling around. "He got into it as much as Jordan did," Troy says.

As Troy and Jordan advanced a grade or two, their rivalry cooled. During their summers, they rarely were seen apart. Rather than joining Cub Scouts or Little League or the 4-H Club, they devised their own style of play. The basement of Jordan's house became their hangout, a sanctuary where they could explore their curiosities and act out their fantasies, without embarrassment. There, they created a world of make-believe. Troy and Jordan would borrow their sisters' clothes and play dress-up—donning swimsuits, sweaters, designer jeans, high-heeled boots, whatever they could find. They would wrap towels around their heads to imitate long, flowing hair, or drape bedsheets around themselves to substitute as dresses. They would stage talent contests, fashion shows, and beauty pageants, employing a sister to act as a judge as they walked an imaginary runway across the basement carpet. They would learn cheerleader routines, borrowing pom-poms from their sisters. They would re-create scenes from movies—*The Wizard of Oz* or *Friday the 13th*—and mimic characters from soap operas: Jordan would take the part of Mindy and Troy the part of Roxy from the soap *Guiding Light.*

The play-acting seemed second nature. "We never really said, 'Well, should boys do this or should boys do that?'" Troy says. "We just went with it. We just wanted to do it, so we did."

One afternoon, when Troy was eight or nine, he put on a pink flowered skirt and white boots that he had discovered in Jordan's basement. Jordan dared him to walk through the public golf course. So he did. "And this man almost hit me with a golf club," remembers Troy. "He said to me, 'Oh, I'm sorry, little girl.'" As Troy ran laughing from the fairway, his sister and Jordan's sister came riding by on bicycles. Troy ducked under a playground slide to hide, then raced home to ditch the wardrobe.

"The only thing that bothered me was the possibility that someone would see me," Troy says. "Otherwise I didn't care."

Jordan's mother didn't seem to care, either. She saw the boys' play as a creative outlet, so much harmless fantasy. Jordan's father, though, had doubts, and tried to temper Jordan's interest in Barbie dolls by buying him "superhero" action toys.

The beauty pageants, fashion shows, and poms-poms didn't sit well with Troy's mother, either. "Boys shouldn't be playing house," she told Troy, crossly. "And they shouldn't be playing with dolls." She blamed Jordan for influencing her son, and tried to stop Troy from playing with him. Troy protested. And whenever his friend would call, he would duck out of the house to join up with him. Troy's father, divorced from Troy's mother and living on his own in Charles City, seemed to be amused by the boys' gender switch. He never made much of it, says Troy, and never tried to discipline or "correct" his play habits.

"He would just laugh," Troy says. "He used to buy me Barbie dolls, actually. He never second-guessed it or told me it was wrong. Never. He was real lenient with me, the most perfect father," says Troy. As the boys grew older, he would drive them to a shopping mall in Waterloo, an hour from their home, so they could shop for clothes that were more fashionable than what they could find in Charles City.

Troy lived with his father for two years during his mid-teens. A tall, thin man, Troy's father served in the army overseas in World War II, and then worked in a manufacturing plant in Charles City after the war. But diabetes got the best of him and put him out of work before Troy was born. Troy has a vivid recollection of his father standing in the kitchen every morning, dressed in bib overalls, injecting himself with insulin. He died of kidney failure in April 1989, the day after his sixty-fourth birthday. Troy was sixteen.

Troy entered Charles City Junior High School a hopelessly alienated thirteen-year-old, careful to steer clear of the bullies and unsure whom to look to for acceptance. He tried out for track but lost interest long before the end of the season. He had given up on the baritone horn, an instrument he had played since fourth grade. He held down a solid C average but had little drive to excel academically. What grabbed his imagination from sixth grade on were his chorus and acting classes. Like the secret performances in Jordan's basement or singing in his church's choir, acting in a school play and singing with the school chorus unlocked his creativity and allowed a freedom of expression that he'd always longed for. But unlike Troy and Jordan's basement productions, school performances were sanctioned by his peers and his parents. He could dress unashamedly in a costume as Little John for a performance of *Robin Hood,* or sing background vocals in *Bye Bye Birdie,* publicly and without mockery. And in this crowd, he saw a set of potential new friends.

But his enthusiasm was short-lived. No matter how hard he tried to find his place, his effeminacy drew even more belligerence in junior high, and the hostility slowly ground him down. Along with Jordan,

Troy again was tagged as the class sissy. Guys as well as girls would pass him in the hallway and spew a string of insults—*fag* and *queer* and *sissy*. Two boys in particular became his daily tormentors, Troy recalls: Matt, "this big, overweight, stocky wrestler that nobody messed with," and his sidekick, John. Matt would corner Troy and poke at him with his finger, laughing and calling him names, humiliating him in front of his classmates. Amazingly, Troy never was physically harmed. He remembers standing near his school bus one day, watching as the junior-high toughs beat up a grade-schooler, shaking him down for his pocket change. How strange that *I* never get beat up, he thought. Me, the most hated kid in school.

To avoid the relentless badgering, Troy withdrew. By eighth grade, he had stopped auditioning for school plays. He remained friends with only one or two classmates, distancing himself even from Jordan, in order to lessen the chance of being labeled and picked on.

To demonstrate to his peers that he wasn't as different as they believed, Troy dated girls, taking them to the movies or parties or school dances, holding hands and kissing on the playground, where they were sure to be seen. He was a steady "boyfriend" of a girl named Penny for nearly two years in his early teens. "I liked her a lot," Troy says. But he knew it was a charade, long before he identified himself as gay. Girls were yet another way to try to fit in, another way to normalize the "sissy" Troy Herman, so that maybe, finally, the resentment would end.

Something remarkable happened to Troy Herman in high school. When Troy was sixteen, a new kid named Michael had moved into town from, of all places, California. Blond-haired and blue-eyed, he dressed and behaved unlike any of the other students. He showed up at school one day wearing brightly colored shorts and an Ocean Pacific T-shirt, reading books that seniors were reading and boasting about his West Coast childhood. "He had the total surfer look. Absolutely," Troy remembers. He was impressed.

Michael lived with his family in a big house on the edge of town.

Although he was short for his age, Michael played running back on the junior varsity football team.

In their junior year, when they were both sixteen, Troy and Michael got jobs at the Hy-Vee grocery store, sacking groceries and stocking shelves. The two frequently worked the late shift together, from 3 P.M. until midnight, shelving shipments of merchandise and clowning around after the store closed. They would play football in the aisles, passing rolls of paper towels and toilet paper over the produce and pet food. Troy's former girlfriend, Penny, worked as a cashier during the days. And one night, when Michael and Troy were the only ones in the store, Michael posed a question:

"So I hear you used to go out with Penny?" he asked. "You gonna go out with her again?"

"No. She's not my type anymore," Troy answered. "She moved on to other people. And I'm looking for someone else."

"Well, what type of person are you looking for?" Michael said.

"Someone I can just have a good time with, who likes the same things I do," replied Troy.

"Well, what would you think of *me*?" Michael asked, brashly.

Troy was mute.

"I've known about you for quite a while," Michael went on. "The whole school does."

Troy laughed. "Yeah? That's no surprise."

And in the after-hour privacy of the Charles City Hy-Vee, a friendship took root, a relationship that seemed to validate Troy's sexual orientation. There had been no denying his attraction to boys over the years. But Michael was the first young *man* to express a romantic interest in Troy, now a young man himself. That night, the two talked for hours about their childhood, about growing up "different." Though Troy never used the word *gay,* Michael was the first person he ever came out to.

Troy was in heaven. He and Michael talked on the phone every day after school and made plans to meet at the movies or at a park. Michael owned a car, and they would spend hours driving the county highways and gravel roads outside Charles City, contemplating their futures. Would Troy go to college? Would Michael move back to California? What would their parents think if they found out about their relationship? Late one night, Troy sneaked into Michael's basement bedroom while his parents and sister slept upstairs. For hours, they lay together in Michael's bed, hugging, kissing, and touching each other. Usually, it was the park or Michael's car where they would make out, masturbating each other and having oral sex. They didn't use condoms, and instead abstained from sex that they thought would be unsafe, Troy says.

"Michael was the first guy I ever messed around with." Never was he ashamed of what he was doing, Troy maintains. "It was exciting. It was sort of like I just wanted to get on a big loudspeaker and start yelling at the whole town: 'This is what we're doing, so fuck you!'"

But their encounters were discreet, oppressively discreet. Passing in the hallways or sitting near each other in a classroom, they would never chance more than a furtive glance at each other. An occasional "Hi" was all they would venture, fearing that someone would somehow suspect them of being "faggots" and they'd be banished forever from their school and community.

The constant hiding began to eat away at their relationship. Michael became increasingly fearful of being found out. As if to build a ready defense against any insinuation that he was gay, he started making vicious remarks about homosexuals and telling "fag" jokes. With his friends, he began to turn on Troy, pointing and laughing and calling him a "faggot," too. Troy, devastated, didn't understand. Although Michael insisted he was just trying to protect himself, Troy thought the act was hurtful and hypocritical.

Troy was heartsick. The masquerade became so ponderous that he finally threw in the towel. "It was just too much," he says. "So I just told him it was not working out. . . . It took me a long time to get over that." They broke up at the end of eleventh grade, after "going out" for nearly eight months.

▲ ▼ ▲

Troy was weary of leading a double life. He hated being forced to mask his true identity, of hiding in the closet. Once the most talkative child of the Herman bunch and the loudest young voice in the Sunday choir, he now barely spoke at all. His personality had been stifled and his social development crippled by the scorn he had endured. It was no surprise that Troy thought he was defective.

Troy's failed relationship with Michael convinced him that he could never live an openly gay life in Charles City. The town was too homophobic, the closet was too oppressive. "I couldn't feel safe," he says, looking back. "I just hated that town. People that live there believe they're so exempt from things. I just hate that small-town mentality. I just hate it."

One day, he overheard his brother-in-law mention a gay bar in Minneapolis, the Gay 90s. Troy and Jordan had rekindled their friendship, with the help again of Troy's cousin Jackie. So Troy persuaded Jordan into driving up to the Twin Cities to give the bar a look. Turned away at the door because they were underage, they instead discovered a couple of downtown clubs that catered to gay youth—the Second Story, a dance club, and the Saloon, a gay bar that opened its doors twice a week to anyone eighteen and older.

It was their first glimpse into the gay community. And they liked what they saw. They no longer felt invisible, irregular. Instead, they were a part of something, something that was at once exhilarating and liberating.

SIDEBAR:

The Roots of Homosexuality

Craig's first hint that he was gay came at the age of eleven, when he was in Boy Scouts: "We would go on camp-outs and there were these other boys that I felt attracted to. There was nothing physical about it or sexual about it. When I look back on it now, I had crushes on them. Then later it started to develop into something physical and sexual. In eighth grade I started thinking, Well, gee, maybe I'm gay."

Craig had no explanation for what he felt. Where did these attractions come from? Why didn't his friends feel the same? Would he always feel this way?

Chance or choice, nature or nurture, the cause of homosexuality remains a riddle. In the absence of a definitive explanation, myth and conjecture have substituted, making homosexuality a lightning rod of our times.

It's commonly thought that people become homosexuals by choice or as a result of experience and upbringing. Some of the more popular notions include the beliefs that:

- homosexuality is the result of childhood sexual abuse or sexual contact with other homosexuals.
- homosexuality is a passing phase of adolescence that eventually is outgrown.
- homosexuality is a deviance that is learned.

- homosexuality is caused by an overprotective mother and absent or detached father.
- homosexuality is a mental illness.

While widely held, these beliefs are regarded as untrue within the scientific community. Although the origin of sexual orientation continues to be a mystery, a string of studies completed in the past decade has brought researchers closer to a consensus. If not conclusive, these studies suggest that a person's sexual orientation is influenced at least in part by genetic and biological factors.

The once-accepted belief that homosexuality is a disease was discarded by the American Psychiatric Association in 1973, and subsequently by the American Medical Association and the World Health Organization. In 1991, the American School Health Association passed a resolution calling for the end of discrimination against lesbian and gay youth. In 1993, the American Academy of Pediatrics revised its policy statement on homosexuality and adolescence to reflect "a growing realization that sexual orientation is something inherent in people." And in 1994, the AMA reversed a thirteen-year policy that supported treatment aimed at changing the sexual orientation of gays, declaring instead that "aversion therapy" is "no longer recommended for gay men and lesbians."

The medical and psychiatric communities generally reject the notion that homosexuality can or should be changed. Studies dating back to the 1950s have shown that homosexuals have no greater propensity for mental illness than heterosexuals. Gays and lesbians lead healthy, well-adjusted lives, mentally and physically.

"You don't cure something that doesn't need curing," says June Reinisch, director of the Kinsey Institute for Sex Research from 1982 to 1993. "Would you say that having a bubbly personality could be cured? Or having a certain kind of temperament? There is no evidence that this is abnormal. The evidence suggests that having same-sex partners has gone on throughout history. It's been around since the beginning of time, as far as we can gather, in all societies around the world. It appears to be a natural alternative."

Dr. Robert Deisher, professor emeritus at the University of Washington's medical school, helped found one of the first counseling centers for gays and lesbians in Seattle in the late 1960s. In the decades that he has worked with gay and lesbian adults and adolescents, he has never seen any indication that homosexuals can change who they are, he says. "You can't 'cure' anyone from being homosexual any more than you can 'cure' a heterosexual to make them homosexual," says Deisher. "You aren't going to change people's identity. This is not a choice."

Various treatment programs have claimed to be successful in turning homosexuals into heterosexuals. But the treatments are largely dismissed as having no potential effect on changing sexual orientation.

"There's no evidence that sexual orientation through therapeutic efforts can be altered," says John Gonsiorek of the American Psychological Association. "If you badger people enough, you can behaviorally suppress their sexuality. But that's not a therapeutic endeavor. That's group pressure and brainwashing. It feeds into the tendency to doubt oneself and hate oneself, which is common among most oppressed groups. Most of those 'change programs' focus on isolation from community as an important component. And that is known as a risk factor for almost everyone."

Dr. Richard Isay of Cornell Medical College agrees that homosexuality, or any other sexual orientation, for that matter, is permanently fixed, and constitutional in origin. "Sexual orientation is well formed in a youngster long before his or her adolescence," he says. "Homosexual behavior can be altered for short periods of time for some highly motivated men, [but] with great emotional costs—depression, anxiety and severe injury to self-esteem. . . .

"You can reverse *behavior* for brief periods of time," he adds, "but certainly the sexual orientation cannot be changed. For many years, by different techniques, people have been attempting to reverse the behavior through negative conditioning—electric shock, drugs, castration, as well as psychoanalysis—with limited success in terms of the behavior. But I have never known or heard of anybody whose sexual orientation has been changed."

Defining Sexual Orientation

According to conventional wisdom, based on studies on sexuality by American biologist Alfred Kinsey in 1948 and 1953, about one out of ten people is a homosexual. More specifically, Kinsey found that 13 percent of men and 7 percent of women had engaged mainly in same-sex behavior. Today, that rule-of-thumb one-out-of-ten estimate is subject to endless debate, as gay-rights activists, opponents, and researchers alike tangle over politics, methodology, and the very definition of homosexuality. The percentage of gays and lesbians in the population can be a crucial piece of information when setting (or limiting) public policy on issues such as domestic-partnership benefits or AIDS research, for example.

Researchers generally are comfortable with a range of estimates showing that 4 to 6 percent of all males and 2 to 3 percent of all females are predominantly homosexual: that is, they have held same-sex relationships through much of their adult lives. Yet recent studies have pushed that range higher and lower, depending on how homosexuality was measured.

In a 1993 report on the sexual behavior of men, the Battelle Human Affairs Research Centers in Seattle found that only 2 percent of sexually active adult men have had any same-gender sex within the past ten years, and only 1 percent reported being exclusively homosexual.[1]

However, a 1994 study combined same-sex attraction with same-sex behavior when measuring the incidence of homosexuality. Released by the Harvard School of Public Health and the Center for Health Policy Studies, the report found that between 16 and 21 percent of males and 17 to 19 percent of females had same-sex attractions or behavior since the age of fifteen. An examination of behavior separately showed that 4 to 11 percent of males and 2 to 4 percent of females reported having sexual contact with people of the same sex in the past five years.[2]

Because of the societal pressures that compel lesbians and gays to conceal their sexual identities, accurately gauging the number of homosexuals within the population is an improbable task. Even defining homosexuality can be controversial. Therefore, the process of determining the root of homosexuality is far from complete. In order to separate fact from theory from myth, it is important to first appreciate the complexity of sexual orientation itself.

Kinsey measured sexual orientation on a seven-point scale, placing men who were exclusively heterosexual on one end of the continuum and those who were exclusively homosexual on the other end. In the middle were those who were equally heterosexual and homosexual, or bisexual. Devised in the 1950s, the scale was based on more than ten thousand interviews conducted about sexual behavior and partnership.

Since then, Kinsey's definition has been fine-tuned. Today, sexual orientation can be more strictly defined as a consistent pattern of arousal toward persons of the same and/or opposite gender, including fantasies, conscious attractions, emotional and romantic feelings, as well as sexual behavior. Or, as sexologist James Weinrich puts it, it's whatever turns your head. "There are several different definitions of sexual orientation, so part of the battle is which aspect of the phenomenon is going to become the definition," says Weinrich, a psychobiologist at the University of California at San Diego. "The definition I prefer is: One's sexual orientation is defined by the sex of the person whose naked body shape is most arousing to you."

Simon LeVay, one of the leading researchers on homosexuality and the brain, recognizes sexual orientation as multidimensional, consisting of psychological as well as behavioral components. LeVay defines sexual orientation specifically as "the direction of sexual feelings or behavior toward individuals of the opposite sex (heterosexuality), the same sex (homosexuality), or some combination of the two (bisexuality)."[3]

Still other definitions focus on more than sexual attraction, arousal, and fantasy. Tossed into the mix are elements that are impossible to calibrate, intangibles such as cultural affiliation, passion, and love.

"Sexual orientation has to do with whom you fall in love, with whom you feel sexual passion, with whom you feel romantic," says the Kinsey Institute's Reinisch. "It has to do with the kind of partner that you associate with when it comes to romance, love, passion, sexual arousal.

"Sexual orientation has little if nothing to do with the way that you present yourself," she adds. "People often confuse gender identity and gender role with sexual orientation, and they are independent. People have the belief that if somebody is homosexual they will therefore be effeminate if they're a male, or masculine if they're a female. That is gender role. That's not sexual orientation. . . . Actually, it's probable that the majority of homosexual men are as masculine as the average heterosexual man."

The Harvard study in 1994 became the first of its kind to include sexual attraction with sexual behavior when measuring the prevalence of homosexuality. "We want to show that homosexuality can be considered as other than simple sexual behavior, and that when sexual attraction is measured along with sexual behavior, a larger population is identified," read the report.[4] "We further argue that by only using sexual behavior as a measure of homosexuality we would ignore respondents that report no sexual contact over the five-year period studied. We cannot assume that all persons who do not report sexual behavior do not have a sexual orientation."

Rather than plotting sexual orientation on a linear scale, another definition paints it as a sphere, with various dimensions of sexual orientation—fantasies, behaviors, levels of arousal, passion—intersecting within the sphere. "There is more than just a linear spectrum between heterosexuality and homosexuality," says pediatrician and researcher Dr. Gary Remafedi, who, through the University of Minnesota, surveyed more than thirty-four thousand junior and senior high school students in 1991 on issues of sexuality. "What we found was, we could measure each of the different dimensions of sexual orientation, but when we tried to put them together, we were tapping into different populations." For instance, some people reported having homosexual fantasies and heterosexual behavior, while others reported having homosexual and heterosexual attractions yet no sexual behavior at all.

Each dimension of sexual orientation can be measured on a continuum, Remafedi explains. Yet rarely is a measurement identical for any two people, whether self-identified as homosexual, heterosexual, or bisexual. "You could be 100 percent homosexual in your fantasies, 50 percent homosexual in your behaviors, et cetera. If you have a continuum for each of these dimensions, and they are lines intersecting at some point, finally you create a sphere. Our sexual orientations are not just one, two, or three—heterosexual, homosexual, or bisexual—but they are infinite permutations."

Growing Evidence

Defining sexual orientation can be complicated enough. But explaining *why* people are gay, straight, or bisexual—or something in between—is a scientific quest still in its infancy. Recent research has encouraged theories that say the foundation of homosexuality is in some way inborn and not learned. At the same time, the studies have served to intensify the debate.

Some of the more well publicized studies have focused on genetic as well as anatomic differences between homosexuals and heterosexuals.

- Research by a team of geneticists at the National Cancer Institute uncovered a region at the tip of the X chromosome that could hold a gene or genes for male homosexuality.[5] According to a report published in July 1993, Dean Hamer and colleagues studied the genetic material from 40 pairs of gay brothers. Of the 40 pairs, 33 shared identical material on the end of the long arm of the X chromosome, a region dubbed Xq28.

  The link, Hamer said, was not due to chance. Statistically, there is less than 1 percent probability of such a match turning up randomly. Nor does the match of the 33 pairs of brothers prove conclusively that one site on the X chromosome is responsible for all homosexuality, said Hamer, noting that something as complex as sexual orientation and behavior probably cannot be determined by a single gene. Yet the finding adds a huge piece of evidence to the theory that the origin of homosexuality includes an inborn component.

If there are genes that contribute to sexual orientation, they could take years to isolate. It's estimated that hundreds of genes—most of them unidentified—exist in the Xq28 area of the chromosome.

• In a study released in August 1992, neuroscientists Roger Gorski and Laura Allen of the University of California at Los Angeles found a significant difference in the size of a brain structure between homosexual men and heterosexual men and women.[6] The scientists examined brain sections from 193 deceased men and women—34 men who were identified as homosexual from their medical records, 75 men presumed to be heterosexual, and 84 women also thought to be heterosexual. All but six of the deceased gay men in the study had died of AIDS, which may have skewed the results.

The researchers found differences among all three groups in the size of the anterior commissure, a small cord of nerve fibers that is believed to play some role in communication between the two halves of the brain. The structure is not thought to directly influence sexual behavior, yet the researchers saw the findings as yet another sign that sexual orientation has a biological basis.

Critics were skeptical of any connection to sexual orientation and faulted the study for relying on brain samples from AIDS patients, arguing that some of the opportunistic infections associated with HIV have measurable effects on brain cells.

• A study of 167 gay men and their brothers was published in December 1991, again drawing an important connection between genetics and sexual orientation.[7] Michael Bailey, a psychologist at Northwestern University, and psychiatrist Dr. Richard Pillard, of Boston University's school of medicine, surveyed 56 pairs of identical twins (who share the same genes), 54 pairs of fraternal twins (who are as genetically similar as any siblings), and 57 pairs of adoptive brothers (who had no genetic similarities at all). In each pair, one brother had identified himself as gay.

According to the findings, 52 percent of the identical twin brothers of the gay subjects were also gay, compared to 22 percent of the fraternal twin brothers and 11 percent of the adoptive brothers.

The higher frequency of homosexual brothers among the group of identical twins offers proof that genes in some way influence sexual orientation, said Bailey, who led the study. At the same time, as Bailey and Pillard noted, not all of the identical twins turned out to be gay, indicating that there is an environmental influence as well.

"The conclusion of the study is that it appears to be a matter of both, but genes are certainly important," Bailey says. It may be possible, he adds, that a cluster of genes related to homosexuality exists, and that men with some but not all of the "gay genes" may be more susceptible to environmental influences—a certain hormonal exposure while still in the womb, for example. "The relative environmental factors, whatever they are, are the type of factors that even identical twins don't share."

• A study published in August 1991 by neurobiologist Simon LeVay at the Salk Institute in La Jolla, California, looked to a section of the human brain for an explanation of sexual orientation. Previous laboratory experiments had cited the hypothalamus as the region of the brain that generates male sexual behavior. In his research, LeVay found that one isolated node within the hypothalamus was nearly three times smaller in homosexual men than in heterosexual men, indicating an anatomic difference between men of different sexual orientations.[8]

LeVay also revealed that the anatomical shape of the node, about as big as a grain of sand, is remarkably similar in females and gay males and substantially different in heterosexual males.

Brain tissue was obtained through routine autopsies of forty-one persons who died at several hospitals in New York and California. Nineteen were homosexual men who had died of complications of AIDS, sixteen were presumed to be heterosexual (of whom six were intravenous drug users who had also died of AIDS), and six were heterosexual women, one of whom had died of AIDS.

LeVay acknowledges that his study was problematic. Because more than half of the subjects had died of AIDS, questions again arise as to the effect the virus might have had on the brain structure. Moreover, samples from homosexual women were not included.

But at the very least, LeVay argues, the research documents a physiological difference between gay men and straight men, and "illustrates that sexual orientation in humans is amenable to study at the biological level."

• Research also has shown that homosexuality can run in the family. Released in August 1986, a study conducted at Boston University found that brothers of male homosexuals were more likely to be homosexual than were brothers of heterosexual men.[9] Fifty-one gay men and fifty straight men were surveyed by researchers Richard Pillard and James Weinrich. While most of the brothers of both groups were heterosexual, the gay men reportedly had four times as many gay brothers (22 percent) as the straight men (4 percent). The familial tie again lends support to the view that some genetic or biological influence is responsible for homosexuality.

None of the studies excludes the possibility that the cause of homosexuality could also have an environmental component. In fact, most scientists agree that sexual orientation is likely shaped by a combination of genetic, biological, and environmental influences. The question is, what are those specific influences and when do they affect the brain? Before birth? After birth? During childhood?

"I feel that there is not one route to an orientation, but there are multiple ways to become homosexual, heterosexual, or bisexual," says

Reinisch, formerly with the Kinsey Institute. "Even if there are biological aspects, it doesn't mean that it is determined or programmed. Human beings are more complicated than that. . . . It's almost impossible to separate environment from biology. Learning changes the brain. Experience changes the brain. It changes it in biological ways. So there is the constant interaction."

Human development, both prenatally and postnatally, is an extremely long process that's subject to many untold influences along the way. Scientists theorize that there may be a genetic predisposition to be homosexual that's stronger in some people than in others. A yet-to-be-determined environmental influence could "push" people toward or away from their innate bent.

That environmental influence could possibly be prenatal. Some researchers surmise that intrauterine hormones coursing through the developing brain of an unborn fetus could determine whether the fetus's genetic predisposition toward homosexuality will be realized.

"The weight of evidence is that sexual orientation is determined either before birth or very early in life, in very early childhood," says the University of Minnesota's Remafedi. "I believe that sexual orientation is biologically based, and that environment simply influences expression."

He uses height as an analogy. Environmental influences such as diet, for example, can determine whether an infant lives up to its genetic expectations in height as an adult. A baby boy who is malnourished may not develop into the strapping six-foot-tall young man that his genes have programmed him to be. Likewise, an infant predisposed to be homosexual may not get the environmental push—whether before or after birth—that would cause him to grow up gay, says Remafedi. Or he may have the correct combination of influences that would contribute to a homosexual orientation.

A study at the University of California at Los Angeles by psychiatrist Dr. Richard Green suggests that the environmental push could occur after a child is born, as his or her personality develops. Green followed a group of forty-four effeminate, or "sissy," boys from childhood into adulthood. During their childhood, their play habits included gender-atypical behavior, such as playing with dolls, dressing in girl's clothes, or taking the role of the mother when playing house. Green found that three quarters of the boys grew into gay or bisexual adults.[10]

Was the influence born or bred? For now, the best researchers can do is to say that sexual orientation is caused by a complex and mysterious interaction of genetic, biological, and environmental influences. "When we find out why someone is heterosexual, it'll be a lot easier to find out why some people aren't," says University of Washington pediatrician Deisher.

Anthropologists have detected homosexuality in many if not all societies, though an intolerance in some societies inhibits the expression of homosexual behavior. Biologists and zoologists have observed same-sex behavior among animals—western gulls and stump-tailed macaques, for example—suggesting again that sexual orientation is genetically based.

"In my opinion the smart scientists are realizing that biology is not zero," says psychobiologist Weinrich. "There are some scientists who would continue to fight tooth and nail the idea that the genetic contribution might be anything other than zero. But they are very much going out of fashion. They have no data to support their point of view. That position is rapidly crumbling."

The Ramifications

For some, the argument over the cause of homosexuality is pointless. As gay and lesbian teens repeatedly ask, Why would someone choose to join a group that nearly everybody hates? Their only "choice," they say, is choosing whether to be out or not.

Some gay activists see research into the origin of homosexuality as potentially dangerous. Isolating "gay genes" could lead to an insidious practice of genetically "fixing" or aborting homosexual fetuses.

Still others maintain that if homosexuality were found to be largely inborn, opponents of gay rights would be stripped of their credibility and long-held justifications for discrimination would become moot.

"If they find out that homosexuality has a biological base and therefore the person is not responsible for its development, that would be enough for some people to take another look at it," says psychologist Evelyn Hooker. Now eighty-seven, Hooker has been called "the Mother Teresa of gays and lesbians" for her 1957 landmark study that showed no pathological differences between homosexual men and heterosexual men on psychological tests. Her early work led the American Psychiatric Association to remove homosexuality as an illness from its diagnostic handbook.

"I think the evidence seems to be increasing that there is a genetic or biological contribution to this," she says. "But even if the basis is biological, that doesn't make the problems for the individual any less. To say, 'Oh well, it's biological. Let's not be concerned about it,' that is throwing the children to the wolves."

Evidence leading to a conclusion that homosexuality is partly innate may be enough to change the minds of some people, Hooker says. "But a lot of people will say, 'It doesn't make any difference. They should not *act* on it.' For many reasons, all those people on the extreme right are going to take that position, no matter what happens. If it's biologically determined, that doesn't make any difference to them. But it will help enormously for reasonably minded individuals, who really seek to understand what this phenomenon is.

"Nobody knows what the basis of homosexuality is today," Hooker reasserts. "Whatever the basis, it's a steady and impossible pattern to change."

7

Michele I:

Just Too Busy for the Boys

As a girl, Michele Boyer had the world on a string. She'd been granted all the necessary benefits a kid would want in life—two loving parents, an army of close friends, and a natural gift for schoolwork and athletics. Her life was blessed. Or so it seemed.

Michele was the older of two children in the Boyer family. Bright and talented, she learned to play the piano at age eight and brought home straight A's consistently in school. Sports became her passion, year round. By age ten, she was a medalist in downhill skiing competitions and a standout on a city football team. In junior and senior high schools, she was a starting guard on the girls' basketball squads. She graduated from high school as salutatorian in 1984 and was accepted into a private liberal-arts college in Minneapolis on a full academic scholarship.

With all that she had accomplished and all the support she had garnered along the way, the passage from adolescence to adulthood should have been a vitalizing and adventurous time for Michele. It shouldn't have been such a strain for the self-assured young woman to simply be herself. But as with many lesbian and gay teens, Michele was gripped by an unaccountable ambivalence as she came of age. As her sexual identity emerged, she was torn by society's fixed yet conflicting rules on gender and sexual affection. Traces of an inner dissonance surfaced first in junior high and then manifested again in her abuse of alcohol in high school. A panicky confusion flared up late in her first year of college as she struggled to sort out her sexuality. By the time she was a college sophomore, her world had turned doleful and colorless. Racked by self-doubt and engulfed by depression, she finally was admitted into a hospital for treatment.

Joe and Colleen Boyer met in Pittsburgh, Pennsylvania. Joe was a traveling salesman for a manufacturing firm based in downtown Pittsburgh, where Colleen worked as a secretary in the advertising department. A lover of the North Woods, Joe had moved his base of operations to Menominee, Michigan, just across the Wisconsin border on the western shores of Lake Michigan. Menominee was a tourist center and paper-mill town of barely seven thousand people. So when Joe and Colleen married in 1965, Colleen reluctantly traded the hustle and bustle of Pittsburgh for the slow-paced serenity of Small Town, USA. She abandoned her career. Her children became her life's devotion.

The Boyers owned a large two-story house on the good side of town, one block from the frosty northern waters of Lake Michigan's Green Bay. They were an active and carefree family. Michele and her younger brother, Joe Jr., enjoyed ski trips each winter to the family's log cabin and excursions with their parents each summer to Pittsburgh to visit their grandparents. "It felt like we had everything we needed," recalls Michele.

As a girl, Michele spent every clement day outside playing with her neighborhood friends, biking to the corner Dairy Queen, swimming in the lake nearby, or kicking a football around Triangle Park. She was called a tomboy, and didn't mind the label. Rather, she wore it with pride, cognizant that a greater value was placed on the activities of boys than on the activities of girls.

In third grade, Michele joined the YMCA football league—the only girl to sign up. Her father coached. Playing running back and defensive end, Michele was cheered for succeeding in a male-dominated role, praised for exhibiting masculine qualities. And she welcomed the high regard. Being singled out as the only girl to play an organized sport boosted her self-confidence and validated her self-worth.

"I kind of bought into the idea that boy stuff is better than girl stuff," Michele says. She felt somewhat superior to girls who didn't excel in sports, superior to her more feminine friends—girls *and* boys. She knew through observations that effeminate boys were held in low esteem by peers and adults as well. "*Sissy* had a much more negative connotation than *tomboy*," she says. Being recognized as having "boyish" attributes was gratifying.

As she grew older, her masculine gender identification set her apart from most of the other girls. But she was comfortable with the distinction and defiant of any suggestion that she should change. "I think people expected me to outgrow it, but I thought, Why? This is how I am," she says. Her father, meanwhile, encouraged her to join not only the boys' football team but boys' Little League baseball as well. And though her mother tried to persuade her to put on a dress or play with a doll now and then, she never berated Michele for rejecting the play habits that were associated more traditionally with girls.

When she was ten, Michele was profiled in the *Menominee Herald-Leader,* the local newspaper. The article focused on her status as the sole girl on the YMCA's football team. Under the headline "Michele Boyer: Earringed gridder," the story included a quote by Michele's mother:

"One day Michele said, 'Mom, I'd rather be a boy. They can do so much more than a girl,'" said Mrs. Boyer. "I told her a girl can pursue anything she really wants."

Colleen Boyer's feminist outlook made a lasting mark on her daughter. *"Girls are as good as boys,"* Michele echoed proudly in the article, *"and should have the same freedom to try."*

Sixth grade threw Michele for a loss. She had graduated from elementary school into junior high—a grade level with a whole new set of expectations for a girl on the brink of puberty. Her girlfriends had discovered boys, a subject she had no interest in whatsoever. To complicate matters, there were no girls' sports teams in the sixth grade, and consequently no easy avenue to conformity. Her years playing football in the Y league were over. And for the first time in her life, Michele felt alone, unpopular, and uneasy with who she was.

"I felt dorky," she says, looking back. "Socially, I felt lost. I was always a popular kid in elementary school. I didn't know how to feel included, and I never had to try before. It was such an effort. I didn't know why what had once seemed so easy now seemed so foreign. I felt very out of touch." Her girlfriends had replaced their jeans and ponytails with dresses and perms. "And I remember thinking, Oh my God, what am I going to do? I don't even own a curling iron. I was uncomfortable with this new girl culture. But I don't think I had any awareness as to why."

Conversations with girls at school inevitably would center on boys. "I'd heard there was one boy who wanted to go out with me," says Michele. "And I thought, Uh-uh, and just kept putting him off."

Her identity crisis passed. In seventh and eighth grades, Michele made the girls' basketball team as the starting point-guard and regained her self-esteem through team sports. She was relieved to have something to focus on other than hairstyles and boys. Once again, she had a set of friends with whom she shared a common interest. "I felt part of a group. I felt like people were getting to know me," Michele says. "I had a place."

With Michele leading the way, the eighth-grade Menominee Maroons finished their season undefeated and captured the conference championship in the season finale by beating their crosstown rivals by one point. The championship game and the net-cutting celebration afterward highlighted a glorious year for Michele, a year in which she cemented new friendships and gained rank as a first-rate young athlete.

Yet, like some recurring illness, the fleeting feeling of alienation that had shaken the core of her identity in junior high school would visit her again in her later years of adolescence.

Michele couldn't believe her eyes. She was standing at her locker between classes, waiting for her friend and basketball teammate, Tammy, to come by. And suddenly there was Tammy, across the hall—kissing a boy.

Michele was brokenhearted. Since winning a starting position on the Menominee High School girls' varsity basketball team—as the team's only sophomore—Michele had been living in the company of heroes. Tammy was one of them. Michele idolized Tammy, a senior and the team's star center. She was tall and lean, with long brown curly hair, a flaky sense of humor, and a wild streak that infatuated Michele. On and off the court, Tammy liked to tease Michele, not maliciously, but in a playful, flirtatious way. But all of a sudden Tammy had a boyfriend. And Michele was jealous.

"It was really hard to see her show affection to someone else, because she had shown affection to me," Michele says. Yet she couldn't reconcile her hurt feelings. She had no good justification for her jealousy, so she let it pass and buried it away.

When Michele was old enough to drive, her parents bought her a used Buick Skylark. The huge car became a party-on-wheels for Michele and her friends. They would cruise the back streets of Menominee on their way to a dance or a party, often with a six-pack of beer or a bottle of syrupy liqueur on the front seat. Alcohol released Michele from her inhibitions. She would become the life of the party, animated and comical, and completely at ease in social settings.

"More and more, I was using alcohol to try to avoid uncomfortable parties and things, where I knew there would be boys," she says. She drank a lot, more than most of her friends. "I took the first sips and made sure I had the last."

In her four years at Menominee High, she went out with only two boys. Her first "boyfriend" fizzled out after only a few weeks. As a junior, she began dating Jim, a shy young man the same age as Michele. Jim and Michele occasionally would go to parties and movies together. They kissed "maybe four times," recalls Michele, and never came close to having sex. By then, her parents were resigned to the fact that Michele, for whatever reason, was just not interested in boys. Her mother had formed a credible excuse: "She's so active in sports, she's just too busy for the boys."

When Jim asked Michele to the senior prom, she obliged him, feeling pressured to comply with the norms of adolescence. With little enthusiasm, she gave in to each of the high school customs. "It was the epitome of heterosexual ceremony," Michele says. She picked out a formal dress, had her hair styled, pinned a corsage to her gown, and posed with Jim for the standard before-prom photographs. "It was really hard," she says, "because there were expectations for me. And I really didn't know what those expectations were." Before the dance, they sat in Jim's car in the high school parking lot and guzzled a bottle of cheap champagne.

Despite the moments of discomfort and doubt, high school by and large had been a satisfying time for Michele. She had made a name for herself as a champion athlete and had won wide acceptance in her school and community. By earning sterling grades, she graduated second in her class. Her triumphs made her parents proud. When she decided to go to an out-of-state college, they backed her wholeheartedly. Michele was chosen as one of seven recipients of the President's Scholarship at Augsburg College in Minneapolis, a small Lutheran school in the heart of the city.

"I was ready to go," she says. "I didn't ever want to come back to Menominee. I was ready to go to Minneapolis and *stay* in Minneapolis." Prince's movie *Purple Rain* had just shown at Menominee's only movie theater. It depicted Minneapolis's club scene and glamorized the life of the androgynous rock star. And somewhere, Michele had heard about a gay bar in downtown Minneapolis that had a small lounge just for lesbians. Though she admitted to nothing, the bar represented a beacon of sexual freedom that she never had encountered in her hometown.

On a balmy evening in May during Michele's first year of college, a friend named Shelly invited her to go to a softball game. Shelly was a good friend of Dena, a pitcher on one of the teams. Through the grapevine, Michele had heard that Dena was a self-identified lesbian. Michele wanted to meet her. She knew that after the ball games,

Shelly and Dena often went to a St. Paul bar called the Castle that was known to be a hangout for lesbians. Michele was curious to get a look inside.

Michele had been playing softball herself during her freshman year at Augsburg College, and there had been rumors that her coach was gay. But they were only rumors. None of the half-dozen women she knew who were suspected of being lesbians were "out." Except for Dena.

After the game, the three women decided to go out for a drink. Shelly drove, with Dena in the front seat and Michele riding in back, carefully committing to memory the route to the Castle. The women shared a six-pack along the way.

The Castle was built into the side of a steep cliff above the Mississippi River near downtown St. Paul. Inside, fake stalagmites and stalactites extended from the floor and ceiling, giving the place the eerie appearance of a cavern, with tables set into dark, small catacombs throughout.

This is what gay bars are like? Michele thought. Pretty weird.

Days earlier, Michele had broken up with a man whom she had been dating seriously for nearly five months. John was three years older than Michele, a transfer student from the University of Illinois in Chicago who was studying philosophy at Augsburg. Tender and introspective, John opened new doors of awareness for Michele. The two would stay up all night in John's dorm room, drinking wine, listening to jazz, discussing religion, psychology, politics—things she had never contemplated back home in Menominee. John was unlike anyone she had ever known. She was fascinated by his intellect and maturity, and thought she was falling in love.

But from somewhere within, an emotional roadblock sprang up. John was looking for commitment from Michele. The two had had sex, but never intercourse, and Michele could see that their relationship was heading that way. But the idea of such intimacy with John made her squirm.

"I wasn't attracted to him," she explains. "He started picking up on that and felt hurt." She began giving him the same bogus excuse her

mother had used years before: She was too busy for an intimate relationship—"too busy for the boys."

After dodging John for several days, Michele finally told him she
was breaking off their relationship. When asked for a reason, she
couldn't supply one—to John or herself. Here's a guy who's *perfect,*
she pondered. Intelligent, good-looking. Why am I not attracted to
him?

Part of the mystery was revealed that night at the Castle. Something had been rising in her for years, something tenuous and fright-
eningly vague, yet undeniable. The signals had become hard to
ignore—her strong infatuations with other women, her inexplicable
rejection of John. She knew she was on the brink of an awakening.

"The minute I walked into that bar, I knew it was for me," Michele
recalls. "I saw women dancing with women, and it looked so natural. I
felt really comfortable. It was like, *I'm home.*"

Michele ran into a woman she knew from Augsburg, an older student who also was purported to be gay. She confided in Michele,
telling her that, yes, she was a lesbian. But as they talked, she tearfully
described the emotional turmoil she had experienced since her roommate spread the word that she was a lesbian. She was desperately
afraid of what her parents might do if they found out and had decided
to take a year off school to recover from the trauma of being "outed."
It was absolutely necessary, she said, to hide her sexual orientation,
even from close friends.

Michele's experience that night was a slap in the face. On the one
hand, she was relieved to have confronted the internal quandary that
had been gnawing at her for so long. But on the other hand, taking
into account the dismal reports she had been hearing about women
who were lesbians—and the dark impressions at the Castle—she saw
the lifestyle of lesbians as tragic and oppressive, hardly something to
celebrate. The message became clear: If you're gay, stay quiet, stay
hidden, stay invisible.

The next day, news that Michele had been to the Castle reached another Augsburg student, a woman named Robin. She caught up with
Michele in a park on campus with a ready question:

"Is it true where you went last night?" Robin asked.

"Yeah," said Michele.

"Well, I've been there too," Robin confessed.

And suddenly, just weeks before the end of the school year, Michele found herself among a tiny group of Augsburg lesbians—all of them closeted. Robin became her closet confidante. She spent hours discussing her homosexuality with Michele, recounting her own coming-out experience. Though Robin had come out to herself two years earlier, she still kept her sexual orientation private. And, like Michele, she had no contacts within the lesbian community—with lesbian organizations or support groups or other resources.

Michele needed to know more, more about homosexuality—and herself. Questions began to fester: Was this her destiny, to live a life filled with secrecy and guilt? Were her feelings toward other women normal? Would she ever find acceptance for being gay? Could she face her parents with her discovery?

With her first year of college at an end, Michele left Minneapolis for the summer. Back home in Menominee, she visited the local library one day. After thumbing nervously through the index cards, she located a thick, dog-eared book entitled *Understanding Homosexuality*. She stuffed the book into her backpack and smuggled it out of the building.

8

Tara I:

"Ode to a Gym Teacher"

Tara Lumley wants nothing to do with labels. Too limiting, she says. Too conditional. When it comes to sexual identity, about the only label she'll settle for is "queer."

Tara has had a long and loving relationship with a man. And she's had several long and loving relationships with women. Does that make her a former heterosexual? A current homosexual? A bisexual?

She remembers wanting to be just like one of the boys when she was a kid. She recalls having intense teenage crushes on women gym teachers and high school friends. And she thrills at the memory of being in the company of thousands of women at the 1993 Michigan Womyn's Festival. If that fits the definition of a lesbian, well, fine, she says. But she also went to the high school prom with a young man and later came very close to marrying another.

"I'm more queer than straight," she allows. "There's absolutely no way I could see myself marrying a man. And there's no way I could go back in the closet. The only reason I would consider myself 'bi' would be, if I fall in love with someone, there's not going to be any physical boundaries of who that person is. . . . If I meet someone, I don't care who they are—male, female, black, white, green, blue—if I love 'em, well, fine."

Tara Lumley grew up in Clearwater, Minnesota, a small town an hour and a half from Minneapolis and seven miles down the road from the city of St. Cloud. When a freeway was built, splitting Clearwater in half, a strip mall went up and the Main Street businesses died, putting many of the residents out of work. Tara's family lived on the poor side of town. Her mother took a job as a cashier at a truck stop, while her father worked as a factory machinist just outside of Minneapolis. Tara, an only child, spent her days roaming around with her collie mix, her cousins, and the neighborhood "welfare babies," as she calls them.

In 1979, when she was six, her parents separated and divorced, and Tara and her father moved in with her grandmother on a farm two miles out of town. Her father had grown up on the farm and began farming again, planting soybeans and raising hogs. Tara's mother, meanwhile, moved into an apartment in St. Cloud.

Tara still played with the friends she had made in town. "I preferred to hang out with the boys more than playing house, and I don't know if that was because they were older or more interesting." Her Christmas toys were miniature John Deere tractors, semi trucks, and Hot Wheels cars. She favored her Ken doll over Barbie.

When she was seven or eight, the games of the older boys turned sexual. "I was doing a lot of sexploration," she recalls, "even at those young ages"—playing doctor or Dracula, coming home with hickeys on her neck. "It kind of got carried away in the course of being in contact with those boys." At age nine, she found herself in a closet with a couple of boys who were trying to talk her into having sex. "They wanted to have intercourse," she says. "I remember they had their penises out and they wanted to try it. I don't remember any penetration or anything, but we tried."

Sex was something she had always known about. At age seven, after Tara walked in on her father and his girlfriend while they were having sex, her mother sat her down and "had the little talk," Tara says, explaining precisely how babies are made.

If she was a precocious child, Tara was also an inquisitive student. She was especially good in her reading class. But again, her impetuous nature would get her into trouble. She was a playground tough in grade school, getting in fights during recess, almost always with a boy.

When she was in fourth grade, Tara and her father moved into a mobile home outside of Clearwater. Placed in a new school, it took her a while to make friends. But when she began playing team sports, she found acceptance among her teammates.

At her new school, Tara again fell in with "a trouble crowd"—a cousin, a girl classmate, and some "loser boys" who were three or four years older than she was. They would all cut school and bike down a dirt road alongside a river to smoke cigarettes and drink beer.

Puberty came early for Tara. At age eleven, she was the tallest and most shapely girl in her class. "I couldn't fit through the monkey bars anymore because I was getting hips and breasts," she says. "I have this great picture of when I was eleven, playing with Matchbox cars in my bra and underwear."

She could later joke about it, but at the time, Tara was dreadfully self-conscious about her changing body. It was not fair, she complained. "Me, of all people, who really didn't want to be a girl, who really didn't want to wear a bra—I felt like I was being forced into it. Why did I have to look like a girl when I didn't do girl things?"

Tara lost her virginity during the summer after sixth grade. Other girls were also having sex at the time, she says. It was what all the kids were doing. But her first time would be the only time until later in adolescence.

Tara's early physical development proved to have one big advantage: It turned her into a solid young athlete. By seventh grade, she was the star shortstop on her fast-pitch softball team. Junior high school had thrown her interest suddenly to women's athletics—and, just as suddenly, to other women. There were four gym teachers at her school. "I had a crush on two of them, the two females." Tara would hang out in the gym or tag along with them between classes.

"They were women that I could have some kind of contact with, who would give me some attention," she says. "But I wanted more attention."

Years later, Tara could identify her crushes in the lyrics of the song "Ode to a Gym Teacher," by Meg Christian:

She was a big tough woman
The first to come along
That showed me being female
Meant you still could be strong
And though graduation meant that we had to part
She'll always be a player on the ballfield of my heart

Tara divided her time between her home with her father and her home with her mother. Her parents had both remarried, and her mother lived with her new husband in a huge four-bedroom house with a hot tub in a suburb of Minneapolis, Elk River. Tara had her own bedroom and half the downstairs to herself.

But going into eighth grade, Tara again was at a new school, and again without any friends. But this time was harder. The students in junior high had already formed their cliques. And outsiders weren't very welcome.

"I didn't fit in with the party crowd anymore," Tara says. "I didn't fit in anywhere." She began throwing herself into her schoolwork, and scored A's in all of her classes. "That's when I found out that learning wasn't such a bad thing. I pretty much did a one-eighty." She was named student of the week on several occasions in science and in social studies.

Yet she was a girl with a past. Stories circulated, most of them originating with Tara herself, about her exploits at previous schools. "If I talked about my experiences, kids were like, 'Oh my God!'" She was shunned because of her reputation and picked on for not wearing fashion designer clothes.

But midway through the year, another new kid appeared, Emily. She sat behind Tara in math class and also was unpopular with the cliques. Tara and Emily started hanging out together. "We were buds," says Tara.

Tara never wore dresses in school. Emily, on the other hand, was very feminine. She wore lots of makeup, frilly blouses, and often came to school in a dress. Tara was intrigued by Emily's looks and had a serious crush on her, but never dared to tell her. One night when she stayed over at Emily's house, Tara noticed with alarm that she was becoming aroused while giving Emily a back rub. But again, she never mentioned it to Emily.

"We hung out over the summer and I got to know her a lot better. We had a lot of fun," Tara says. "I don't know why I would even think that my feelings for her were anything sexual. I just did. I wanted to kiss her. But I definitely knew that she wouldn't be comfortable with that. So that bothered me. If she would have had those feelings too, then I wouldn't have thought anything about it. But I knew that the feelings weren't right, because they weren't mutual. And it wouldn't be the same as having a crush on a boy that didn't acknowledge you."

Tara also was enamored of her softball coach, who was supportive and complimentary of Tara's athletic talents. Tara was flattered by the praise, and charmed by the older woman. "I knew that my feelings for her were definitely sexual," Tara says. "I would fantasize about being a man so I could kiss her." She had a vivid dream that she was a tall man with a mustache, wearing a suit, drinking a glass of wine, and embracing the coach.

Tara would find excuses to talk to her coach about sex. She once mentioned to her that she was considering going on birth-control pills and asked for her advice. But the conversation was only a ploy for Tara to ask about issues of sexuality.

"I think she knew about these feelings I had, even though I didn't know what they were." Tara had no concept of what it meant to be a lesbian. "To me, that lifestyle didn't exist."

In ninth grade, life began to spin too fast for Tara. Too much seemed to be happening at once. She played on the girls' volleyball team in the fall and planned to try out for softball again in the spring. Her grades were still straight A's, and she was nominated to the National Junior Honors Society. But her moods were erratic. She couldn't calm down. "Sometimes I felt like I had too much to handle going on inside."

One day, Tara told Emily she desperately needed to talk to her.

They artfully told their band instructor that they had left their instruments at home and couldn't practice, then huddled in the back of the band room, talking above the din. Class ended, the students filed out, and Tara and Emily stayed behind, skipping their lunch hour. "That's when the talking really started," Tara says.

Sitting on the risers, Tara told her friend that she felt anxious, but couldn't explain why. She was confused and afraid, she said. Emily didn't understand. She pressed Tara for more information. "What do you mean, confused? What's the matter? What are you feeling?"

Tara had an explanation. But she was embarrassed to say the words. "What?" Emily pushed. Finally, Tara let it out. "I think I'm gay," she said.

Emily jumped back three feet and stared at her friend in disbelief. Tara started crying.

"Well, I didn't mean it like that," Emily apologized. "I was just . . . surprised. I'll still be your friend."

"Well that's not all," Tara said, looking into Emily's eyes.

"You have feelings for *me?*" asked Emily.

Tara was humiliated. "If I'm gay, I'm gonna kill myself. It's wrong."

Emily told Tara that she didn't think it was wrong. Her parents had two gay friends, she told her. And they were okay.

But Tara wouldn't be consoled. She never had known anyone gay. "I just thought that gays were hated people," she remembers thinking. "And if that was the case I didn't want to be hated, I didn't want to be evil. I didn't want to be gay."

Over the summer and into the fall of tenth grade, Tara gradually drifted away from Emily. She didn't feel comfortable around her after divulging her secret. The two never again talked about Tara's revelation. Though they had mutual friends, they each went their separate ways.

"I think I was trying to push her away and push away the fact that she knew something about me that I didn't want to know," Tara says. "Every time she was around, I would do something that was really straight, like talk about a guy or someone I was seeing. I definitely wasn't ready to be out."

Tara tried to put any thoughts about women out of her mind. But one day, while flipping through the TV channels, she happened upon a tennis tournament. Martina Navratilova was playing, and Tara paused to watch. She had heard somewhere that Navratilova was living with a woman lover.

"At that time, I had never really heard about her and had never watched tennis," Tara says. "But I was just so intrigued by her."

A world-class athlete, a woman, a lesbian, a hero—"She was everything," Tara says. She was a role model.

9

CODA:

A Mother's Lament

*Raising a gay son, Judith Ulseth was turned into an activist.
She served as a member of the Minnesota Task Force for Gay and
Lesbian Youth for five years, as secretary of the national
Federation of Parents, Families and Friends of Lesbians and
Gays (P-FLAG). But her activism was hardly automatic. Only
after two attempted suicides by her son, Julian, in his early
teenage years did she fully come to know him. Ulseth lives with
her family in a rural community south of the Twin Cities. This is
her story, as she tells it publicly to church groups, in schools, and
at rallies for the rights of gays and lesbians:*

Our son growing up was a mystery to us. He was a mystery. . . .
As soon as he started talking, our son seemed to be quite talented.
He could carry on a conversation even with adults at two and a half.
He used big words in sentences. And he was quite agile. He could ride
a bicycle without training wheels before he was four.

When he would get excited or angry, he would have feminine hand
movements and his voice was quite high-pitched. He was very excitable and very, very active, always. . . . When we noticed he was effeminate, it became a nightmare. Other people noticed it before I did.
I didn't notice it until he was about six or seven. To me, he was perfect. He was an exceptional child. To other people, he was feminine.
We were quite concerned. We even heard adults say that he was a
"fairy" and whatnot. So, after he was six or so, we started to worry
about his behavior.

I remember, Julian was a natural athlete, a backyard gymnast. . . . But there was a day that marked the end of his athletic abilities. We were roller-skating and my husband told him that none of the other boys were skating with their hands, and couldn't he skate more like the other boys? He was so self-conscious about moving like a girl, he never participated again unless we insisted that he participate. He's never forgotten that.

At first Julian loved school, he loved learning. But he lost more and more interest as each year came along. He was very unhappy. He came home one day and asked me what "queer" meant, why kids were calling him a "queer." It started in kindergarten. First it was older kids on the bus that would say that about him. To make matters worse, he had one real good friend, and she happened to be a girl. Of course, when the older kids starting calling him that, then the younger kids picked it up. We always told him, "Well, that'll stop. As children get older, they get over those silly name-calling things." But we were wrong. It got worse.

We're not strict parents. I was quite free with Julian. But when he started having trouble, we tried to teach him to be more like the other kids so that he wouldn't be hurt. The way he walked and the way he carried himself was more like a girl. But he was determined to be himself. . . . It never occurred to me that it was a simple matter of him being homosexual. My husband and I didn't know anything about gays. . . .

When he had to have his school checkup—I suppose he was six—my husband said, "Why don't you ask the doctor whether he may be lacking in male hormones?" And I thought it was a funny request. The doctor said that he was a perfectly normal, very intelligent child, very artistic, and not to worry about him. He said that if there was any shortage of male hormones, there would be nothing he could do about it anyway.

For his eleventh birthday, he had a party at our house. And my husband decided that he should learn how to play touch football. So they went out in the front yard. My husband and Julian were both near tears the whole time. It was very painful to watch. It's just like a photograph in my mind. . . . My husband tried so hard to teach him and get him to enjoy it, and my son tried so hard to enjoy it. And he just didn't.

Julian was so stubborn. He was stubborn because he was confident in himself. It was the rest of the world that was crazy. . . .

It escalated. By the time he was to start seventh grade, we decided to move. And one of the reasons was to give him a fresh start. That was a big mistake, because we moved to a rural area, and it grew worse. The first day of school they tripped him on the stairs and called him names—"queer," "faggot." Even the teachers. If he complained about how he was treated, they said, "Well, if you didn't act that way, they wouldn't treat you that way." Like he was doing some behavior on purpose, when he was only being himself.

It took Julian about a year, he was fourteen then, to come out and tell us he was gay. The news was a revelation to me because I suddenly knew that we had been fighting something that could not be fought. Oh, sure, I was upset and didn't know what to do next, but at the same time it was the piece of information we needed to understand why Julian was so troubled. He was still the same little Viking that saved his allowance and bought me a house plant, who read stories to his little sister and made sure she was safe, who was narrator for the Christmas program at church. . . .

He attempted suicide once that I didn't know about. I heard about that later. He said he tried to hang himself. But I didn't know. The next time, I believe, he was maybe fourteen or fifteen. He felt quite isolated, even though we took him to a youth group and we were really trying to support him. He wanted to go see a friend who lived in the Twin Cities. I had three children and it was twenty-five miles to drive him there. And I just said, "I cannot do it now." Well, he must've been having a terrible day. He went right upstairs and swallowed a bottle of codeine that I had in my medicine cabinet and slit his wrists with a razor blade.

I came upstairs. He told me what he did and he made himself throw up. I found a pool of blood in the bedroom. . . .

I was terrified. But I tried to be very calm so that he wouldn't know how upset I was. I could tell that he didn't need to go to the hospital.

He had just done it so quickly. He had gone straight upstairs and done it. He was saying: We have to do something different. Look at me. The message to me was that I had to do something else. What we were doing wasn't good enough. I planned to find someplace else for him to go to school.

He was sorry. He didn't know why he did it. After that, we talked a lot more. We kept trying to make sure that he saw his friends often, the ones that he could talk to. And we really listened to his needs. That's when we went for counseling, the three of us, with a gay psychologist. We had to take him out of school to do that.

The next thing I noticed was that Julian's expectations for himself had changed. He believed all the stereotypes about gay men. He actually thought he had to be promiscuous and all the other stereotypical garbage that is so untrue. That's when I knew that he absolutely had to have our love and support to help him understand himself and to keep him from seeking help from strangers who might take advantage of him.

> But the emotional deprivation had taken its toll on Julian. Soon after, he dropped out of school and transferred to an alternative high school run by Quakers in Northern California. He later moved to San Francisco.

Now that he lives in California, he says there's days go by that he doesn't even think about being gay. He is so comfortable in his life that being gay isn't a big issue. He's just himself. He just doesn't think about being gay all the time. . . .

He had to be out. When you start attempting suicide and stuff, you have got to make changes in your life. And he had to be himself. But he couldn't be himself here. So he had to leave. When you're fine with who you are, you have to be who you are. And that's the way it was for him. He had to leave so he could be himself.

10

INTERLUDE:

Voices of Courage

No two coming-out stories are alike. Though a common thread runs through each tale of disclosure, the act of coming out is as distinctive as the person behind the secret.

Some choose to "crash out," telling everyone they know as fast as they can. Others are more oblique, divulging their mystery by letter or proxy. Still others "leak" the information gradually through telltale signs and actions. Many never get the chance to say the words at all. They're "outed" by others or found out accidentally or forced out through personal inquest.

But no matter how abrupt or subtle the technique, with the simple statement "I'm gay" or "I'm a lesbian," a secret is uncovered and a life is changed forever.

JAMES   The first person James came out to was his high school counselor. He was a senior. But long before then, he knew he was somehow different than the other kids.

"I remember in the first grade, I liked little boys, not little girls," he says. "You just know. You know all your life. But you're scared, 'cause everyone tells you you've got to be a heterosexual, you've got to produce kids, man and a woman."

When James had graduated from high school, he figured he'd tell his mother he was gay—over the telephone. He got a little drunk, then dialed her home, long-distance, in Oklahoma.

"That was the hardest thing I ever did," he says. "I remember when I told her, I started crying. She called me a faggot and a queer. She was crying, so I hung up on her. . . . But I called her back."

SUSAN   Susan was thirteen when she told her therapist she thought she might be a lesbian. Her therapist panicked and called Susan's mother. "She outed me to my mom," says Susan. But her mother, a registered nurse, handled the news well and told her daughter that she had known all along.

Her father, on the other hand, refused to believe Susan. "He said I was looking for a label and just rebelling."

JOSEPH   Joseph came out to his family—and the world—on a public-television talk show about sex and teenagers. He was a senior in high school.

"My mother was shocked out of her wits," says Joseph, with more than a little vengeance in his eyes. "And she was really a bitch about it. She treated me like I had AIDS."

Joseph doesn't go out of his way to spare his parents any discomfort. His spite and antagonism is payback for what he sees as abuse and persecution because he's gay, he says. He's bitter that his parents won't accept his gayness. "I'm me and I'm not going to deny it anymore," he says. "I'm sick of acting every day, twenty-four hours a day, every day of the year."

During the school year, Joseph packs his days with hours of extracurricular activities to take himself out of his home and away from his parents. He competed on the school speech team, sang in the school choir, and acted with theater groups at his school and church. He's a junior assistant scoutmaster with the Boy Scouts, and lives for Saturday afternoon episodes of *Star Trek: The Next Generation*.

Joseph says he has known he was gay since long before puberty. He believes the suppression of his sexual orientation—by his parents and himself—has contributed to a raft of emotional problems and psychological disorders that have led him to treatment centers and even a brief stay in jail in his eighteen years.

"My mother called them 'Joseph problems,' " he says. "I call them family problems." He has taken medications, mostly for depression, and tried to kill himself several times, he says, once by eating rat poison.

His family problems became serious during the summer between his junior and senior years. Joseph was arrested for scuffling with his mother and charged with fifth-degree assault. He spent a couple of days in jail. A judge removed him from his home and ordered him not to contact his mother for six months. He moved in with his great-grandmother.

VICKY "I was attending junior high school," Vicky relates. "I was thirteen. I had never had a crush on anyone, but one night I had this incredible dream about a girl in my class. All that happened in the dream was that our palms touched. But upon awakening, I was instantly, irrevocably in love. I had never felt like this before. I hardly knew the girl. We had some classes together, but never talked. In fact, she disliked me. Until this point, I hardly thought about her. I knew that my feelings of wanting to kiss her and be with her every waking moment were what lesbians did. I knew that this also meant I wasn't supposed to share these feelings with anyone. . . . At this early point, I didn't decide that I was a lesbian yet. I just decided not to think about that part of it. I hoped it was a passing phase."

Then came the next crush, and the next, and after a number of "serial crushes" on girls in junior and senior high school, Vicky was convinced by age seventeen that she was a lesbian. But she decided she had to keep it to herself.

"My family was fundamentalist/apocalyptic Christian, very religious, and didn't even encourage me to date boys," she says, "so I just rode my bicycle around town for hours every afternoon, hoping to accidentally see one of the girls I had a crush on mowing the lawn or going out to her mailbox."

The isolation was excruciating. "I was desperately afraid that I would never be able to be happy as a lesbian," Vicky says. "I knew that my family would disown me. I even thought maybe God would punish me. For a few years I toyed with the idea that either I would kill myself or be a lesbian. I knew that I could not live the straight life and get married to some guy. I had absolutely no attraction to boys, and the thought of marrying one was terrifying. Everyone in my church was getting married at seventeen, eighteen, nineteen. My sister was getting married to a guy we'd grown up with."

While still in high school, she had an affair with a teacher. "She was forty-four and had a daughter who was a year younger than me, who went to my *school*. Needless to say, it was all very confusing, but exciting as well. The moment right after we kissed for the first time, I ran to the mirror and looked at myself. I was ecstatic. I thought I would look different. I said in a barely audible whisper, 'I'm a lesbian.' About six months later, we stopped being physically sexual, at my request. I was racked with guilt feelings and knew that it was out of control. I was terrified of someone finding out. . . .

"I decided during the end of my freshman year in college that I would *not* kill myself, but that I would be a lesbian. The next step was coming out to my family. But I didn't have to, because my mother read my diary. I was finally having a relationship with a woman I'd been trying to seduce for months, and I'd written about our lovemaking in minute detail. My mother must have read it all because she looked like a ghost when she approached me. She said, 'I finally know who you really are.' But I was the same exact person she always knew and loved, only happier, stronger. It broke my heart. I had been very close to my mother, her favorite. . . . Nothing between us has ever been the same.

"It's been about seven years and my family still won't have anything to do with me, although my mother does call me about once a year (she only lives twenty-five minutes away) to see if I am okay. She won't hug or kiss me. It's really painful. I've let her go quite a bit since it happened, but it still hurts tremendously. My sister is the same, only she won't talk to me at all, and won't take my phone calls. . . .

"I never apologized for being a lesbian and never denied it after that night. And I'm thankful for that, for being strong enough at that point to avoid that shame."

CHRIS   Chris came out when he was eighteen. It was traumatic for his parents. His mother blamed herself and cried for days. She asked him to go to a psychologist to make sure it wasn't a phase.

His stepfather said his announcement was like hearing his son's death sentence, that he would surely become infected with the AIDS virus.

"My dad said, by accepting this, they were nailing the lid on my coffin."

GARY   The first time Gary used the word *gay* to describe himself to his father was in a seven-page handwritten coming-out letter, written years after he had come out to himself. Gary knew the announcement was long overdue; and his father lived only thirty minutes away, but he felt most comfortable putting pen to paper and sending it through the mail.

"You must understand that I am happy," he wrote. "I am secure with myself. I have been in touch with my feelings, emotions, and thoughts for years. I am healthy and in no 'risk groups,' as the media may label, and due to my extensive knowledge, I'm *not at risk* for infection of HIV. I'm saying this because this letter is, in no way, an attempt to seek approval, educate you, perpetuate any fear, defend myself or try to make you become less prejudicial. . . . I'm assuming, Dad, that you have had prior education on 'Gay/Lesbian 101' and what it is to 'come out.' With some basic, accurate knowledge, we have a good chance of being closer. . . ."

Shortly after sending the letter, Gary received a card in the mail, signed by his father and stepmother. It read: "We love and support you in any of your decisions in life."

LIZ   "Well, *this* one won't have grandchildren" were the first words out of the mouth of Liz's mother when Liz told her she was a lesbian. Her grandmother insisted it was a phase. Her aunt and uncle wouldn't allow her near her three-month-old niece. "And I have another uncle who won't even speak to me."

Rejected by her family, Liz found acceptance at a teen center for gay and lesbian youth, where she began volunteering her time.

PHILIP   Brought up by parents who were Jehovah's Witnesses, Philip knew he would have a tough time coming out to his family. And he was right. After telling his folks he was gay at age fifteen, he says, he was physically chased out of his home by his father and mother. He hopped a bus for Seattle.

Philip lived on the streets for six months, squatting in an abandoned apartment, nailing up plywood in the door and open windows to keep out the rain and cold. He drank a lot and took drugs, he says, as an escape. But after tracking down a social-service agency in the gay community, he eventually went back to school, got his high school GED certificate, found a job, and enrolled in a community college.

Philip occasionally talks to his parents, but their relationship is strained, largely, he says, because their religious beliefs condemn homosexuality as sinful.

"My mom says that I should be celibate and devote myself to God. And I know that that's not possible," he says. "If you live your life, doing what you think is right, God's going to see that, see what you truly believe inside, in your heart. And if you live your life doing what you don't believe in, what you think is wrong, God's going to see that too.

"I'm sure that my mom loves me, and I love her too. But if she wants to be part of my life, she has to be part of all of it, not just the parts that *she* likes."

DAVE   "My mom wasn't too happy about it. But after I was able to show her what homosexuality truly was, she got a lot better attitude about it. When my mom first found out, she immediately told my sister, without my permission. My sister has a twelve-year-old son that I'm around a lot, and she totally freaked. She thought that I had molested her son. Her exact words were: 'I swear to God, if you ever touched my son I'll kill you!' I'd never do something so terrible as molesting a child (which is what I see him as), and I assured her of that. She lately has been making up sorry excuses for him not to be allowed to spend the night over here."

BRANDON Brandon told his mother he was gay when he was fourteen. "My mom was fine with it," he recalls. "She's an ex-hippie."

The word got around quickly in school that Brandon was gay. Once, when he was on his paper route, a couple of classmates knocked him off his bike. Out of self-defense, Brandon bit one of his attackers, he says, and police required him to take a blood test for HIV.

He was in the ninth grade. Police took no action against his attackers.

KAREN Coming out didn't begin for Karen until after adolescence. "I was kind of going along, assuming I was heterosexual," she says. "But looking back, I see little warning signs, like in junior high when I would go to the beach with my friends, I would always look at the women. . . . I assumed that all the other girls I was with were doing the same thing and no one was talking about it."

It wasn't until she was twenty-two, a senior at a Lutheran college and living in the campus ministry house, that she fully recognized her attractions to other women. She was having lunch one day with a gay friend, and a woman came by to bum a cigarette. Karen had seen the woman around campus before, and wanted to get to know her. But she didn't know how to approach her.

"And my friend said, 'I heard that she's a lesbian.' And the minute he said that it just clicked. I realized, Oh. I have a crush on this woman. That's what it is." She eventually got up the courage to ask the woman out, and thus began a relationship that lasted for a year and a half.

"Finally, for the first time, I felt like who I was," Karen says. "I finally felt like I found myself. Whereas all through high school and college I was trying on all these different hats and things to see who I was. It wasn't until I came out that I felt like I found the hat that fit."

Karen describes herself as a "femme lesbian." Throughout her girlhood and adolescence, she played with feminine things, exhibited feminine mannerisms, and wore feminine clothes. "In high school, I was on the dance line. That's a pretty girlie-girlie thing. We had pompoms and everything," she says. "I had taken dance lessons starting when I was five, ballet and tap and jazz lessons. I always liked that. I competed in figure skating. I played softball when I was in fourth grade and I was terrible at it. I tried it, but it just wasn't for me."

After coming out, she had a tough time finding acceptance within the lesbian community because of her inclination to follow feminine gender roles. "I had a harder time coming out as a femme in my own community than I did coming out as a lesbian to my friends," says Karen. "It was a really hard struggle. I felt like I came out so I knew who I was and I was happy about that, but there was still something that was unsettled.

"It was some of the real subtle things," she explains. "People would make jokes about the typical role of women and how women should look. Those types of things—making fun of cheerleaders or being weak, like that was selling out. Which to me is a direct slam. But they didn't make that connection, because they assumed only straight women were like that. Butch women will make jokes about those things and they don't realize that it's offensive to me, that's part of how I identify. It was hard to come to terms about feeling okay about being femme. We would joke around with it, but I always felt like I was lesser of a person. Like I wasn't a real lesbian if I was femme."

She felt self-conscious wearing earrings or makeup or dresses and regarded the label "lipstick lesbian" as a put-down. "Femme is kind of equated to straight women, because they kind of look the same," Karen says. "And so then you hear: 'You're not as strong. You're selling out. When times are tough, you'll switch.' Those kind of things.

"When people look at you, they don't know that you're a dyke, and that's not good enough, because we all have to be out and we all have to be visible. We all need to be out and counted. There's a part of me that believes we *should* be out and visible. So I try to wear queer things, pink triangles or whatever. But this is how I am; this is how I was born."

THOMAS Thomas was in the sixth grade when a rumor ran through his grade school and neighborhood: Thomas was a "faggot"; Thomas was a "fairy"; Thomas was a "queer." The behind-the-back stories petrified him, made him afraid to go on to seventh grade.

A crush on a boy in junior high confirmed his own suspicions and filled him with guilt and shame. Why can't I be straight? he would ask himself. Why do I have to be this way?

Dejected and alone, he hated junior high. But in high school, he found refuge—and courage—in a support group for gay, lesbian, and bisexual students. When he was a sophomore, he came out at home and at school, sure of who he was, unconcerned of the consequences. Part appearance, part attitude, he began wearing dangling earrings and a dozen GAY PRIDE buttons on his clothes and backpack wherever he went.

"For me, it was really good to come out in high school," Thomas says. "I wish I would've come out in junior high or grade school."

But his openness also made him fair game for harassment. One afternoon, his mother's boyfriend scribbled FAGGOT MAGGOTS on his bedroom wall.

Thomas hung a poster over it.

"Whenever he's home I just try to stay in my bedroom," Thomas says, "because I don't want to deal with him."

DENNIS One of three siblings, Dennis has two older sisters who are lesbians. He came out to his family when he was sixteen.

"At first, my mom didn't want to believe it. She thought I was doing it because my sisters were. But now she's fine with it."

Dennis's father is also gay, and separated from his mother when he came out to his family. "It's kind of a family joke: We all say how sorry we are for our mom . . . because she's the only one left out."

ALLEN Allen grew up in a small Wisconsin town north of Milwaukee. He felt his first attraction to another male when he was six. He remembers seeing a man in church and thinking he was beautiful. But he also believed his feelings were out of line at the time.

Allen describes himself as the classic overachiever. In high school, he was president of his class, president of the student council, first trumpet in the band, and active in the German club.

But when it came to dating, he was just going through the motions. He went out with girls, but the dates were never intimate. Deep down, he felt hollow, lonely, and depressed.

When Allen went to college, he remained closeted throughout his first year, ashamed of his same-sex desires. Frequently, he felt suicidal. He checked into a hospital to talk to a mental-health worker.

"I went in hoping there was some kind of medication that would take care of my sexuality in general," Allen says. "I would have liked to have been neutered and gotten it over with."

Instead, he was given information about sexual orientation and put in touch with organizations within the gay community. He attended a summer Gay Pride parade, and for the first time felt whole.

Eventually, he came out to his friends and family. His mother took the news well, he says, though her initial thought was that he should join the priesthood. His father too was understanding, and told Allen that his deceased uncle had been gay.

Allen says his parents don't treat him any differently because of his orientation. But there still are times when he feels second best. When his mother talks about his three brothers getting married someday, Allen is left out. There's never any questions about his love life.

"We really don't talk about it anymore."

BARBARA   Barbara was raised by devout Roman Catholic parents. "I grew up with priests and big prayer meetings and a lot of spiritual music," she remembers.

When Barbara came out at eighteen, a close cousin, who was twelve days younger than she was, had already announced that she was a lesbian. "For that reason, my coming-out process was very comfortable," Barbara says. "It was exciting, liberating."

After seeing the movie *The Joy Luck Club,* a story about the mother-daughter relationships within a San Francisco Chinese-American community, Barbara decided to share her own story with *her* mother. Her parents were living in Alaska at the time, so she called her mother on the phone to share the news.

"Well, I'm not surprised," her mother said.

"You're not?" answered Barbara, incredulous.

"Oh no. You're father and I have known for years." She told Barbara to be happy with who she was. "We love you. We support you. And we'll defend you to the death."

Part II

Disclosure

*F*or gay and lesbian teenagers, two things are happening at once—growing up and "coming out." The process of coming out begins internally, as teens recognize and investigate their homosexuality. They must then decide if and when they will come out to others.

Taking that step can be the most frightening—and consequential—move a young gay or lesbian ever makes. Sharing the secret with a friend or a teacher or a parent can begin to lessen the burden of invisibility and isolation. In the best circumstances, coming out can be a self-affirming rite of passage. But in the worst cases, it can lead to rejection, blame, and harassment.

Youth advocates say that lesbians and gays are coming out earlier than ever, some as young as thirteen and fourteen years old. It's a courageous decision. But without a wide safety net of support—at home, at school, and in the community—it's also a potentially dangerous one. Being scorned or ignored at such a precarious stage of their lives can throw open a door to many risks—from physical violence to homelessness to acts of self-destruction.

11

Dan II:

A Good Intensity

Although Dan Birkholz had found sympathy from two or three high school teachers, he continued to cry out desperately for understanding. For an assignment in a high school English class, Dan wrote a poem of self-discovery, a distillation of his life from his childhood to his adolescence, filled with reproach toward his parents and anguished pleas for help. Written as if he were describing someone else, Dan's untitled poem was a simple but insightful account of his struggle as he came of age:

> *He grew up smarter than most of his friends.*
> *Sure he could read, couldn't everybody?*
> *No?*
> *"I guess I'm pretty lucky then, aren't I Mommy?*
> *I'm five and I can read."*
> *He got to his first day and was scared.*
> *Mommy cried.*
> *Why?*
> *It was only kindergarten.*
> *He went to school and played with the other kids.*
> *Some were nice,*
> *Others, not.*
> *"The teacher was nice, Mommy."*
>
> *"Daddy, why would parents teach hate to the children?"*
> *Daddy didn't know.*

This disturbed the boy.
He cried.
He cried so hard and didn't know why.
He couldn't understand why they wanted to hate.
And if they didn't want to
Why didn't they stop?

He woke up one morning and was in the seventh grade.
This will be a nice chance to meet more people.
He was wrong.
"PIZZAFACEMORONJERKNERDASSHOLEFAGGOT!"
The words still sting.
"GODDAMNSONOFABITCHQUEERNERD!"
He was different and he knew it.
He was humiliated into knowing it.

"Dad, they say things that hurt."
"Get used to it, life sucks."
"But I want to cry . . ."
"Don't be so fuckin' sensitive!"
"Mom, they say things that hurt."
"Just ignore it, they'll leave you alone."
"But I want to cry . . ."
"Just ignore it."
"Guidance counselor, they say things that hurt."
"It's only natural in junior high."
"But . . ."
"I'm sorry, there's nothing I can do."

He woke up again and he was in a new city.
OhGodohGodohGod
New people, new city, new house.
But a new start.
He went into school.

"FAGGOTCOMMIEBASTARDFUCKHEAD!"
Just ignore it.
It'll go away.
He ignored it.
His soul went away.

When he was thirteen
He discovered that
He was all too different
From the other kids.
He didn't know how,
He just knew.
Fag!
There were words running through his head
Faggotfaggotfaggotfaggotfaggotfaggotfaggot
That he tried in vain to ignore
Queerqueerqueerqueerqueerqueerqueerqueer
But he tried.
He tried his damnedest
Fagfagfagfagfagfagfagfagfagfagfagfagfagfagfag
But a lone battle against oneself is doomed to fail.
He failed in the battle.

At fourteen,
He moved to a different city.
The people were somewhat nicer
But much dumber
Than in his old city.
They had such antiquated ideas
About what a man is,
About what a woman is.
He tried to tell them they sounded silly,
But they just laughed at him.
And so the cycle started again.

He grew up quicker than he would have liked.
But how could he not
With such heavy things on his mind:
"When will you grow up?"
"What's wrong with you?"
"Why can't you accept a little responsibility around here?"
"GROW UP!"
He took his parents' advice
And ignored it.
His soul withered more.
He could ignore his parents,
But he could not ignore himself.
THEY'RERIGHTYOU'RENOTHIN'BUTAGODDAMNQUEER!
His self-image was virtually nonexistent.
FUCKIN'FAGGOTYOUDESERVEWHATALLYOUGETAIDS!

At fifteen,
He told his parents:
"I'm having trouble here.
"I think I'm gay.
"I've found a group with others my age
"Who are going through similar problems.
"It's in Minneapolis."
"MINNEAPOLIS?!" they said.
"What are we supposed to do in Minneapolis
"While you're off gallivanting with those
"Those
"People?"
They told him "No!"
He ignored the pain.
He was hurt anyway.
He wanted to hurt them.

At sixteen,
After a year of acting out,

Just to anger his parents,
He asked for help again.
He wanted to die.
He just wanted to take those two bottles
Of Nuprin
And get it all done.
He didn't.
He ignored the pain.
But nothing withered further,
He had gotten so used to ignoring it,
He sometimes didn't even feel it. . . .

Dan's parents separated when he was sixteen, claiming "irreconcilable differences." His mother moved into an apartment near the hospital where she worked as a nurse, leaving Dan and his younger brother to live with their father in the tiny town of Zimmerman, Minnesota.

"He had more money and he could take care of our needs better," Dan explains, matter-of-factly. But he and his brother bitterly resented their parents' decision. They saw their mother's actions as selfish and lashed out at her for "abandoning" them, for leaving them with a father who could hardly speak to his sons without getting angry, who would scream so loudly that the window glass would shake. "I was so mad at my mother I couldn't see straight," says Dan.

Dan's father eventually sold the house in the country and moved the boys to a subdivision in St. Francis, a bedroom community north of Minneapolis. They had lived in St. Francis before and attended schools there. But for Dan it still was beyond the edge of his definition of "civilization."

Although Dan had told his parents that he thought he was gay, Jerry and JoAnn Birkholz were unable and unwilling to accept his disclosure. His requests for books on the topic of homosexuality went unanswered, and pleas to join a Minneapolis support group were dismissed with little discussion. They were reluctant to talk to him or anyone else about his sexuality, and quickly changed the topic whenever Dan brought it up. "They were hurt," he says, "and they expected me to take responsibility for their hurt."

Dan and his brother began family counseling sessions with their father to overcome the resentment they harbored toward their separated parents. In a one-on-one session, Dan informed the therapist that he was gay, thinking a professional would be best suited to offer an impartial explanation of Dan's sexual orientation to his father and brother. But instead, the therapist was disapproving. He told Dan that his homosexuality was likely a result of being raised by an overbearing mother and an uninvolved father. Dan challenged the classically faulty theory. If my parents are responsible for my homosexuality, he asked the therapist, why isn't my brother gay too? The therapist had no reasonable response, Dan says. He dropped out of the counseling, galled and disgruntled.

In the summer of his seventeenth year, after resorting to personal ads and long-distance "fantasy" phone lines to meet other gay men and following an off-and-on relationship with a man twice his age, Dan finally persuaded his parents to drive him into Minneapolis to attend a popular weekly support group for gay teens—Lesbian and Gay Youth Together. As he had done the previous summer, he sat them both down and told them he was gay and needed some help. This time he was emphatic and wouldn't let them off the hook. And this time they listened. "I wore their resistance down," he says.

His junior year had been one of his better years in school. His grades were good. He was writing for the school newspaper. He had won several trophies for performances in statewide speech tournaments. And he had major roles in the Dylan Thomas play *Under Milkwood* and in an excerpt of N. Richard Nash's drama *The Rainmaker.*

From the years of being tagged a "faggot," he had become cavalier about revealing his sexual identity. Deadened by all the slurs he had endured, he came out to a few more classmates at school. "I had survived so much that I didn't really care anymore," he says. "It didn't even concern me. I didn't care if people knew I was gay or not."

Yet Dan still was unendurably lonely. He had no gay friends in school at all. His sexual relationship with Tom, the older man he'd met through a newspaper ad, had run its course after turning emotionally empty. Without a driver's license, it was nearly impossible for Dan to get to the Twin Cities to meet anyone of his age. Joining the peer group was essential, he told his parents, and long overdue. "It was two years too late," he says.

Dan's father begrudgingly agreed to make the hour-long Sunday-afternoon drive to deliver Dan to the support group. "I had my dad drop me off a block away," Dan recalls. "I wanted to do this alone. I wanted to do this as independently as I could."

The two-hour meeting was held in a large, bright room adjacent to the offices of the Minnesota AIDS Project. The group was led by a handful of youth advocates from a number of community social service agencies. Sitting in a circle of metal chairs were about twenty-five young people, most of them men, ranging from kids in junior high to college graduates. "I found the room, sat down, and pretty much stayed there," Dan remembers. "I was scared. I'm not a very outgoing person. People pretty much have to knock me down to drag a hello out of me."

But no one did. Why the hell am I here? Dan thought, second-guessing himself. When introductions were made, he was choking with angst. "When it went around the room and came to me, it was: 'Hi. My name is Dan. I came out to my parents. I really need to talk.'"

Through the course of the next year and a half, Dan found a place for himself among a group of young gay men his age. For the first time in his life, he could talk about his resentment toward his parents, about the "fag" jokes in school, about his adolescent sexual desires—and have someone really understand. It was comforting.

Still, the support group was far from perfect. Dan had hoped to meet other gay teens who were looking for a relationship, emotionally, sexually, and intellectually. But it seemed to Dan that many of the young men had already turned eighteen and came to the group only to socialize before the Sunday night "Boys Night Out" parties at a downtown gay bar.

"I had hoped that I might be able to meet someone there," he says. "There was one guy who was so nice," he adds, rolling his eyes. "But he didn't even notice me." And Dan was too shy and unsure of himself to strike up a conversation.

Yet he continued to attend. "It was a nice way to get out and into the city," he says. "And I got to meet a lot of interesting people, mostly the facilitators." Each week, an adult guest speaker addressed the group on topics such as gay culture, domestic violence, and safe sex. With each presentation, Dan met another gay role model and took another small step into the gay community. He even joined in a "kiss-in" protest at the Minnesota State Fair with the group Queer Nation, targeting the welcoming booth of U.S. senator Dave Durenburger with a couple of dozen "queer" activists. At home, at school, and now in public, Dan was slowly shaking off the binds of the closet.

On the long drive home each Sunday night after group, his father fell silent. Not once did he ask Dan about the discussions he'd had or the people he'd met.

Dozens of students paced the hallways and talked to the walls of a rural Minnesota high school, reciting noble lines about life and death, love and hate, glory and defeat. They were rehearsing for the regional speech tournament, practicing orations and soliloquies, plays and poems by some of the most prominent writers of the day or by the students themselves. Without lighting or music, without costumes or props, they would perform solo before judges and peers, competing for awards and stature as amateur orators.

Dan nervously inspected a tournament schedule that was taped to a classroom door. He had come with the team from St. Francis High School, thirty miles away, to compete in the "serious drama" category. His selection was a dark departure from some of his more humorous monologues of past tournaments. But Dan's humor had soured in his senior year. He yearned desperately for acceptance, and couldn't wait to get out of school and move away from home. His life had become a mire of anger and frustration. And his choice of material for the day's tournament fit his temperament perfectly.

Dan would perform eight minutes of dialogue from *Torch Song Trilogy,* by gay playwright Harvey Fierstein—eight stormy minutes of confrontation between a gay man and his mother. Dan had won numerous awards in past tournaments for other, more popular performances, but, against the advice of his coach, who was concerned about the subject matter, chose Fierstein's play "to exorcise some ghosts," Dan said. Fierstein's pared-down dialogue seemed foreign and out of context in this rural school. But in many ways, it defined the very moment of Dan's life—and probably countless others like him.

Dan was the last to perform in the second round. He watched intently as his competitors presented fragments of dialogue from Peter Shaffer's *Equus,* Tennessee Williams's *Suddenly, Last Summer,* and Arthur Miller's *Death of a Salesman.* As his turn neared, Dan stared unblinkingly at the dull surface of his desktop, psyching himself up. When the judge finally called his name, he mechanically removed his glasses and class ring, and stepped to the front of the classroom to make his introduction:

"For gay men and lesbians everywhere, coming out to their parents can be the most stressful and trying time of their relationships. The same holds true for Arnold Beckoff and his mother. . . . *Widows and Children First!,* by Harvey Fierstein."

Dan's fingers stabbed the air, his eyebrows arched and fell as he brought the two characters to life. Arnold Beckoff and his mother are embroiled in a bitter argument over his homosexuality. The mother laments the fact Arnold is gay, and pleads with her son not to "rub my face in it." She would rather just forget about his homosexuality and continue to love him for the "good" and "sensitive" person that she raised. But Arnold refuses to yield to her denial, and challenges her to accept him for who he is, a gay young man.

The words were all too familiar to Dan. He had found himself in identical arguments with his own parents. He was always put on the defensive, always forced to explain himself and his gayness.

As Dan neared the end of the drama, he stumbled on a line and seemed to lose his grip for a second. But he quickly recovered and charged toward the conclusion with an anger that he had hurled at his own parents a hundred times before.

ARNOLD: *Ma, look. I am gay. I don't know why but that's what I am. For as far back as I can remember. Back before I knew it was different or wrong. . . . I know you'd rather I was straight, but I'm not! Would you also rather that I had lied to you? My friends all think I'm crazy for telling you. They'd never dream of telling their parents. Instead they cut their parents out of their lives. And the parents wonder, "Why are my children so distant?" Is that what you'd rather? Listen, Ma, if you want to be a part of my life, I am not going to edit out the things you don't like!*

MA: *Can we end this conversation?*

ARNOLD: *No. There's one more thing you've got to understand. . . . There is nothing I need from anyone except love and respect. And anyone who can't give me those two things has no place in my life. You are my mother, and I love you. I do. But if you can't respect me . . . then you've got no business being here.*

The performance was powerful, arresting. But Dan, forever the self-critic, was disappointed in himself. He returned to his seat and scribbled on a pad of paper: "I sucked!"

But the judge handed a written critique to Dan as he left the room, praising Dan's performance. "Arnold has a good intensity!" read the note. Yet his offering fell short of winning a prize.

Dan's parents had never seen him perform this declamation. And he doubted that they ever would.

Their loss, he decided.

Dan and his parents had reached a stalemate over the issue of his homosexuality. His mother seemed preoccupied with her own concerns and indifferent to Dan's. His father was annoyed by his son's admission and tried to persuade him to keep quiet: You can't tell by *looking* at you that you're gay, he would say to Dan, so why stir things up? Why does everyone have to know? But Dan was losing his patience. They had denied his sexual orientation for so long that it hurt.

One day, after Dan returned home from an overnight stay at a friend's house, his father began interrogating him, demanding that he justify his whereabouts and accusing him of "whoring around." Dan was furious. He assured his father that he was behaving safely and responsibly. And in a spasm of frustration, he stomped into his bedroom.

"I went into my room and just started throwing everything out of my closet," he recalls. "Everything." Shirts, socks, underwear, all his clothes were heaped in the middle of his bedroom. His closet was empty, the doors wide open.

"It was like some weird symbol of my life or something."

As a small but symbolic measure of growing acceptance, Dan's mother took him to a shopping mall one evening to get his ear pierced. Because she thought an earring in the right ear was a sign that a person is gay, she insisted that Dan pierce only his left. She was paying the $11 charge for the piercing, so Dan felt obligated to comply. But he vowed to someday get the right one pierced too—when he could afford to pay for it himself.

12

Troy II:

Born This Way

Late in his senior year of high school, Troy Herman began making regular visits to Minneapolis with his boyhood friend Jordan—the only other gay teenager he knew. They both had heard that the Twin Cities had one of the largest gay and lesbian populations in the country. Exploring the gay bars, gay newspapers, gay bookstores, gay movie festivals, and Gay Pride parades in Minneapolis and St. Paul became a deep breath of fresh air to the young—and closeted—friends.

Troy and Jordan made their first three-hour drive to Minneapolis to visit the Gay 90s, a renowned gay bar on Hennepin Avenue. Driving along the downtown streets, they pulled over to a telephone booth to call the bar for directions.

"Is the Gay 90s a gay bar?" Troy asked the man who answered the phone. "I don't mean a happy bar, I mean a *gay* bar," he repeated.

Yes, Troy was assured, the Gay 90s was a bar for *gays,* for *homosexuals.* Jordan and Troy were thrilled. But when they marched up to the flashing marquee lights of the "90s," they discovered they were too young to get in. Unsure what to do next, they followed the suggestion of the doorman and checked out a teen club around the corner called Second Story. The club was like nothing they had ever seen back in Charles City. Spotlights in the ceiling washed the room in color. A deejay played tapes of loud, pulsating industrial music. And on the dance floor, young men and women their age paired off with partners of the same sex. Second Story became an instant hangout and a safe haven for Troy and Jordan.

After a couple of visits to Second Story, they heard of another club called the Saloon, a gay bar down the street. Every Thursday and Sunday night, the Saloon admitted teens eighteen and up from 10 P.M. until closing. Drawing young gays from all around the Twin Cities, the Saloon and Second Story became homes away from home for Troy and Jordan—and easy entree into the Cities' community of gay youth.

The car drives to Minneapolis soon became a weekend routine for Troy and Jordan. They both held jobs at a nursing home in Charles City, working the 6 A.M.–to–2 P.M. shift. Each Thursday after work, they would stash their "gay outfits" in Jordan's car—dress shirts, short pants, and black shoes—then drive pell-mell to Minneapolis, changing clothes at a rest stop along the way or in the bathroom of the Saloon. Having nowhere to stay, they would sleep in the car or drive straight back to Charles City early Friday or Saturday. Troy's mother frowned upon the weekly jaunts. But he promised her that he would call his aunt, who lived in a Minneapolis suburb, if he ever got into a jam.

Later that summer, a family friend, Barry Nelson, returned home to Iowa from Minneapolis for the wedding of Troy's sister, Brenda. Barry, seven years older than Troy, had grown up in nearby Nashua, Iowa, and was close to Brenda and her fiancé. At the wedding, Barry filled Troy's head with alluring stories of what it was like to live in the Twin Cities. He talked of wild parties, downtown clubs, exotic restaurants, fancy stores. Troy was envious. "It just made me want to live in the Twin Cities even more," he said.

That fall, a cousin of Troy's got married in Minneapolis. Barry had invited Troy and his sisters to spend the weekend at his Minneapolis apartment. After the wedding, and more than a dozen rum-and-Cokes, Barry took Troy aside.

"Can I talk to you?" Barry asked.

"Well, about what?" Troy wondered.

"I want to tell you something."

"Sure. Go ahead."

Barry paused. "I'm gay."

Troy laughed. "I'm supposed to believe this?" he said, his jaw hanging open.

As proof of this declaration, Barry instructed Troy to take a look in the bottom drawer of his dresser when they returned to his apartment. Later that evening, in an apartment filled with his family, Troy pretended that he had to use the bathroom and slipped into Barry's bedroom, unseen. He hurriedly slid open the bottom dresser drawer. Inside were dozens of *Playgirl* magazines and gay newspapers. Surprised by his friend's disclosure but impressed by his candor, Troy went back to Barry with his own admission. But Barry told him he already assumed Troy was gay. He just knew, he said.

Troy suddenly had an ally in the Twin Cities—a gay ally, a gay role model. He and Jordan began hanging out at Barry's apartment often, partying with his gay friends, reading the gay papers, watching GAZE-TV, a local cable show for gays.

"We never knew so much existed," says Troy. "A small town is so limited. I just didn't want to stay in Charles City." They were sure they were ready to leave Iowa behind. So when Barry's roommate moved out and he suggested that Troy and Jordan move in, they jumped at the offer. They began checking employment listings in the newspapers, and by spring both had lined up jobs as nursing assistants at a suburban nursing home.

The bright-light enticement of the city, and the sizable reputation of Minneapolis's gay community, made moving to the Twin Cities the right thing to do for Troy. He always knew he would someday live in a big city. His dreams and ambitions stretched far beyond the borders of Charles City. He had plans to go to college someday to study nursing or music or acting. Though he had fond memories of growing up in a small town, he had no regrets about leaving. His hometown was too dull, too confining—not to mention homophobic. Charles City was just no place to be "queer."

So, on a Monday morning in April, Troy packed all of his worldly possessions into Jordan's Honda—clothes, stereo, television, books, tapes. They both were ready to make the leap.

The family goodbyes were long and emotional. The night before they left, Troy desperately wanted to tell his mother he was gay. But he couldn't muster the nerve to say the words face-to-face. Instead, he scribbled a note on a piece of paper:

Mom: The reason I'm moving up to Minneapolis is, I'm gay. You may not accept it. You may never accept it. But this is who I am. I'll miss you. I'll always love you. If you love me like a mother should love her son, you'll accept it.

He placed the announcement on a towel stand in the bathroom, where she would be sure to see it, and left home, making the familiar drive to Minneapolis for good.

Troy called his mother later that evening from his new apartment to tell her he had arrived safely. And to check her response to his note.

"Well, have you done any cleaning?" Troy asked, nervously.

"Yeah . . ." she told him, giving away nothing.

"Did you clean the bathroom?" he pressed on.

"Yeah? Why?" she asked.

"Well, did you find my note?" he said.

"Yep," she snapped, and quickly changed the subject. When would he be coming home next? she asked. Could he shop around for some toys for the grandkids?

"I kind of expected that," he says, recalling her reaction. "I just wish Mom wasn't as reserved as she is. If I had my way, I'd have her jump right into it and learn all she could."

Four months after relocating to Minneapolis, Troy went home for his sister Linda's twenty-first birthday and a family reunion. By then, his coming-out note had been thoroughly discussed by everyone in his family. Tears were shed, blame was cast. His lifetime secret was out.

Troy's sisters had told him they suspected he was gay all along, and accused Jordan of corrupting him. Troy patiently tried to explain that there was no one to blame. He was who he was. And he wanted to live his life without secrecy or shame.

"If people can't accept me the way I am, they have no place in my life," he asserted. "I love men the way straight men love women. It's not sick. I was born this way."

Since moving to the Cities, Troy had grown confident and comfortable with his gayness. "It's easier to live my life," he said. But he was anxious about returning home. He was torn between his new life and his roots, the past and the present. He missed his family and knew that they missed him. In the few months since he had moved away, he had become a city-wise baby brother in the eyes of his three older sisters and a favorite long-distance uncle to eleven nieces and nephews. He enjoyed regaling them with stories of his new life in Minneapolis, stories of his job at a nursing home, his apartment, his friends, his *experiences.* But he grew tired of being put on the defensive by his mother and sisters. Too often he had to make absolutions for his gayness. Over and over, he felt obligated to explain his actions and feelings. When one of his sisters learned he was gay, for instance, her first concern was that he would molest her young sons. He had to explain to her that the vast majority of sexual-abuse cases are committed by heterosexuals, not homosexuals. To allay his family's worries and convey a few fundamental lessons on homosexuality, he passed out copies of *Loving Someone Gay,* a collection of true-life stories of gay and lesbian children coming out to their parents, and *Now That You Know: What Every Parent Should Know About Homosexuality,* a personalized how-to account of raising a gay child by two mothers of gay children. Troy's mother eventually read *Now That You Know.* But, except for a cursory look at the manuals, none of his sisters read them.

On a humid Saturday in August, Troy's family waited for his arrival at the home of his sister Linda and her husband, Lenny. Troy burst into the kitchen with a flourish, his arms filled with presents. A towheaded nephew marched up and asked for a kiss, and a niece promptly crawled onto his lap.

"Love you," said the girl.

"Love you," returned Troy.

Troy handed Linda a gift he had wrapped, a T-shirt from Camp Snoopy, an amusement park in the Mall of America just outside of Minneapolis. "I bought it big so you can tuck it into your pants and it'll still be baggy," he said to her. "Baggy is in."

Linda thanked him, and held it up for everyone to admire. Troy had always been generous to his family. With a decent-paying job in Minneapolis, he was able to help out occasionally with his mother's living expenses. Once, when he still lived at home, he donated his babysitting money to Linda so she could buy diapers for her baby, and often pitched in for her children's clothes.

For much of the day, Troy sat around the kitchen table chatting with his sisters and mother over birthday cake, ice cream, Diet Coke, and cigarettes. The floor was sticky underfoot from the brood of soda-pop kids banging in and out of the screen door. Troy's two brothers-in-law came and went, too, pulling cans of beer from the refrigerator and then retreating to the garage to listen to rock music. The kitchen coffee conversation drifted to small talk and family gossip. The sisters knocked Troy about his big-city habits, his new clothes, his new talk, his new hair. They swapped opinions about men, music, and Madonna, and laughed about their pasty white legs, an apparent family trait.

"I figured out why you've had so many problems, Troy," his mother said, out of the blue. "You had to have a blood transfusion when you were born." Though she left it unspoken, Jane Herman had come up with what she thought was a plausible explanation for Troy's homosexuality, the missing piece in her son's puzzle.

"Whatever," said a dubious Troy, lighting a cigarette. He would be patient. She'll deal with my sexuality in her own way and on her own time, he thought.

Troy's oldest sister, Vicky, held up a drinking glass with a line drawing of a bare-breasted woman etched on its side.

"See this, Troy?" she teased.

"She's not my style," Troy parried, blowing smoke at the ceiling. "Doesn't do anything for me. Not a thing."

It went this way all afternoon—his family talking *around* his homosexuality, never addressing it, never affirming it. His sisters traded jokes about condoms, snickered about oral sex, and offered to take Troy to an all-male strip joint nearby. Troy withstood the playful banter. Again and again, he invited questions about his sexual orientation, dropping hints about his gay friends and his current boyfriend. But no one took the hint. No one spoke the word *gay*.

"When the kids and I are all together, we never bring up Troy's lifestyle or anything," his mother later admitted. "It was pretty hard for me to accept it at first, and now I accept it. I love Troy. But like I told him, I won't accept it in my house. And Troy can go along with that." She laid down a few ground rules for her son: He could bring home a boyfriend, but she would not allow the two of them to sleep together, kiss, or hold hands in the company of family.

The next day, the Herman family would hold a reunion in a municipal park. It would mark the first time Troy would see his relatives since he had come out, and he was worried. He was sure the word that he was gay had circulated. And he foresaw a confrontation. He expected a disapproving aunt or uncle would grill him about his sexual orientation, about his boyfriend, maybe even his sex life.

"I'm not going to give any details on what we do or anything like that," Troy vowed, "because that's not any of their business."

The night before the reunion, as he unpacked his suitcase, Troy showed his mother the shirt he had bought especially for the occasion, a loud purple-and-blue rayon shirt.

"Ma, what do you think of this?" he said, holding it up to his chest.

"Where'd you get *that?*" she said, clearly not impressed.

"At the Mall of America. *This* is the shirt I'm wearing tomorrow."

"Oh God."

"What? It's *nice,*" he insisted.

She groaned. "You can go in the basement and get one of my T-shirts and wear that." She didn't say it, but Troy could read his mother's mind. He knew she thought the shirt was "too gay."

The next day, at the local Kmart, Jane bought a replacement— a button-down dress shirt, equally as loud, but not nearly as gay, in her eyes.

Some seventy-five members of the Herman family congregated in Charles City's Wildwood Park for their first family picnic in more than six years. Kids were everywhere, chasing each other around trees as the men of the family played horseshoes and the women prepared the barbecues.

Troy—the "new Troy"—received mixed reviews at the reunion. Dressed in a pair of khakis and the shirt his mother had picked out, he didn't socialize much. He didn't recognize many of his cousins. They had grown up so fast. He passed much of the afternoon with his sisters and mother. But as he anticipated, one of his aunts cornered him. He was bouncing his baby niece on his lap.

"You're not going to have any kids of your own now, are you?" she chided, sarcastically.

"Yeah, I want to have kids," he shot back.

She shook her head.

But later, another aunt from Mason City took him aside. After some idle talk about his move to the Twin Cities, she asked cautiously if he was seeing anyone special.

Yes, Troy told her proudly, "I have a boyfriend. His name's Bob."

She smiled. "Well, that's good," she said. "That's all I want to know. Let's go back and eat."

Whenever he goes home these days, Troy stands out among the locals. The gold cross dangling from his left ear and his dyed auburn hair, combed back and gelled down, attract double takes. His big-city clothes cause him dirty looks and disdain. But he's not about to have a makeover for the benefit of his hometown.

"I'm not sick, I'm not perverted. I was born gay and I'll die gay," he says, defiantly.

Sitting with his mom and sisters at a Charles City bar one night, Troy was approached by a distant cousin, a long-haired redneck railroad worker who hadn't seen Troy for years.

"Who's that?" the cousin asked Troy's sister, Linda.

"*That* is my brother. Troy," she said.

The cousin didn't like Troy's hair, and told him so.

"How do you make your hair do that? Do you spray it?" he asked.

"Gel," answered Troy, patiently.

"*Why* do you do it?" he demanded, staring Troy down. "Why do you *look* like that?"

The cousin was a menacing character, a jail-time barfly, the kind of person who for no good reason would gladly cause somebody harm.

Troy said nothing, and put up with the put-down. It was a sobering reminder of the reason he had left home in the first place.

SIDEBAR:

Coming Out

You could call coming out a stepping-stone in the personal development of young gays and lesbians, a vital transition between childhood and adulthood, a life experience that's startling and exhilarating and galvanizing all at once.

But it's seldom like that. Most gay and lesbian teenagers are alone in their journey through adolescence, ignored or condemned, driven to secrecy out of fear of being turned away by family and friends. Not only are they in the midst of growing up, but they're compelled to grapple with a sexual orientation that they probably know very little about.

Lesbian and gay teens often tell of feeling regretful as they come to recognize their homosexual orientation. They know that being gay means losing certain freedoms and privileges. In most cases, they can't walk hand-in-hand down the street, can't take same-sex dates to prom.

By definition, coming out is the process by which gays and lesbians come to terms with their homosexuality—their same-sex attractions, affections, fantasies—and decide to incorporate it into their social and personal lives. The term itself has a dual meaning. Typically, lesbians and gays first come out internally to themselves and subsequently come out to others, announcing that they're homosexual.

To a large measure, the coming-out process spans a lifetime, extending from stages of self-awareness to self-disclosure to self-acceptance and beyond, as lesbians and gays choose to reveal their sexual orientation incrementally—to other lesbians and gays, to families and friends, to co-workers, to the public at large—throughout their lives. But at the outset, coming out is a complicated time of turmoil and uncertainty, a taxing process on all fronts—emotionally, psychologically, socially, spiritually, sometimes even physically.

"When you're a teenager, heck, that's when you think about dating or you flirt with someone or you look at pictures and you share them with your friends, and you say, Isn't this person cute? Isn't that person cute?" says Virginia Uribe, founder of Project 10 in Los Angeles. "A gay or lesbian kid really can't do that. They have to hide all this."

For all of the underlying trials that gay youth face in the coming-out process, they also must deal with growing up. In many ways, the developmental tasks of coming out parallel the tasks of adolescence in general. A teenager must establish a sense of identity, develop self-esteem, and work toward intimacy and socialization—through friendships, peer group associations, sexual relationships.

"Gay and lesbian youth are much more like other adolescents than they are like gay and lesbian adults," says Dr. Gary Remafedi, a pediatrician at the University of Minnesota's Youth and AIDS Projects. "And they go through the same struggles as all young people do."

Yet for the gay or lesbian adolescent, there are detours and barriers along the road to adulthood that are unique to their sexual orientation. For all teens entering adolescence, sudden hormonal changes stir feelings of sexual attraction and fantasies. But for gay and lesbian youth, attractions to people of the same sex bring a recognition of just how different they are from their peers, which can cause profound inner conflict. During middle and late adolescence, alienation from family and failure to connect with gay and lesbian peers can interrupt or postpone normal social development, causing a developmental "lag" that threatens relationships, education goals, even career plans. Oftentimes, the tasks of adolescence get postponed until adulthood.

But a deficiency in their social development doesn't mean their sexual orientation is undeveloped. Their homosexuality no doubt has been determined long before they realize they're gay. Rather, the lag is a result of the cold rejection that greets them as they come out. If they have no one to talk to and nowhere to turn for support, they're left to wrestle with their puzzlement on their own.

A Model

There are a number of theoretical models of the coming-out process within social-science literature. While the stages are different for each individual and can stop, start, or stall along the way, most models describe remarkably similar patterns of change and growth as the homosexual identity forms. Adapted from some of the more notable models,[1] the process generally goes like this:

• *Sensitization-Insight:* Before puberty, gays and lesbians experience certain social episodes and personal sensitivities—often described later in life as indistinct feelings of "differentness" during childhood—that serve as a basis for their emerging self-perceptions as homosexuals in early adolescence. In this pre-coming-out stage, kids usually are not consciously aware of feelings or thoughts about same-sex people.

All kids begin to feel some sexual attraction to those of one sex or the other at about age nine, ten, or eleven, notes Dr. Robert Deisher, who pioneered research of gay teens at the University of Washington. The attraction fades in and out in early adolescence. But because opposite-sex attractions are reinforced by society and same-sex attractions are not, most gays and lesbians in their early teens are reluctant to admit to a recognition of their sexual affinity.

"They're not going to put a label on themselves for a while," Deisher says. "Usually, it's not until they're fourteen, fifteen, sixteen before they're going to say, 'Gee that could be me.' "

• *Identity Confusion-Isolation:* Adolescents begin to personalize the notion of being gay or lesbian as they recognize that their thoughts, feelings, and behaviors fit the definition of homosexuality rather than heterosexuality.

"That's a very frightening point for many adolescents—when they have to admit to themselves that this is what they're feeling," says Frances Kunreuther, executive director of the Hetrick-Martin Institute, a social-service agency for gay and lesbian adolescents in New York City. "I think that is really a key turning point, psychologically. They are carrying a very big secret. . . . And often they see it as a terrible secret."

Framed against a backdrop of social stigma, the realization that they "might" be gay can bring a flood of emotions—from fear to dread to sorrow—and a flurry of reactions. According to several theoretical models, lesbian and gay youth respond to this inner dissonance by adopting one or more of the following tactics: They deny their homosexuality and cultivate a heterosexual image; they attempt to change or alter their homosexuality (through psychological counseling, for example); they avoid or rationalize their homosexual thoughts, feelings, and behaviors (claiming, for instance, that their gay behavior is only a passing phase); or they accept their homosexuality.

Avoidance is especially common, and shows up in a number of techniques. For example, gay and lesbian teens can date members of the opposite sex to "prove" to themselves (and perhaps others) that they're not homosexual; they can attack homosexuality, again to demonstrate that they're not gay; they can limit their exposure to information on the topic of homosexuality; and they can escape, by dropping out of school, running away from home, abusing drugs and alcohol, becoming pregnant or, in the worst cases, committing suicide.

• *Identity Tolerance-Disclosure:* Lesbian and gay youth come to acknowledge that they are "probably" homosexual and, to lessen their alienation, begin sharing the news with others, typically with other lesbians and gays or trusted heterosexual adults first. It is during this stage that adolescents might begin to experiment sexually and explore gay and lesbian culture, as a gay-positive attitude slowly develops. They might tell a teacher they're gay, ask a gay classmate out on a date, or join a gay and lesbian support group—acts that start to pull them out of the closet yet set them even farther apart from their heterosexual counterparts. In effect, they live "double lives," actively seeking out other gays and lesbians while still passing as straight.

This phase, as teens begin to "go public" with their sexual identity, can be a particularly risky one. Hasty or impulsive disclosures can bring negative responses—lost friendships, family crises, even physical harm. Without some preparation or support network, coming out can leave a gay or lesbian teen alone and vulnerable to an assortment of risks.

A two-year study at Horizons, a Chicago social-service agency for gay and lesbian youth, by anthropologist Gilbert Herdt and developmental psychologist Andrew Boxer, detailed the progression of the coming-out process.[2] Interviews were conducted of 202 self-identified gay and lesbian youth (147 males and 55 females), ages fourteen to twenty. First same-sex attraction was reported on average at age 9.6 for boys, 10.1 for girls. First same-sex activity was reported at age 13.1 for boys, 15.2 for girls. And the age at which youths first disclosed their homosexual orientation to another person was sixteen, for both sexes.

• *Identity Acceptance-Socialization:* Teens now accept rather than tolerate a gay or lesbian self-image. They venture further into the gay and lesbian cultures, which serves to validate and "normalize" homosexuality as a way of life. Same-sex love relationships develop; friendships with adult gay and lesbian role models grow.

Adolescents in this stage might make public their "queer" identities—by attending a Gay Pride celebration, for instance— yet an inner tension still exists. To reduce the chances of confrontation, they might limit their contact with family or heterosexual peers.

• *Identity Pride-Commitment:* Confident in their homosexual identity and aware of society's prejudices, adolescents form a solid connection and commitment to the gay and lesbian communities, which fosters a strong sense of belonging.

At this stage, public identity is brought in line with private identity. Less energy is spent by teens on concealing their homo-sexual identities, and confrontation becomes a way to defend homosexuality as an acceptable and normal way of life.

Marked by slogans such as "gay and proud," a teen's sexual orientation becomes the most important thing in his or her life. This is where separatism and political activism might arise, as self-pride and defiance of heterosexual conventions intersect. Their homosexuality is not only accepted, but it becomes pre-ferred to heterosexuality.

• *Identity Synthesis:* Adolescents integrate their homosexual orientation into all elements of their life, as the "us against them" philosophy diminishes. Homosexuality becomes just one of many elements in the definition of self. Similarities are recog-nized between gays and their straight peers, and contact with heterosexuals is seen as less threatening as young gays and les-bians feel confident enough of their identity to come out to the world.

Between a Rock and a Hard Place

For some lesbian and gay teens, coming out is effortless, right from the start. Those fortunate few generally tend to have exceptional cop-ing skills, a supportive circle of friends, extraordinarily accepting families, and some exposure to the gay culture—through friends of the family, siblings, neighbors—prior to their coming out.

But teens of that sort are a rare breed. For the majority, coming out is greeted with ambivalence or outright negativity. In more subtle forms, their reactions can turn to an emotionally debilitating self-hatred or "internalized homophobia" or, in more overt forms, self-destructive behavior.

Much of the coming-out drama is played out in school, a battlefield of fragile egos and identities vying for recognition and approval. By the time they reach high school, most teens are drawing away from their parents and redefining themselves within the context of their peers. But if their peers are judgmental and intolerant of homosexuality, the expectations of a self-identified lesbian or gay will be crushed.

"Certainly for many young people, their primary arena of support is the school system," says Rea Carey, coordinator of the National Advocacy Coalition on Youth and Sexual Orientation in Washington D.C., an umbrella group of youth advocacy and service agencies from around the country. "And we're finding . . . that school systems are either passively or actively discriminating against gay and lesbian youth." Counseling services and sensitivity training for teachers are scarce. And, in some areas, gay-positive curricula are being shelved by anti-gay school boards. In the New York City borough of Queens, for example, a neighborhood school board in 1992 refused to adopt the "Children of the Rainbow" curriculum because it included a section on teaching first graders respect toward gays and lesbians.

Scant information is provided on adolescent homosexuality through the schools or the community. Sex education in most classes offers only the bare minimum. So gay and lesbian youth form their understanding of sexuality based on societal definitions and images that frequently are distorted and emotionally freighted.

More often than not, the social environment for gay teens—whether at school, at home, or at church—is discouraging and ill prepared to serve their unique needs. "It's not going to be a supportive one, and this is what puts the stress on these kids," says the Hetrick-Martin Institute's Joyce Hunter, offering a notice of precaution: "If they don't have the emotional support, the correct information, and the opportunity to interact with their peers in an open environment, they're going to have problems."

When to Tell

On top of all of the other struggles they endure as teenagers, young lesbians and gays find themselves on the horns of a dilemma: Should they or shouldn't they tell someone they're homosexual? And if they do decide to tell, just *whom* do they tell, and *when*?

There's no consensus as to when lesbians and gays should come out to others. What might be a life-affirming event for some could be a disastrous mistake for others. In the perfect world, stepping out of the closet should be a liberating, self-fulfilling experience. But in the real world, coming out can be a great risk—a risk of repudiation, discrimination, even physical harm, often by the people they regard as their main source of comfort and trust. Because of the hazards, some gays and lesbians stay closeted until well into adulthood.

"The vast majority of gay adults did not come out in adolescence," says Mary Jane Rotheram-Borus, a professor of social psychology at the University of California at Los Angeles. "The numbers are very small."

Most gays and lesbians put off telling anyone until they have the resources and wherewithal to live independent of their families. Usually, there's less risk of negative repercussions when they're of college age or older. "It's not so clear to me that waiting is bad," adds Rotheram-Borus. "The younger that they come out, the harder it is on kids."

Coming out as an adolescent is not the same as coming out as an adult, agrees Project 10 founder Virginia Uribe. "Most students are not self-supporting and . . . coming out can be a very perilous thing. Parents can throw them out. That happens more times than I care to think about.

"If I were to characterize the coming-out process for a teenager in our society now, I would say that it is more perilous than it is positive," she says. "Even if they come from supportive families, they still have to deal with being part of a stigmatized group. And that doesn't change even though the world is changing and things are evolving and there are positive role models. You're still part of a stigmatized group if you're homosexual, and you still have to work through that."

Perhaps the greatest fear among teens who are about to come out is the fear of being rejected or renounced by their families.

"When we have young people who come to us and say they're going to tell their families, we do not counsel them to tell their families very readily," says Mitzi Henderson, president of P-FLAG and the mother of a gay son. "We ask them to think very carefully before they come out, to make sure they have a good sense of what the family's reaction might be and to have a fallback in case it's a bad reaction—a friend they can stay with, a place they can live, some kind of financial support.

"Their repertoire of resources is so small," Henderson continues, "and the ability to plan and look toward some sort of self-support is practically nil. Many of these kids have had trouble in school or dropped out and don't have the educational training that's necessary."

Coming out is an unsettling task, because no one can predict the response. Even confiding in people who teens believe they know well can seem chancy, which makes a less-than-ideal outcome even more devastating to them.

"It seems to me that it's terribly important for a gay or lesbian person to show some patience, which is very hard for young people," Henderson adds. "They want immediate reaction. They want to tell you *today* and have you say 'okay' *tomorrow*, and then that's it. But that *isn't* it. Families and friends have to go through a process too, and they need the youngster to help them through that process."

While the outcome may not be immediately positive, coming out will be rewarding in the long run, she says.

"It frees the gay or lesbian or bisexual person to be themselves, to be honest. And it frees the family to understand and be a part of that person's life, to continue to celebrate their joys and commiserate with their problems. Coming out for families is just as liberating as coming out for young people. . . . Your perceptions change, your understanding changes. The world changes."

The Next Generation

Buoyed by advancements within the gay-rights movement, recognized by a growing number of support services, and defiant of societal conventions, gay and lesbian youth are coming out younger than ever. A decade ago, youth workers say, young gays and lesbians might have waited until college to break the news to a friend or a parent. But today, they're speaking out in high school, and sometimes as early as junior high.

Secrecy is less necessary. While the topic of homosexuality is still taboo in most sex education programs, HIV/AIDS awareness has compelled schools to at least broach the topic, opening the door for gay teens to reveal their sexual orientation. Professionals—school nurses, teachers, counselors, social workers, therapists, doctors— have become more trained at identifying gay youth and responding to their needs. Public awareness of issues of sexuality overall has accelerated.

As conditions progress for gays and lesbians in general, today's generation of gay teens reaps the achievements that began with the birth of the battle for gay liberation in the late 1960s. An alliance between gay and lesbian youth and gay and lesbian adults has grown. Where gay bars once were the predominant community link a generation ago, youth now have a wider network to look to for interaction with other gays and lesbians, through coffeehouses, teen centers, support groups, social clubs, churches, bookstores, magazines, newspapers, and computer bulletin boards.

Still, the implications of this trend cut both ways. While coming out at an early age may be a helpful survival lesson for facing the slings and arrows hurled daily at gays and lesbians, it can also be potentially harmful for youth who are unprepared for the consequences or unable to find support. Indeed, teens coming out at a younger age pose unique challenges for schools and child-welfare agencies.

In an ideal world, there wouldn't be a closet, and gay and lesbians wouldn't have to come out at all. Like their straight counterparts, they would be accepted for who they are by their parents, their friends, their teachers, their coaches, their pastors—without judgment or ridicule.

"I think discrimination against gays and lesbians could disappear tomorrow if all of us came out of the closet and society saw that we were just people," says Uribe. "I'm a lesbian myself. . . . I never was harassed, because I always hid it. So I never had the experience of having people calling me 'dyke' or 'faggot' to my face, because I just sort of insulated myself. . . . Some of the younger kids nowadays, they aren't doing that anymore, and I've got to hand it to them. They're trying to be who they are at a very young age, which to me is remarkably courageous."

14

Tara II:

Women Seeking Women

Tara Lumley had found a hero and a role model in Martina Navratilova. Yet she didn't want to be gay. She tried to put any attractions she had toward other women out of her mind.

Tara was sixteen and working behind the counter of a small-town grocery store when she met Andy. He would stop in regularly for supplies and they would strike up a conversation. Andy was nearly twice her age, but Tara didn't mind.

"I thought he was cute, everything about him," she says.

One day, Andy dropped in to return a rented videotape while Tara was working, and the two made small talk.

"Well, I can't think of anything I need," he said, glancing down the aisles as he was leaving the store.

"You can take me home."

"Well, what time do you get off work?"

Tara had just turned seventeen when they started dating. She knew her parents would disapprove of Andy's age, so she didn't tell them about her new boyfriend. Her parents were divorced and lived in separate towns. Tara lived with her mother during the week and with her father on weekends. But on some weekends she'd tell her dad she wouldn't be coming over, and she and Andy would sneak out of town together for a night or two at a lake resort or in Minneapolis.

Andy was raised in the city. He was a divorced father, an easy man to talk to, Tara says. Yet he tended to be a loner, a nonconformist. He wasn't into partying, but instead put in long hours running a construction company in a rural suburb of Minneapolis.

Andy was Tara's first true love. "He was someone I thought I could see spending my life with. We got along great. He cared for me a lot, and I cared for him a lot."

Any affections she had for other women remained buried deep, at least for the time being.

After eleven months of secretly dating Andy, Tara decided to tell her mother about their relationship. Her mother took the news hard. She was furious. She grounded Tara, took away the keys to her car, and threatened to have Andy arrested for statutory rape. She gave her an ultimatum: Stay away from Andy for one month and think about what you're doing with your life, or sacrifice your college fund.

"For the month that I wasn't supposed to be seeing him, I saw him every day, even if it was for twenty minutes," Tara says. One night, five days before her eighteenth birthday, she came up with a bogus excuse to get out of the house and met up with Andy and some friends at a fancy restaurant to celebrate her emancipation. When they came out of the restaurant, a note was lying on the front seat of her car. It was from her mother: "I can't deal with your lies anymore," it read. Heaped in the backseat were plastic trash bags filled with Tara's clothes.

Tara moved in with her grandmother.

From her grandmother's home in Clearwater, where Tara grew up, she drove forty-five minutes to and from school each day. Her softball coach, a new biology teacher at school, lived not too far away, and occasionally the two would carpool. The coach was young and congenial, and one evening they decided to have dinner. Tara proceeded to tell her coach all about herself, about her childhood, her family, her boyfriend.

"Well you know almost everything about me now, except for one thing," she said. "Only Emily knows about that."

But with a little prodding, Tara told her coach of her sexual feelings toward Emily.

"So how do you feel about that?" she asked Tara.

"I don't know." Tara still was bewildered by her same-sex attractions.

The coach told Tara of lesbian friends she knew from college and assured her there wasn't anything wrong with women loving other women. She suggested that Tara read some books on gay issues and contact the local gay and lesbian organizations.

"At that point I hadn't really connected to being queer," Tara says. "It was always a big joke. I had this friend at school, and we used to joke around in the lunchroom, and I would sit in her lap and run my fingers through her hair. That kind of thing."

Near the end of her senior year of high school, the name Martina Navratilova came up in conversation between Andy and Tara. Andy mentioned that she was a lesbian, and Tara told him how fascinated she was by the tennis star. She was her hero.

"Do you fantasize about sleeping with her?" he asked.

Tara was floored. He had read her mind. "I denied it at that point," she recalls, "but later I admitted to him that I did." Andy told her that he understood, and remarked that he had sexual feelings toward another boy when he was a teenager.

The topic of homosexuality would come up frequently, usually at Tara's prompting. She had a head full of questions for him about lesbians and gays. "He knew more about being queer than I did, being from the city," Tara says.

One day Andy put a question to her. "He just said: 'So you want to sleep with a woman?' And I said, 'Yeah.' And he said, 'Well, I can get you a prostitute.' And I was like, 'No, that's not what I want.' I was thinking more of a relationship."

Tara knew of a girl on her school softball team who seemed to be gay. "She had a girlfriend in her junior year. And I *knew* that, because of the way they stood together in the hallway, and her girlfriend would come to her games. I mean, I knew she was queer. And I wondered if it could happen to me."

A few weeks later, Andy suggested that Tara place a personal ad to meet a lesbian or bisexual woman. "We were talking about marriage," says Tara, "and we both agreed that it was something that I should sort out before we went ahead with it."

Tara graduated from high school and was spending most of her time at Andy's place. "Right after I graduated, it seemed like it was something I had to step up and take," she says. "My whole interest in this thing wouldn't quit. I thought about it a lot."

Andy gave her a copy of *Gaze,* a gay and lesbian newspaper from the Twin Cities. "I hid it under my bed," she remembers. "I was just awed that there could be a paper like this."

At the end of June, an ad appeared in *Gaze* among the "Women Seeking Women" listings: "Exploring sexuality. Short blond hair, 5-foot, 4-inches, 130 pounds. Interested in bike riding, reading, sports. If you share any of these interests, please respond."

A week later, a letter appeared in Andy's mailbox, addressed to "Woman of Mystery." Tara tore open the envelope and read the short note inside:

"This is the first time I ever responded to a personal ad, because it could have been written by *me.* . . ." A telephone number was printed below.

"I called her like forty-five minutes later, and we talked," Tara says. "She called me the next night, and we arranged to meet. We met on a Monday, the fifteenth of July."

Andy drove Tara into Minneapolis and dropped her off at Lake Calhoun. Waiting for Tara was a woman named DeAnn. She was wearing a yellow hat. "She was really beautiful," Tara remembers. "She had a really beautiful smile. And she smelled really good."

DeAnn was two years older than Tara and lived with two roommates—a married couple—in an apartment just outside of the city. She was an English major at the University of Minnesota and worked part-time at a group home for mentally ill patients.

Tara and DeAnn sat in a park along the lake and talked until sunset, sharing their thoughts on everything from religion to families to favorite movies. Later that week, they decided to see a ballet together, *Romiet and Julio.*

"It was a queer ballet," and Tara had already seen it with Andy. "But I wanted to see it again."

She stayed in the city the night of the ballet and slept with DeAnn at her apartment. "As soon as I slept with her, I was totally whipped," Tara says. "If there's anything like love at first sight, it was possible with her. She made me feel so good, and not just sexually. We had a real good time. All the doubts that I had about what being gay were like, gone. . . . It felt so right. It pushed all the negative thoughts out of my head immediately. It just felt so right."

Their night together was the first time either of them had slept with a woman lover. DeAnn told Tara that she often would hang around a gay coffeehouse, reading the personals in the gay newspapers, dreaming about meeting another woman. "Like every young lesbian, she would sit and hope that someone would come up to her and ask, 'Are you a lesbian? You look like a lesbian. I'm a lesbian too. Let me show you around the city.' "

Tara was sure she had found a partner. But she couldn't just walk out on Andy. They had been through too much together. She was set to begin classes in a few weeks at the College of St. Benedict, a Catholic all-girls' school in the small town of St. Joseph, Minnesota, nearly ninety minutes from DeAnn's apartment. She thought she'd be spending less time with Andy when school started.

"He was security, emotionally, financially, just everything," Tara says. "He was just always there for me. And DeAnn was so independent, she wasn't somebody that I could just throw myself into and be safe about it. Even though I wanted to be with her and not with him hardly at all, he was just secure. I had a lot more power in that relationship."

But Tara was torn by the situation, and by the end of summer, she needed someone to talk to about her feelings. "I wasn't sure how I was supposed to be dealing with it emotionally. There were a lot of changes going on, I just thought some professional help wouldn't be a bad idea."

She asked her mother for a list of health-care providers one day. "I'm thinking of going into counseling," Tara told her.

"Why?" asked her mother.

"Well, I'm just going through some things right now, and I'm not sure I want to tell you."

"You're not pregnant, are you?"

"No, and I don't think I will be."

"I think I know why."

"Why?" Tara was surprised to hear that her mother had suspicions.

"I'm not going to say."

"Well *say* it."

"No, *you* say it."

"Mom . . . I'm gay."

Her mother didn't buy it. "I don't think you're gay," she told Tara. "It's probably just a phase you're going through."

Tara didn't push the issue. Let *her* deal with it, she thought. She wasn't especially close to her mother at the time, she says, and felt indifferent to her mother's reaction.

"I didn't have a reason *not* to tell her," Tara says. "She was the safest one for me to come out to, because I just thought if she disowned me it wouldn't be that big of a loss."

Tara moved into a dormitory at St. Benedict's in the fall of her eighteenth year. She was majoring in sociology and secondary education. She wanted to teach someday.

Once a week, she would make the drive to DeAnn's apartment in the city, and once a week, DeAnn would drive to her dorm for the night. Meanwhile, Tara was still holding on to her foundering relationship with Andy. She couldn't let go. "I would spend at least a night a week at his place too, and he would sneak into my dorm. . . . But I really didn't want him to be there."

Sex with Andy had become unpleasurable, even painful, she recalls. "I think the pain was all in my head. I was so emotionally uncomfortable sleeping with him that it was causing physical pain, too. Every time I was with him, it was so tense and miserable for both of us."

Neither DeAnn nor Andy realized that Tara was sleeping with both of them. Tara had misled DeAnn into believing that she had broken up with Andy, and had quelled Andy's suspicions by telling him she was losing interest in DeAnn. He assumed that her same-sex attraction had run its course.

Tara had come to a crossroads. She had lingered too long in her dwindling relationship with Andy. It was a convenient arrangement, and she was confused about how to get out of it. She didn't want to be pressured to make a choice—Andy or DeAnn? Man or woman? Straight or gay?

But the choice was made for her. Her deceit didn't hold. Andy caught her in her lie when DeAnn had come over to visit. Confronted by both Andy and DeAnn, Tara ran out of Andy's house crying.

Andy was resentful of Tara's scheming and, over the next several months, began making phone calls to her family. Hoping to somehow spoil Tara's relationship with DeAnn, he told her mother, her father, and her grandmother that she had a lesbian lover, "outing" Tara to her family.

"I was mad," Tara says, "because at that time I really believed that I was never going to be out to my dad." Her mother ignored the news, figuring it was Tara's personal business, and her grandmother refused to believe it. "My dad just kind of went along with my stepmom, because she convinced him that it was just a phase that every woman goes through. But then when he saw that it wasn't a phase, he started coming around."

The "outing" ended her relationship with Andy, and Tara gravitated toward DeAnn. They began to grow close, spending as much time together as they could. Shortly after Tara ended her first year of college, they decided to get an apartment together in Minneapolis.

Rent was cheap—$65 a week—in the condemned old house on Pillsbury Avenue that Tara and DeAnn called home. A toilet upstairs leaked water through the ceiling of their one-room efficiency. The bathroom was down the hall. There was no kitchen. Meals could only be cooked in a microwave or on an illegally installed hot plate.

"You had to wear shoes to take a shower, the bathtub was so filthy," recalls Tara. But they didn't care at the time. They were living the true urban experience. And they were in love.

Tara sees her partnership with DeAnn as a junction in the shaping of her sexual identity. "It was weeks into my relationship with her when I thought, I would rather spend time with another woman than a man. It was like a turning point in my development—physically, sexually, spiritually."

Discovering the lesbian and gay community was exhilarating for both Tara and DeAnn. It was the first same-sex relationship for both of them. They would hang out at "queer" coffeehouses, sneak into "queer" bars, get invited to "queer" parties. They attended their first Gay Pride parade that summer. "It was just amazing," Tara says. "It was like, Where are all these people on any other day?"

Her mother came to accept her relationship with DeAnn, the more she saw of her. "She and her husband decided that if they wanted to keep me in their lives, they were going to have to accept my friends into their lives," says Tara.

As fall approached, Tara and DeAnn became homebodies, a happy, infatuated lesbian couple, stuck on each other like Velcro.

"I was totally wrapped up in DeAnn," Tara says. "Pretty much, she and I were what queer was."

15

SIDEBAR:

Identity

When a teenager says he's gay, he'll typically be asked: "How do you know?" It's not an easy question to answer. While young gays and lesbians try to explain that they "just know," they often use sex to furnish the "proof" of their sexual identity. Because they've mistakenly been led to believe that homosexuality is defined solely by sexual behavior, they look to sex to validate themselves.

"There is a feeling out there that you can't know you're gay until you've had lots of negative sexual experiences with persons of the opposite gender and lots of positive experiences with persons of the same gender," says Dr. Gary Remafedi, a specialist in adolescent medicine. "So the message from society implicitly is, use sex as a litmus test for your sexual orientation. The reluctance to acknowledge gay teenagers leads to a tacit encouragement for them to have lots of sex."

It's also conventionally believed that gay and lesbian teens are merely youths who are temporarily "experimenting" with homosexual behavior and will eventually return to a "normal" heterosexual lifestyle. Yes, say researchers, many teenagers *do* experiment with sex. But it cuts both ways. Just as heterosexuals may try homosexual behavior, homosexuals also experiment with heterosexual behavior, sometimes forcing themselves into opposite-sex relationships in order to disguise their gay attractions.

"Many adolescents do experiment with homosexual behavior," says psychiatrist Dr. Richard Isay, a member of the National Lesbian and Gay Health Association. "But the pressure is on the gay adolescent to conform with heterosexual behavior, and not the reverse. . . .

There's a lot of pressure to conform with the expectations of their peers, which is terribly important to all adolescents."

Gay and lesbian teens should be allowed to openly explore the same passions and crushes and loves that their straight peers experience, Isay says. But seldom is that the case. Instead, most gay and lesbian teens are compelled to hide their feelings and impulses, out of fear of being ostracized by their peers.

The many risks that gay and lesbian teens face as they come out flies in the face of claims that they are trying homosexuality just to be trendy. The potential for ridicule, harassment, physical harm—the price for being identified as homosexual—can hardly be regarded as a boost in social status.

"All of my data would indicate that if you're exploring being gay, you're not changing," says Mary Jane Rotheram-Borus, of the University of California at Los Angeles, who has worked with gay youth for more than a decade. "There's little reward. These kids are stigmatized, punished, ostracized. There are such negative social sanctions against it. No one is trying it out to be chic. . . . The kids that are coming out are not changing back to straight. This is not some little flirtation that they then change from."

People might experiment with their sexual practices, but it's not possible to experiment with their sexual identities. "It isn't something that people simply go out and choose, like you choose vanilla ice cream," says Project 10's Virginia Uribe. "It's part of your whole development. Everybody has a little homosexuality in him. If people knew that, they might not be so scared about it."

Bisexuality

Valid explanations or gross misconceptions?

- Bisexuality is just a phase, a stepping-stone to homosexuality.
- Bisexuality is a cop-out used by gays and lesbians who are afraid to come out of the closet.

- Bisexuality is an excuse used by reluctant gays and lesbians in order to gain heterosexual privileges.
- Bisexuality is a pretext used by gays and straights alike in order to experiment with sexuality.

Serious research into the area of bisexuality has been meager, particularly of bisexual women. What is known is that there is little known. Bisexuality is enigmatic, regarded with doubt and suspicion by the straight as well as the gay and lesbian communities, who view bisexuals as "fence sitters," confused or dishonest about their sexual identity. Even agreement on the definition of bisexuality can be elusive.

"If you define it by saying that anybody who has ever had both kinds of partners is bisexual, then there are a lot of those people out there and there is a lot of bisexuality," says the Kinsey Institute's June Reinisch. "If you define it by saying a person has to have both a same-sex and an opposite-sex partner at the same time, then there are very few people that fit that definition.

"There are a lot of people that we would identify as *behaviorally* bisexual—that is, they have had sex with both kinds of people in their lives more than once," says Reinisch. "If you ask them, the likelihood is, they're not going to identify themselves as bisexual. Most will identify themselves as either gay, lesbian, or heterosexual.

"It turns out that there are some people who, in fact, are able to fall in love with both kinds of people," she adds, persons who are aroused and passionate with same-sex as well as opposite-sex partners.

As with Reinisch's explanation, most definitions of bisexuality tend to focus on more than sexual behavior. As researchers point out, behavior alone is not the sole determinant of sexual identity. Factors such as desire, arousal, and fantasy also play a large part in the equation. Someone is truly bisexual, says Isay, if his or her sexual passions and fantasies are more or less evenly divided between men and women.

James Weinrich, a sexologist at the University of California at San Diego, uses this determination: One's sexual orientation is defined by the sex of the person whose naked body shape is most arousing to you.

"If you use that definition for men, there are no bisexuals; that is, there are no men who are sexually aroused by looking, let's say, at pictures of naked men and naked women to about the same degree," Weinrich says. "That does not mean that someone who is gay by that definition cannot get married and have kids or cannot notice that he's aroused by some women. . . . So some gay men who are totally 100 percent gay by that definition can nevertheless discover that they're very much in love with a woman. And if they start having sex, they are very much turned on by the interaction. Bisexuality does exist in that case. So sexual orientation is not just what you tell a scientist what you are. It is what your genitalia do in response to stimuli of naked men versus naked women."

It's not uncommon for gay and lesbian teens to first identify themselves as bisexual as they're coming out. "For some people, bisexuality during adolescence is a transition point," notes Remafedi. "It may be a label applied to themselves until more information is available. And then there are the people who will eventually see themselves as being bona fide bisexual. So I'm theorizing *two* forms of bisexuality—one being bisexuality which is an actual reflection of what is a true sexual orientation, and bisexuality which is a transition point between identifying oneself as heterosexual and the way to homosexuality."

In studies that he has done, Remafedi says, there have been no detectable psychosocial differences between boys who said they were bisexual versus boys who said they were gay. "Once again," he says, "we get back to the profound questions of, What is sexual orientation? And what [do] the labels that people apply to themselves mean? There is no universal understanding of that."

As the executive director of New York's Hetrick-Martin Institute, Frances Kunreuther has listened to hundreds of coming-out stories. "I think there are real bisexual youth. I think there are some youth who are confused about their sexual orientation and will probably be much more primarily gay or primarily straight. I think that there are some youth who find it more acceptable to say they are bisexual than to say they are gay or lesbian—acceptable to others and to themselves, probably. And I think that's fine. That is part of adolescence. We shouldn't be putting them down. We shouldn't be categorizing them, anyway. My belief is young people can categorize themselves. And that categorization may change as it changes in adults. I know plenty of people who are married and then came out. I know people who have been out and then get involved in heterosexual relationships. I think that our sexuality is probably more fluid than we'd like to admit."

Perhaps the most decisive explanations of bisexuality come from bisexuals themselves:

Bisexual activist Victor Raymond defines bisexuality this way: having an attraction for members of both genders; feeling equally comfortable, or equally not *un*comfortable, in a romantic relationship with a person of either gender; or being blind to gender altogether.

"The basic thing that people need to understand is that being bisexual is not the same as being confused," he says. Bisexuals are *not* waiting to make up their minds about their sexual identity. They're *not* sex-starved opportunists, dissatisfied with only one sex. "We're people whose hormones flow for both genders."

Victor came out as a bisexual when he was seventeen. He had not had sex with another man at the time. But based on attractions he had to men, and several satisfying relationships with young women in school, he came to the conclusion that he had a sexual-emotional affinity to each sex. He has since been in long-standing relationships with women and with men, and considers himself a confirmed bisexual—for life.

Part of the misunderstanding about bisexuality hinges on society's need to hang definitive labels on people, Victor says. But when it comes to something as complicated as sexuality, labels become onerous, and comparisons to heterosexuals and homosexuals become unconvincing. "Self-definition must be respected, because once you let other people start defining who you are and what you are, that's when the game starts being played against you."

Victor is a national coordinator with BiNet USA, a bisexual advocacy group. He sees the bisexual movement experiencing the same kind of growing pains that the gay liberation movement did in its early years. "Bisexuals are in about the same place that gays and lesbians were in twenty years ago," he says. The 1987 March on Washington brought the discussion of bisexuality out of the closet and into the public realm, he says.

"This isn't merely a movement about one group getting a set of recognitions. What we're talking about is a movement of sexual liberation, getting people to fully realize the complexities of human sexuality. And that's very frightening to a lot of people."

By all accounts, Susie Knoll was living the life of a typical heterosexual teenager. She indulged herself in things feminine—lipstick and makeup and strapless dresses. She was prom queen in high school. She dated boys, had a steady boyfriend, and eventually had sex. It was pleasurable, she says. There was nothing unnatural about it. "It felt right."

Yet, off and on, throughout her adolescence, she felt "twinges" of attraction toward other young women, she says. She was infatuated by a girl in her middle school geography class. She was enthralled by the older girls on her swim team. In the locker room, her admiring glances would linger on their lean, athletic bodies. And at the local YMCA, she was intrigued by a woman who was known to be gay. "I was always watching her. I don't know why, but I was very aware of her."

In college, Susie befriended a small group of gay men. She became curious about the gay community and issues of sexual identity. She started reading gay newspapers and books on homosexuality, and slowly, she began to understand her same-sex attractions. Yet she was bewildered by what she *didn't* feel.

"I didn't feel like I was lesbian. I didn't feel I was straight. I didn't know who I was." At the campus Womyn's Center, she was introduced to a woman who identified herself as "bi." It was when she listened to the woman describe herself—her attractions, her fantasies, her love interests—that Susie realized she too was bisexual. It was her epiphany.

"As she talked, I felt like she was reading my thoughts," she says. "This capsulized what I was. I felt this wall coming down, like I didn't have to be shameful."

Susie came out as bisexual long before having sex with another woman. And immediately came the suspicions. From her straight friends she would hear: "Have you had men and not liked it?" Or: "Go ahead and experiment. Get it out of your system." From her lesbian friends, she would hear: "You just need to have sex with a lesbian. It'll be the greatest thing in the world, and then you can go on."

But sex was not the defining factor, she told them. Her sexual orientation was framed by affections and love for another person, *any* person, regardless of the gender.

When she did have sex with a woman, it was "sweet" and "exciting," she says. And like her past sexual encounters with men, "It felt so right."

"Sex does play a part in it," she says. "But for me, sex goes along with the love and respect I have for someone." She can develop loving sexual relationships that are equally as intense with both women and men. Sexual orientation is a continuum, as Kinsey defined it. And Susie says she is somewhere in the middle.

"I don't see bisexuality as a stepping-stone. I am not questioning; I am not wondering. I have sexual fantasies about both genders. I have loved a man and I have loved a woman—with the same kind of intensity that makes your shoelaces start on fire. I know it's there. I know I have that capacity."

Susie has lived with the myths: that bisexuals have the best of both worlds; that bisexuals are promiscuous, and crave group sex. "I don't want to be with more than one person," she says. "I don't want to have sex with a man on Monday, sex with a woman on Wednesday, and sex with another man on Friday."

She does know bisexuals who are in bisexual non-monogamous relationships who concurrently have partners of both genders. "It's not something that I aspire to, yet I don't see it as morally wrong. Non-monogamous relationships are not specific to the bi community. People get to make choices about those relationships and how they play out. And if it works for them, who's to judge?"

People shouldn't be so eager to rush to judgment about a person's sexual identity, she says. "You need to respect people for whatever they are labeling themselves. And right now, that place for me is that I'm bisexual. I have no doubts. I'm not sitting on a fence, waiting. It's something that I just know."

Gender

Gays and lesbians are often grouped together, for sheer convenience and sometimes for political expediency. But they're more different than alike. Gay men generally have much more in common with other men than with lesbians. And lesbians generally have much more in common with other women than with gay men.

"So we're sort of strange bedfellows," says Beth Zemsky, a lesbian psychotherapist. "In fact, we have very little in common except for two things: One is, there's something about the coming-out process that is a rite of passage. There's something that happens to ego development when you go through this process and come out on the other side. . . . And the other thing we share is oppression, although oppression smells and looks different for lesbians than it does for gay men."

At the root of homophobia is a fundamental fear of the violation of gender roles. Throughout childhood and adolescence, boys are taught to be strong, self-reliant, aggressive. Anything less is suspect. Boys who act girlish are seen as sacrificing their masculinity, giving up their masculine potency.

Girls, on the other hand, are praised for being self-assertive and independent. Their masculine qualities are seen as positive attributes, signs of superiority—up to a point. Lesbians are tolerated as long as they're not considered a threat to traditional gender roles. Holding hands or kissing in public between two women is still regarded as radical, an affront to our customs and decorum.

"It's okay to be butch as long as you're not *too* butch," says Zemsky. "It's sort of like, it's okay to be a tomboy, but when you're twelve or thirteen you're supposed to start growing up."

Certainly, the more gender-atypical a young man or a young woman is, the more likely he or she will be ridiculed as an adolescent. Yet there's more of a concern about the transgressions of gender roles by males than by females. Simply put, it's more acceptable for women to behave in masculine ways than for men to behave in feminine ways. Sissy boys wearing dresses and playing with dolls are viewed with suspicion and scorn, whereas tomboy girls wearing bib overalls and playing with trucks are considered cute. As boys grow into adolescents, it doesn't take much—the wrong kind of walk or talk—for them to draw the label "fag."

"They grow up in a society that tells them if they step out of their gender role . . . they will be ostracized, possibly harassed or even victims of violence," says Joyce Hunter, co-founder of the Hetrick-Martin Institute. "If they don't have the emotional support, the correct information, and the opportunity to interact with their peers in an open environment, they're going to have problems."

Gay men appear to take the brunt of the ridicule and violence, particularly if they stray from traditional gender roles. One study cites several factors: Gay men tend to recognize their homosexual orientation earlier than lesbians. They are generally more visible than lesbians and thus more vulnerable to violence. And they have more opportunities to go to public gay-identified locales, such as gay bars, which also puts them at a greater risk for anti-gay violence.[1]

"I think gay men are thought of as vile and disgusting," Zemsky says. "Lesbians are either thought of as sort of a joke or titillating. Either we don't exist or we exist for the pleasure of all heterosexual male fantasies."

Compared to male homosexuality, female homosexuality in many ways is regarded as less forbidden, says Reinisch. "In Western culture, it's more acceptable for women to touch each other, hold hands, hug, comfort each other and so forth. So it's very hard to identify who is lesbian. Women have always been allowed to live together their whole lives, and it's just seen as roommates, companions. Not the same for men."

Historically, lesbians have been allowed a certain measure of leeway because, like all women, they have been overlooked within our society. Traditionally, girls and women—whether lesbian or straight—have been regarded as the weaker, submissive sex, a status that in many ways is the result of how they are raised.

"Girls are more isolated than boys," says Hunter. "They are raised to be more dependent and homebound, not to be as assertive to have their needs met. . . . If parents find out or suspect that their daughter might be a lesbian, they're kept close. . . . Curfew will start earlier with the girls." Consequently, it's more difficult for them to meet or interact with other lesbians. They become secluded, undersocialized, enduring a "cognitive isolation," as Hunter calls it, bereft of role models or any understanding of what it means to be a lesbian.

By comparison boys, who are socialized to be more assertive, enjoy more social freedoms. They're permitted to consort with fewer restrictions. As a result, gay young men stand a better chance of meeting up with each other. But because of the social stigma connected to homosexuality, the places of contact tend to be secretive and their introductions furtive. While there are more outlets and opportunities for today's generation of young gays to meet—through teen centers, high school support groups, and computer bulletin boards, for instance—they historically congregated in "pickup" spots, typically, gay bars. Thus, the context of their introduction has been sexual, and sexual contact precedes social contact.

"I believe young gays are socialized into having anonymous sex," Hunter says. "We offer them no opportunity to interact in any other way."

More often than not, young gay men will look to sexual encounters to define their homosexuality, while young lesbians will express their orientation through emotional and romantic attachments. In other words, men have sex, then fall in love, and vice versa with women.

"If you have gay and lesbian adolescents who haven't had time to romance, they will probably fall back on sex roles to tell them what

to do," says psychologist John Gonsiorek. "And consistent with traditional sex roles, males are more prone to acting out during the
coming-out process, and women are more apt to respond with reflection and self-absorption."

Young gay men have a higher frequency of brief relationships. As a
result, they have been saddled with the reputation of being sexually
"promiscuous." But rather than being promiscuous, gay males are behaving much like heterosexual males. Driven by hormones and instructed by society to be aggressors, they're more apt than women to
follow their sexual impulses, which might translate into multiple
partners. In heterosexual courtships, women tend to limit and measure sexual behavior. Straight teens learn how to date and follow a series of "scripts," with sex as a potential end result. But a homosexual
relationship travels the reverse course. The young gay male is not
bound to the same constraints. Potential partners are not socially
scripted to resist sex, as women are. As Gonsiorek puts it, two gay
men equals "sex roles squared."

"What young gay men are doing is what heterosexual men would
be doing if young heterosexual women tolerated it," he says.

Typically, "women tend to do intimacy before identity," says Zemsky. "It's much more common for women to fall in love, then move in
together three weeks later"—the "date-and-mate" syndrome, as she
calls it. Young lesbians rush headlong into steady relationships, expecting all their needs to be met by their union, while young gay men tend
to play the field.

The dichotomy is universal, regardless of sexual orientation:
Whether homosexual or heterosexual, women generally emphasize
intimacy and personal attachment in a relationship, while men stress
autonomy and competition.

"On many erotic matters, gay men are quite like straight men and
not really like straight women, and vice versa for lesbian women," says
Weinrich. "The stereotype, which, like many stereotypes, has a grain
of truth in it, is that the woman has sex because she's all in love with
the person, and the man has all of his love for the person he's had
good sex with."

Role Models or Recruiters?

Adult gays and lesbians have long endured accusations that they're child molesters. Suspicion is reflected in a public-opinion poll taken in 1994 for *Time* magazine and the Cable News Network: When asked whether gays and lesbians can be good role models for children, 57 percent of those polled said no, while just 36 percent said yes.

The fact is, most sexual-abuse crimes are committed by heterosexuals—usually men abusing girls, and usually fathers abusing daughters. "The vast majority are predators, heterosexual in orientation, and their victims have been of the opposite sex," says psychologist Eli Coleman, director of the human sexuality program at the University of Minnesota.

Along with the onus of sexual molestation, gay adults—men in particular—are encumbered by beliefs that they "recruit" teens against their will into lives of homosexuality. Adults are slapped with the slanderous labels "chicken hawk," "troll," or "bull dyke," and indicted for preying upon unsuspecting, vulnerable minors.

The stereotypes are steeped in myths, which maintain that homosexuals are motivated by uncontrollable sexual desires and prefer children and adolescents to adult partners.

"When people try to understand how someone becomes homosexual, they mostly will *not* believe that we are born that way," says Leo Treadway, a gay man who, as an associate with a Lutheran ministry, began working with gay and lesbian adolescents in the early 1980s. "They might believe, for example, that gays were sexually abused or molested as youths. People conjure up this image of adult homosexuals as predators on innocent children, and through seduction or coercion—probably of a sexual nature—draw them into this 'lifestyle.' "

That erroneous though popular scenario is founded on the myth that a teenager's sexual orientation is still forming. However, a growing body of scientific research suggests that sexual orientation is determined long before adolescence. And by the time teenagers begin identifying themselves lesbian or gay, they are more sure than unsure about their own homosexuality.

It's at this critical point in their identity development when gay and lesbian teens should be meeting other gays and lesbians—both peers and role models—to help walk them through the coming-out process, says Treadway. Because parents usually are unaware or unaccepting of a child's homosexuality, those introductions should be the responsibility of gay and lesbian adults.

He points to the heterosexual community and the roles that teachers, scoutmasters, and ministers have played in intergenerational relations. "Almost everyone would agree that the presence of adults —responsible, caring adults—in the lives of children and youth is a good thing." But rampant myths and misinformation have hampered similar intergenerational support in the gay community.

The notion that gay and lesbian adults are able to sway the sexual orientation of teens strikes Virginia Uribe as absurd. "Everything in our society is geared toward making people *hetero*sexual. All the television images and the book images and the magazine images are heterosexually oriented. Yet despite all that, homosexuals still appear. So, obviously, role models don't have anything to do with it.

"I can't imagine that I have ever influenced anyone into being a homosexual," adds Uribe, a teacher and a lesbian. "That is just something you can't influence, human sexuality. We can't even teach our kids where Canada is, let alone influence them to be homosexual."

Nevertheless, the affiliation between gay adults and gay teens is hindered by fear and self-censorship. Spooked by the spurious reputation as "recruiters," gay and lesbian adults feel pressured to bow out of the role of mentor. "The gay and lesbian community is one of the few minority communities where intergenerational contact doesn't exist," says Gonsiorek. "It's extremely difficult for gay and lesbian youth to find positive role models in an organized way."

The single most important task facing the gay and lesbian community is to create a better world for gay and lesbian youth, he says. "The whole society ought to be shouldering the burden, but society at large doesn't give a damn about the gay and lesbian communities. Nothing ever happens. So the ball's now in the community's court. And people are coming to that realization slowly." Progressively, by helping to organize school peer groups, teen centers, computer networks, and the like, adult gays and lesbians have built a track record that stands up to the charges that they're rapists and "chicken hawks."

But the door swings the other way as well: Gay teens frequently become infatuated with gay adults. "A lot of gay youth are erotically attracted to older men," says Weinrich. "Almost without exception, young men who prefer older men feel that guys their own age are way too immature, too busy playing childish games, and so on."

Some older men do manipulate younger men. And some younger men become attracted to older men for all the wrong reasons. "But it's important for people to realize that the stereotype of older gay men molesting young boys is a false stereotype," adds Weinrich. "There are some who do so, of course, and should be locked up in jail. And there are also some heterosexuals who do the same things with little girls."

The line between intergenerational relationships and exploitation is a fine one. Often within the gay and lesbian community itself, the issue remains off limits.

"As a community, we haven't really openly dealt with that issue," says Kunreuther. "Coming out of the feminist movement, we were very openly talking about how men exploited young women. But in the gay community, we don't talk about how men exploit young men. We pretend it doesn't happen."

Counselors at Hetrick-Martin advise teens that a relationship with a peer is preferable to a relationship with an older person, she says. A relationship with an older adult can be immensely confounding for a young adolescent. The balance of interpersonal power is skewed by the age discrepancy, and the role of the adult can become ambiguous and misleading.

"We have a real struggle with confusing intergenerational relationships and pedophilia," Kunreuther says, "which I think is absolutely clear-cut."

Needed is a clear-cut norm within gay culture that says: Gay and lesbian teens may choose to be sexual with each other, but gay and lesbian adults should not to be sexual with teens, says Gonsiorek. Then the impediments to gay and lesbian adults serving in adult roles with gay and lesbian youth would lessen.

"Clearly, there is a gray area—middle and late adolescence," he adds. As with other cultural norms—from the right to vote to the age limit on drinking—an age cutoff is necessary to separate adolescence from adulthood.

"That's a very hard situation to formulate, because in that group—middle and late adolescence—are varying levels of maturity. Is it inappropriate for a nineteen-year-old to have an interaction with an eighteen-year-old, or a seventeen-year-old, or a sixteen-year-old? I mean, where do you cut it off?"

Some areas, though, are far from gray. "If a forty-five-year-old runs through a fifteen-year-old every three months, that is not true love. That is exploitation, and that is the profile of most of the pedophiles."

16

Amy II:

"Walk Away from Trouble"

On a Sunday evening, a dozen baby-faced teenagers sat elbow-to-elbow around a large table in the back room of the Café Wyrd, the unofficial Minneapolis headquarters for young gays and lesbians. Strains of the Indigo Girls and Ella Fitzgerald drifted softly from a CD player as the set of friends, all clad in black jeans and T-shirts, sipped cappuccino and Italian sodas, sucked on filterless cigarettes, arranged tiles on a Scrabble board, and flipped carelessly through the pages of the local gay newspapers—a touch of bohemia. They were a network, an alliance, a clique with attitude, tight enough to catch each other's inside jokes and know who was dating whom—and who wanted to.

Amy Grahn, free from her parents' home for the weekend, listened to the conversation and laughed. She was dizzy with devotion, enlivened by this newfound kinship. This was her element, these were her "buds," and her type. They knew who she was. And they accepted. "They're the greatest group of friends I ever had," Amy beamed.

In her transformation from country girl to city girl, from tomboy to town girl, Amy had become a regular at "the Wyrd." Employees knew her by name and sometimes took down phone messages for her from her friends or her mother. The coffeehouse, of course, was a great place for her to meet other young lesbians. And lately she'd had her eye on Katie, older than Amy by four years, with black bobbed hair and a droll, urban attitude. The two were introduced through mutual friends and hit it off instantly. Amy was intrigued by Katie's poise and connections within the gay and lesbian communities, while Katie seemed charmed by Amy's country innocence and sense of adventure.

Amy had spent the entire weekend knocking around the Twin Cities. She stayed at the home of a lesbian couple she knew and then went to a tea party on Sunday afternoon at Katie's house before dropping by the Café Wyrd. It was a perfect two days. But as always, the good times were coming to a close. A friend had agreed to drive Amy halfway home, to a shopping mall where her mother would meet her and take her home. And Amy was running late.

Amy's home in the western suburb of Shorewood was barely thirty minutes from downtown Minneapolis. But it might as well have been in South Dakota. She felt trapped, forced to keep her sexual orientation hidden at a high school where homosexuality was still regarded as unmentionable. "I feel closeted, that's a big part of it," she complained. "Nobody's out here. Nobody that I know of."

The contrast between the city and the suburbs was stark. "It's a real culture change," Amy said. "It's kind of like I don't want to go home anymore. I want to be with my gay and lesbian friends. And I can't."

After spending eleven productive months at a school for emotionally troubled students, Amy enrolled at Minnetonka High School near her home. During the fall of the following school year, though, she transferred to South High School in Minneapolis so she could be part of a support group for gay and lesbian students. The group—formed at the insistence of a handful of gay students and run by the school nurse—was the first of its kind in a Minnesota school and one of only a few in the nation. Amy liked South High and loved the city. People weren't as homophobic, she concluded. And she seemed to fit right in with the crowd at South. Through the support group, she was introduced to a handful of lesbian and gay peers and soon began going out with a girl a year younger named Gretchen. She was Amy's first same-sex romance. The two went out together for four months and once slept in Amy's basement bedroom at her home. It was Amy's first sexual experience with another woman.

But her tenure at South High was temporary. After less than a year, Amy decided to return to her school in the 'burbs. Her relationship with Gretchen had ended disastrously when she discovered that

Gretchen was dating another girl behind her back. Moreover, traveling into Minneapolis every morning was disruptive to Amy and her parents. In order to catch an early bus into the city or a ride with her father on his way to work, she had to wake at four-thirty in the morning. Going to school in Minnetonka, just ten minutes away from her home, was much more convenient.

But the change brought a distressing reminder of the loneliness that she had known in her junior high school years. The suburban school and the city school were light-years apart. South High was unique, unlike anything Amy had ever known, an inner city school with a broad diversity of students, from jocks to punkers to gangbangers—and her small group of openly gay friends. Minnetonka High, by comparison, was upper middle class and, to Amy, snobbish. It was a school of conformity, a slice of white-bread America: braces and push-up brassieres, team sweatshirts and starter hats, prom-night fantasies and daddies' cars.

On the drive home from the Café Wyrd after her intoxicating weekend of freedom, Amy sank into a fitful depression. She detested living two lives, a closeted life on weekdays and the high life on weekends with her new circle of friends. She wanted out of Shorewood, out of Minnetonka High School, out of school altogether.

Amy didn't sleep at all that night. She tossed and turned, replaying over and over in her mind those pitiless memories of being ditched by her friends in eighth grade. The next day, she couldn't get out of bed. A migraine kept her home from school. She hadn't sunk so low since she was hospitalized for depression two years ago.

Sue Grahn sensed her daughter's mood swing right away. She had learned to keep a watchful eye on Amy's emotions and could tell when depression was setting in. That afternoon, when Amy's father got home from work, Amy and her parents caucused. They sat around the dining room table to sort things out, piece by piece.

Jim Grahn, former math teacher that he was, pulled out a legal pad to help Amy measure her misery. In one column, they listed her frustrations and problems. In another column, they drew up a set of potential solutions:

Problem: Amy is lonely and isolated at school.

Solution: She would change schools.

Problem: Amy is too dependent on her parents for transportation and spending money.

Solution: She would find a part-time job and maybe buy a cheap car. For the time being, she would be allowed to use her father's car three days a week.

Problem: Amy is boxed in, distanced from the community of gay friends she has made in the Cities, removed from the cafés, the parties, the weekly support groups—and the young women with whom she shares a likeness.

Solution: Her curfew would be negotiable. As she neared her eighteenth birthday, her parents would honor her need for greater independence.

Amy snapped out of her funk immediately. She saw that there were answers to her dilemmas. And she saw that her parents were her allies.

"My dad made me laugh, and we figured things out," Amy said. "And it was okay." Life wasn't so hopeless after all.

With her parents' consent and the school district's authorization, Amy was enrolled in a private, alternative school in the nearby community of Eden Prairie, a program for students who for one reason or another couldn't cut it at a conventional high school. Amy planned to continue classes through the summer and find part-time work.

Her last day at Minnetonka High School was bittersweet, a day of deep regrets and new horizons. Ostensibly, the day was a formality. She had to drop off her textbooks, hand in a couple of assignments, and pick up her locker deposit. She hadn't bothered to tell anyone she was transferring out; she had grown indignant and callous. But secretly she hoped that word of her departure had gotten out and people would flock to her with kind words and best wishes for her future.

There were no goodbyes, no gifts or balloons or silly cards bidding her good luck. As always, she walked the halls by herself, generally ignored by her classmates. *Whatever,* she shrugged, trying to steel herself against the disappointment. She was quite used to the lonesomeness.

Amy ate an early lunch, alone. Three tables away sat her childhood friend, Billy, unmindful of her transfer or her discontent. Billy and Amy hadn't hung out together for years. Except for small talk on the bus or in a classroom, they barely spoke anymore. He too had drifted out of her life. "I miss him," Amy lamented out loud. She gathered her notebooks and hurried off to English class.

English was her favorite subject, thanks to the humor and enthusiasm of her teacher, known affectionately by his students as Mr. Z. A thirty-something hippie with a stubby ponytail, dark beard, wire-rim glasses, and a single earring, Mr. Z had spent a good amount of the semester teaching a section on romantic poetry. For the class's midterm project, students were required to interpret the lines of a poem or song lyric. Not surprisingly, every student in the class chose the lyrics of a rock song.

Accompanied by a taped cassette of their selected song and printed handouts of the lyrics, each student steered the class through a commentary on the imagery, the symbolism, the *message* of the words. One serious-minded young woman with short cropped hair dissected the lyrics to "Black Boys on Mopeds" by Sinead O'Connor. A Tom Petty lookalike attempted to find deep meaning in Petty's song "Free Fallin'," while a shy student in a short skirt dwelled on the gravity of "Candle in the Wind" by Elton John.

Amy's selection was an interpretation of "Luck in My Eyes," by lesbian singer k. d. lang. She stood silently at the front of the classroom, staring down at her lyric sheet, as the portable cassette deck played her anthem of the day. For Amy, the song couldn't have been more poignant:

Gonna walk away from trouble
With my head held high
Then look closer you'll see
Luck in my eyes. . . .
All my trouble

All my troubles gone
All my worries
All my worries gone. . . .

Mr. Z gave Amy a long handshake after class and wished her well. She ended her day by clearing a wad of term papers and stray paperbacks from the bottom of her locker, and then left the building. All her worries, gone.

Amy celebrated her liberation from Minnetonka High at a St. Patrick's Day party at Katie's house. Katie shared an older two-story duplex in Minneapolis with half a dozen friends—gay, lesbian, bisexual, and straight.

Whenever Amy came into the Cities, she would kill time at the duplex, watching videos, listening to music, or just sitting around the huge dining room table talking with whoever wandered in. Katie and Amy had become steady dates. And lately, on weekends, Amy would sleep over, and the two women would share a bed.

The house was furnished economically, like the home of any other group of college-age tenants. A mountain bike, ironing board, and rummage-sale sofa occupied the living room. Lifeless potted plants dangled from the ceiling. A milk crate held a small television. On the walls hung homemade art and a poster of Madonna.

The front door of the house remained open wide all night long for the St. Paddy's Day bash. People came and went, some familiar, some not. Guests clotted in the kitchen, mixing vodka and orange juice. An extra refrigerator in the back stairway was filled with beer and unidentifiable food. A radio played loudly in one bedroom while a boom box played loudly in another. A black light illuminated toothy smiles. Someone banged on a drum set in the dining room, while a Dalmatian—identified by Katie's housemate as a "gay dog"—sniffed for food on the table.

As Amy paraded through the party, wearing a green paper hat turned backward on her head, friends greeted her with bear hugs and high fives. The household had become her happy sanctuary. Her new friends had become her best friends.

"This is the fun I never have!" she crowed.

It had been an enormous week for Amy, a glorious week of coming of age. She had changed schools and made a pact with her parents that allowed her more independence and more room to come out. And she had fallen head over heels for Katie.

In two days, Amy would turn eighteen.

Amy Grahn reached her majority on March 19. On this day, she legally purchased a pack of cigarettes (for her mother), bought a lottery ticket (and lost), and gained the right to vote. As an emancipated adult, she could now call her own shots in life. And maybe most importantly (on *this* night, at least), she would finally be admitted into a downtown gay bar to dance.

But before she was let loose for a night on the town, her parents threw a surprise birthday party. One by one, friends appeared unexpectedly at the Grahns' front door carrying presents: a lesbian couple who had become role models to Amy; a straight friend who had been Amy's peer counselor during her darker days of depression. And Katie.

The party began awkwardly. The occasion marked the first time Jim and Sue Grahn had ever met their daughter's lover, Katie. While they tried valiantly to make Katie feel welcomed, they weren't accustomed to seeing Amy so intimate with another woman. It was uncomfortable to watch the two kiss and hold hands. Somehow, the sheer physicality made the notion that Amy was a lesbian a reality, a finality. Sue was visibly tense. You'll get over this, she told herself. It's just another hurdle. Still, it brought up the question that she had asked herself so many times lately: Why does it have to be this way?

When the introductions were done and drinks were poured, the friends and family sat in the living room to watch Amy open her gifts: A pair of black high-top Converse sneakers, required attire for any eighteen-year-old. A copy of the book *Fried Green Tomatoes at the Whistle Stop Cafe*. As an acknowledgment of her coming-out process, a white

T-shirt bearing the bold black letters GWF—Gay White Female. And from her father, always the sentimentalist, a dozen red roses.

Dinner was served. Katie took a seat at the table next to Amy, then turned suddenly to face Amy's father. She had an announcement, she said.

"Amy is my girlfriend," she said, proudly. It was an engagement announcement of sorts, without the rings, a formal declaration of Katie's affection for Amy.

"I'm not surprised," smiled Jim, nodding his head.

Amy let out a nervous laugh, somewhat startled by the proclamation, and then launched into the story of how they had first met.

The ice was broken. The tenseness dissolved. Over coffee and homemade birthday cake, the lesbian couples shared coming-out stories and tossed bawdy wisecracks across the table. Almost as a test of the Grahns' tolerance, they swapped jokes about lesbians.

But Jim was ready with his one of own: "Did you hear about the new line of tennis shoes for lesbians that just came out?" he asked with a wink. "They're called Dykies, but they had to be recalled. The tongues weren't long enough."

Sue groaned, embarrassed by her husband's crassness. But Amy's friends were hysterical. Jim had won their hearts. And Amy had won her parents' acceptance of her new friends and lover.

"Oh my God, I feel so happy," she said. "This is my best birthday ever!"

17

SIDEBAR:

Parents and Families

When a child comes out of the closet, parents must come out, too —by choice or by circumstance. Ready or not, parents are asked to put aside years of ignorance and prejudice and enter a world entirely foreign to their sensibilities, a world fraught with myth and misunderstanding. No matter how loving and empathetic parents might be, the adjustment is never an easy task. To discover that their son or daughter is gay can knock them off balance and plunge the entire family into crisis.

Coming out is one of the most difficult issues a family may ever have to face. Parents and siblings often hold many of the same unfounded fears and apprehensions about homosexuality as the rest of society. But with the coming out of a son or daughter, a brother or sister, the family suddenly is forced to bear a share of the societal umbrage cast at gays and lesbians.

The response by parents usually is less than ideal. Parents tend to react to the myths rather than the realities. They respond with an array of emotions—denial and rage, dread and disgrace. They feel shamed by the discovery. They feel responsible for their child's homosexuality. And they feel completely lost about an issue that, in their minds, is sure to become problematic.

Connie Bender's son came out when he was twenty-one. The news caught her totally off guard. For months, she tried to hide from relatives and friends the fact that he was gay. But her son resisted being closeted, and he pulled away from his parents. Eventually, he moved away from home.

"Parents are afraid of what other people think. It's real basic," says Bender. "They don't want other people to think that they're bad parents and did something wrong. . . . That's the big hurdle for parents."

The Parents' Response

Before they have much of a chance to sort out their thoughts and feelings, parents are asked first and foremost to form a response to their child's disclosure. It's a critical juncture in the relationship between child and parent, and in the child's maturation process. The way in which the child copes with the recognition of his or her homosexual identity will hinge on the reaction of the parents. If parents are oblivious to the struggle, teens will live in secrecy, left to confront the seemingly contradictory question of their homosexual orientation without family guidance. If parents are ill prepared to help, teens will look elsewhere for affirmation and support, all too often relying on dubious sources. Parents' rebuking and devaluing the child's sexuality can be a profound blow to the child's self-worth and sometimes contributes to a lag in the child's social development itself.

Indeed, parental response to a child's coming out is crucial to a healthy, normal identity, say gay and lesbian youth advocates. "There are certainly many families who are supportive of their young gay and lesbian children, but unfortunately, I think there are many more who are not," says Rea Carey, coordinator of the National Advocacy Coalition on Youth and Sexual Orientation. "Just their very home may not be a safe space. . . . Either they feel like they can't come out to their parents and brothers and sisters, or if they do come out, they fear that they may be kicked out of their homes or suffer physical or verbal harassment from their families. They may end up running away, living with friends or other family members, becoming involved in behaviors to douse the pain, whether that's substance use or having sexual experiences that put them at risk."

While the family may be the safest refuge, many kids are scared to death to tell their parents they're gay. Not only do they face the scorn of a judgmental society, but they risk being forsaken by their family, turned away by the people they love and trust the most. Knowing they're among one of the most despised and shunned groups in society, they see that their sexual orientation must be hidden. In their homes as well, they're forced to live a life of silence and deceit.

"The approval and support of parents particularly is terribly crucial, because without that, young people really feel cast adrift and rejected," says Mitzi Henderson, president of P-FLAG, Parents, Families and Friends of Lesbians and Gays. "Rejection by parents—the people who nurtured you and cared for you and whose love you thought you could count on—is one of the cruelest of all. This is their home base. Even if the relationships with parents are not real good, the feeling that there is that one tie, that one bond, is hard to shake."

P-FLAG grew out of the efforts of a mother of a gay young man assaulted in New York City while he was distributing leaflets protesting the mistreatment of gays. The organization was formed in 1982 with three aims, says Henderson: to keep families in loving relationships; to educate society about homosexuality; and to advocate for gay and lesbian rights. It now has nearly 350 chapters in the United States and Canada, with a membership of more than 35,000 households.

"The worst kinds of reactions parents have are to cut their kids off, throw them out, put their belongings out on the driveway, and say, 'I never want to see you again,' " Henderson says. "Throwing kids out, making it impossible for them to live at home, ragging them all the time, looking through their things, bugging their telephone conversations, imposing curfews, sending them off to a private school—these are not myths.

"Sometimes kids realize that they're different very early," she adds. "They don't have a name for it or a label or an understanding that it's a sexual orientation. But they realize that there's something different and it may not be acceptable. So they strive to be the perfect child, the high achiever, the dutiful son, the dutiful daughter. And that makes their sense of betrayal even deeper when they realize that they are gay or lesbian and their parents may reject them for that."

A Family of Strangers

In a sense, lesbian and gay teens come out to a family of strangers. Unlike other minority groups, they do not have role models in their parents. To the contrary, parents and siblings may be antagonistic toward their sexual minority status and may want to distance themselves from the gay child.

"Lesbian and gay kids are the only ones that have no preparation for their minority status," points out Joyce Hunter, co-founder of the Harvey Milk School in New York City. "They are not born into a family of homosexuals. So they are isolated, and that isolation is the major problem for them. They are at risk for family violence. . . . A lot of these kids run away, and that puts them at risk for drugs and violence and suicide."

Judith Sinclair came frightfully close to losing her son to suicide. When Mike, her only child, was fourteen, he took an overdose of pills.

"He did this in the middle of the night, while I was sleeping," says Sinclair, a secretary. "But fortunately he had second thoughts and came and woke me up, and I rushed him to the emergency room. If he had not changed his mind and come and talked to me, the doctor told me that I would've found him dead in bed the next morning. He had taken twenty-nine antidepressants, about a fourth of a bottle of aspirin and about a half a bottle of Extra-Strength Tylenol or something. And he'd washed it down with a little Southern Comfort."

Sinclair believes it was a combination of issues and events that led to Mike's suicide attempt: His father had died a year earlier, and Sinclair herself had been depressed and unable to devote much time or attention to her son at the time. All the while, Mike was silently struggling with his emerging homosexuality. Though Sinclair suspected her son was gay, Mike didn't come out to her until he was nineteen.

Sinclair says she was accepting from the start. There was little self-blame or teeth-gnashing, and very few dashed expectations.

"I think one of the reasons it wasn't a big deal is, having nearly lost him made all that really unimportant," she says. "Any parent who's ever come close to losing a child better be darned grateful that they're okay. I don't care if they're gay or straight—he survived."

As with most parents of gays and lesbians, Sinclair had to deal with the reactions of her own parents. When Mike came out by announcing that he was moving to Michigan with another man, Sinclair's parents were hardly receptive.

"He came out to them right before he came out to me," she recalls. "And apparently my mother's reaction was, 'Go ahead, move to Michigan with this man, get AIDS and die.' "

Sinclair tries not to hide the fact that her son is gay. "With my friends and relatives that I trust, who are a little more open-minded and a little more liberal, I'm very open about it. I guess I felt this way: If my friends are really my friends, and they really love me and they really love Mike, it won't make any difference to them. If it does, and it changes our relationship somehow, they weren't really my friends to begin with. As it turns out, everyone who I believed were my friends *were,* because no one has turned away, not even my most conservative best friend. She has a little hard time with it, but the thing is, she's known Mike ever since he was a small child and she's always loved him. You know, she might have a problem with others, but with Mike himself she doesn't have a problem.

"My mother's only reaction to me was, 'Well, I'm really glad that you can talk about it with your friends. But you know I really don't want the rest of the family to know or my friends to know. I'm too old to have to deal with this.' "

Role Reversal

In a society that condemns gays and lesbians as sinners and perverts, coming out can be a perilous undertaking. But like other life passages, it can also have positive results. It can be liberating and cathartic for youth, and can provide the context for developing and honing coping skills.

For parents, though, the process is seldom celebratory. Instead of sharing their child's sense of relief and empowerment, parents feel guilt, fear, sadness. Many deny their child's revelation, or try to force their child to stay closeted, or insist that their child be "treated" for their homosexuality, or renounce their child altogether.

"At first, it's like their whole world caved in on them," says Virginia Uribe, founder of Project 10 in the Los Angeles Unified School District. "And their immediate response is guilt. And then they have this sadness. They cry. And they get angry. . . . It's real tough on the parents. And some can never make that jump. Some parents stay alienated from their children forever, which is so sad."

The distress is frequently exacerbated by the belief that their parenting practices somehow caused their child's homosexuality. Parents typically blame themselves for their child's plight.

"There's a sense of alienation, that 'I should have known, I should have been able to see this, I thought I knew my kid, I wasn't a good enough parent to really understand this about my child,' " says Henderson, of P-FLAG. "And it's a shock to realize that you *don't* know your child that well. . . . Parents have the fantasy that they're going to mentor their children into an adult life, an adult role. But when that child is gay or lesbian, suddenly they're no longer the mentors. The *child* becomes the mentor for the *parents,* introducing them into a world that the parents really don't know much about. And that's a role reversal that is very difficult."

Children become the teachers, informing their parents of the gay or lesbian experience, acquainting them with the gay culture, parenting their parents as they make their way through the coming-out process.

Nothing had prepared Dick Barrett for the announcement that his son, Neil, was gay. "It was a real surprise," recalls Barrett, a retired sewage plant supervisor, union organizer, and the father of nine. "He was active in the youth group at church, had a lot of girlfriends, and so forth. For me, it was a real jolt.

"I describe myself as a typical 1950s father, who pretty much ran the world, you know, with some help now and then," he says. "I was in charge. Union, supervisor at work, church. I had this mistaken notion that it was a male structure and we ran it, and I ran my part of it very well."

But his son's disclosure led Barrett to re-evaluate his beliefs about religion, about sexuality and, essentially, about personal values.

"I reflected on how easy it was to tell gay jokes before that, because it was always somebody else," Barrett says. "That came to a screeching halt, because like so many things in your life, once you know a person, you can't really generalize or categorize any particular group. . . .

"I think that's the real struggle with homophobia. We just have such fixed notions in our minds of what should and shouldn't be. I don't have any problem with homosexuality except in the area—and this is where I think most homophobes really struggle with it—the genital-sexual activity of gay people. What really turns a lot of people off, myself included, is public display of excessive affection. Not the normal hug or something. As a straight person, that turns me off with hetero-sexual couples, too. That part of sexuality is a personal, private thing. . . . I generally put everything in that context. Straight or gay doesn't make a hell of a lot of difference. I don't think it's proper behavior for normal adults.

"I was pretty homophobic at the beginning. Frankly, I had a real struggle. Males are more intellectual, I think. They deal from concrete things rather than from their feelings, so my own personal journey was going from the head to the heart. And today I'm somewhere in between. . . . I'm still working on that whole issue of sexuality."

With Neil's permission and help, Barrett and his wife, Beverly, slowly began telling friends and family that they had a gay son. The process took nearly a year and a half. "We eventually started telling Neil's siblings, little by little," says Barrett. "Our oldest son had a real struggle with it. Still does. He's like I was twenty years ago. He's the sole breadwinner, he's a fifties father, even though he's younger. He's everything that I taught him to be, and I can't fault him for that, because that was the role model that I had and I passed it on. . . . It's a strained relationship."

In the course of raising nine children, Dick and Beverly Barrett have endured a disproportionate share of family crises, including chemical abuse by their children and a teenage pregnancy. And just months after Neil came out, another one of their sons was killed, stabbed to death at a party.

Barrett sees unfortunate parallels in being the parent of a gay child and of a murdered child. In each case, he felt denial, anger, and shame, he says. He was afflicted with a relentless sense of guilt—for fathering a gay son, for failing to protect his murdered son. And for years he had a tough time admitting to people that he was the parent of a gay son or a murdered son. It took three years for Barrett to "come out of the closet" as a parent of a murdered child, he says.

In 1992, eight years after Barrett learned that Neil was gay, his youngest child, Craig, announced that he too was gay. "The biggest lesson that I learned from that was what a struggle kids must go through, because it became that hard for Craig to come out in our family, even with a gay brother. He had to go away [to college], establish his own identity, and come back and come out. You must wonder what kids in a family that's really homophobic must struggle with."

Barrett was ordained as a deacon in the Roman Catholic Church in 1990. He has become somewhat of a spokesman in the Catholic Church on behalf of gay rights. Today, he is completely open about being the parent of two gay sons. When people ask about Craig or Neil, usually he tells them they're gay. "It's the easiest way to deal with it. It doesn't make any sense to skirt around it. My general rule is, I'm going to tell you and *you* can struggle with it."

Lost Horizons?

Parents often feel an enormous amount of loss when they discover a child is gay or lesbian—a loss of assumptions, norms, and images of what make up the model heterosexual family. That sense of loss frequently catapults them into something resembling the grieving process.

"They feel as if they're losing a child," says Uribe. "But what they're losing is all their heterosexual expectations of that child. And they're replacing him with a whole new set of expectations. In most cases the parents don't have a clue as to what that means. So it's a real difficult process for them."

The notion that homosexuality is a result of troubled families or bad parenting causes needless guilt and self-blame to parents. "There's nothing to blame themselves about. It's like blaming yourself for your child's eye color," says psychologist John Gonsiorek.

Realigning heterosexual conventions and values is a huge leap for parents to make, which does produce a legitimate loss—a loss of future perceptions. "Parents perceive that their kids will go on a certain course in life and become married and have children," says Gonsiorek. "What is genuinely lost . . . is the anticipated future of what their kids' life course is going to be. And I think that is a psychologically legitimate loss."

Parents will always be role models to their children, no matter what sexual orientations run in the family. And there's a great deal that heterosexual parents have to offer their gay and lesbian kids, says Gonsiorek.

"Relationships are relationships, and parents have a lot to offer kids in that regard, if they're reasonable parents," he says. "A lot of the bread-and-butter issues are just human issues. And I think oftentimes parents forget that."

▲ ▼ ▲

Back in the 1950s, when Barbara and Douglas Taylor were dating, they dreamed of the "perfect" family. "Before we were married, we were sending one another Mother's and Father's Day cards," says Barbara Taylor. "We planned on a family. We were going to do everything right."

So when two of their four children turned out to be gay, their dreams and expectations were replaced by fear and confusion.

Amanda, the Taylors' third child, came out to them while attending a women's college in California. "I always considered us very close," Barbara Taylor says. "Amanda always shared more with me than I wanted to hear about some things." When she had suspicions that her daughter might be attracted to women, she believed Amanda's disavowal. "I'd ask her, 'Well, is this an issue for you? Is this something that's appealing or interesting to you?' " recalls Barbara. "And she said, 'Not for me. I just find it curious.' And so I had totally dismissed it."

But one day, when Barbara was visiting her daughter at school, Amanda conceded that she was lesbian. "And I remember just being blown away," Barbara says. "Because I thought I knew her so well and because she had assured me that this was not an issue for her, I had kind of dismissed it from my mind. So it was very difficult for me."

A big obstacle for Barbara was the sense of loss. "I felt like I knew what it was like to be a woman—and I don't know what it's like to be a man—but I didn't know what it was like to be a woman and be attracted to women. That was just foreign to me. And so the daughter that I felt I knew so well, it was suddenly like I didn't know her at all. We had been very excited about her being a daughter. She was our only daughter. We named her Amanda Bliss Taylor because it was so blissful to have a daughter. She was like a special treat. So there were lots of things that I had hoped to share with her that I just very quickly began to realize I wouldn't share in that same way. I sort of felt like the daughter that I knew had gone away and there was someone else there. I almost felt like there was someone wearing an Amanda suit. I felt real estranged, like, Who is this person? I thought I knew her. And obviously I didn't know her at all."

Amanda's father, Douglas Taylor, found an analogy in the musical stage play *Fiddler on the Roof,* in which a Jewish father expresses anger and disappointment when his daughter marries a gentile. "There seemed to be very much a parallel there, that, here's as if everything that you shared when you were courting and everything that you had hoped for in your family is no longer the case."

The Taylors' second child, Christopher, came out a year after Amanda. Again, the news hit the Taylors hard.

"I cried a lot," Barbara says. "For about two years, I cried. I cried on the freeway, I cried while swimming laps. I just felt like this is too hard, this is just too darn hard. . . . Even though I knew better intellectually, I did have this feeling that somehow I'd failed my kids, there was something I hadn't done that maybe I could have."

Douglas, a professor of mathematics, remembers the words of another father that he met at a P-FLAG meeting. "He said something that I found very truthful. He said, 'The problem is, you can accept your children's sexual orientation, but you can't share it.' That's the thing, that inability to share that feeling. . . . That really struck me."

Even though Barbara had spent years working as a nurse-practitioner and had taught high school students about human sexuality—including homosexuality—she lacked the emotional credentials for parenting a gay child. "Being an educator and talking about something that you're intellectually informed about is far different than when you've spent your life worrying about children's braces, immunizations, whether they can drive safely, and then, all of a sudden, worrying whether they're going to be assaulted on the street or get HIV."

The emotional reconciliation was arduous. "There was an unfolding of emotions over a long time, months," Barbara remembers. "There was this kind of ambivalence about it all. We couldn't get on with it. I was kind of hoping, Well, maybe this isn't true, because then I won't have to deal with it. You go through all these years of raising your kids, and you think, Oh dear, I don't have the energy to learn something this new, this *challenging.*

"This has a lot of impact, because it touches so many things that you're not even aware of, all the expectations that families have of their kids," she says. "I became aware too that the hardest thing was feeling like I was keeping a secret, and there was nobody really to talk to about it."

The Taylors both come from small families of origin. So far, only Barbara's mother has been told that Christopher and Amanda are gay. "And now, Grandma plays these little games with Amanda," Douglas says. "Every time she's here, Grandmother will say, 'Well now, have you found a boyfriend?' Amanda said to me, 'What should I say to Grandma?' And I said, Get angry at her. Tell her, 'Grandma, I told you I'm not interested in boys.' "

Although their road to understanding was often bumpy, Barbara and Douglas say they are as accepting of their two gay children as they are of their two straight children. "I'm proud of them," Douglas says. "I think of their sexual orientation as a little blip in their personalities and their lives. . . . I think by the time Christopher gets to be my age, it's not going to be such a big deal. I hope not."

Barbara was instrumental in forming a high school support group for gay and lesbian youth. She is a long-standing member of P-FLAG, and has marched in Gay Pride parades locally and nationally. Yet sharing the family secret—with friends or strangers—still causes a certain amount of trepidation.

"It still seems big," she says. "It's still not like it's nothing. A counselor I talked to once said, 'You know, you don't have to share this with everybody. You don't have to put your pearls before swine. You can choose who you want to share this with.' It's special because it involves your heart. It's what you care most about. But I feel also if I can say this to some people, then maybe it'll touch someone somewhere. . . .

"I guess the thing that drives me now, besides wanting to be more understanding and more knowledgeable and more empathetic, is the civil rights issue. That does make me want to be more of an advocate. I think the thing that came after all this initial stuff was the feeling that, doggone it, I don't want my kids to be discriminated against. Or anybody else's.

"Because of this," she decides, "my life is certainly destined never to be dull, because new things are happening all the time."

Sibling Rivalry

Parents aren't the only family members forced to reevaluate their expectations. Siblings too are compelled to react when a brother or sister bursts through the closet door. The response of a sibling, though, generally differs from the response of a parent. Rather than shouldering a sense of guilt or blame, brothers and sisters may feel embarrassed, abandoned, even betrayed by a lesbian or gay sibling. They may resent the fact that they also could become "stained" by the stigma of homosexuality.

"Siblings *have* to deal with it," says P-FLAG's Henderson. "They have to decide if they are going to stay in the closet about having a gay brother or sister. What do they say when their friends comment? At what point do they tell someone they have a gay or lesbian brother or sister? Is that going to affect their relationship with somebody who's dating them? In my own family, my older son had a great deal of trouble with it, but we didn't realize it because he was away at school. Five years after our son told us that he was gay, there was a big explosion between the two brothers, a big fight. By that time, my older son was married and his wife said, 'You have a real problem, don't you?' And he said, 'Yeah, I do.' And he had to begin then to work it through. It turned out that he felt it threatened his sense of his own sexuality. If his brother was gay, was there something latent about himself? What did that mean for him? Did he carry those genes? Was there something about himself that he didn't understand? It was scary for him. He couldn't even verbalize it. It was something that had riled him up emotionally."

▲ ▼ ▲

Embarrassment and anger were the first emotions to hit Karen Tvedt when her younger sister told her she was a lesbian—anger because she was the last in her family to know, and embarrassment because she thought it would be hard to admit to the fact that her sister slept with women.

Karen, a teacher, was twenty-one at the time. Her sister, Tina Garrett, was two years younger. Tina already had brought the news to their grandmother, to their parents, who were divorced, and to their younger brother, who was still in high school. But she waited to tell Karen last.

"I made a big to-do about that," Karen remembers. "My feelings were hurt. I felt betrayed that she didn't trust me enough to tell me earlier on, like when she first knew, and maybe we could've talked about it. But she just wasn't there yet. And I understand that today."

But she didn't at the time. "She knew how my response would be—that's why she told me last," Karen says. "I wasn't very understanding about it to her at all.

"I was in Madison, Wisconsin, in college. Tina went to school at MIT [Massachusetts Institute of Technology] in Boston. She called and she said she had to tell me something. I knew by the tone of her voice that it was something important, and then she just said that she was gay.

"One of my first reactions was, What is everyone going to think of me? I didn't consider her feelings at all, about how tough it was for her to tell me or what she was going through at the moment. I was selfish. I was embarrassed. . . . I asked her personal questions that were probably none of my business and I *didn't* have permission to ask, like, who her first relationship was, how did she know—those kinds of questions that I think are silly now. . . . I didn't ask, 'Gosh this must've been painful for you. How are you doing?' I was really questioning it, to make sure that this was what she meant. I was kind of skeptical, and embarrassed, I guess.

"The thing is, I kind of always knew she was gay. She didn't date men. And stereotypical things, like appearances. She looked to me like she was gay. Even growing up she was more masculine than I was.

And so it wasn't a complete shock to me when she called. But she was finally saying it. And I didn't treat her very well."

Karen had never given much thought to the issue of homosexuality. "I adored [a relative] who was gay, I thought he was a neat guy. But I didn't think about it, because it never really touched my life very closely."

But when Tina announced she was a lesbian, it brought the issue home—literally. "Then I thought, Gosh, it's genetic. I thought it was definitely something that ran in the family. . . . It dawned on me after a while, What if I have kids that are gay? Because you never know. It certainly is a possibility."

Tina returned home from college, politically supercharged and brimming with gay pride. "Tina would kind of be in my eyes a little bit preachy about it, and that made it uncomfortable for me," Karen said. "I wanted to kind of accept this on my own time and go through this process on my own, how she went through the process of coming out on her own. She had a problem with that. She wanted us all to get it right away and kind of celebrate her sexuality. And none of us did at first. We needed some time to think. I think she was mad about that, or disappointed anyway. She wanted us all to be really happy for her, because she was really happy, relieved, I think. And she wanted us to be at that same place, and none of us were right away. We needed some time. . . . She wanted me to march with her and things, and I wasn't comfortable with that at this point. It took several years for me to kind of be normal around her, because I was always on guard then after she told me."

Since then, Karen's comfort level has risen. "I don't feel like I've done a 180-degree flip, but I feel I've come a long way. I like the person that Tina's with now, her partner. I go over to their house a lot and hang out with them, like another couple. . . . I guess I'm not at the point where I really celebrate it for them. But I'm comfortable around them, and I'm happy for them. . . . I remember when Tina first told me, I thought, She'll never get married, and she said, 'Why not?' And I said, 'Well you can't. It's against the rules.' And that kind of thing. And now I think that would be kind of fun, actually.

"The big thing for me was when she was in my wedding last year. She hates to wear dresses. She doesn't wear makeup; she doesn't have pierced ears. And I wanted her to be a bridesmaid at the wedding. But I told her she needed to wear this dress that everyone else wore, and nylons and the shoes. And if she didn't, well, that was okay, but she couldn't be in it, because that was the uniform. And she never once complained. She even wore clip-on dangling rhinestone earrings. She looked great. She didn't complain once."

But feeling at ease when Tina was openly affectionate with a woman was another barrier for Karen to overcome. She remembers going to a movie with her husband-to-be and Tina and her date. "I remember spending half the time of the movie looking over my shoulder at them, because they were sitting next to each other with their arms around each other. And it was really uncomfortable for me, thinking of what other people in the movie theater might have been thinking.

"I think the public-affection stuff still bothers me," Karen admits. "Even today, even though I feel comfortable, I have a tinge of, Uh oh, what are other people thinking? I know that they're looking at them and thinking something. When we're at their house for dinner and they hold hands and, like, hug each other, it doesn't bother me.

"At the beginning, when it was all kind of hard, it would've been a lot easier for me if she hadn't been gay. Only for me. But when I got out of the selfish part of the process I went through . . . now I don't wish that. Now it's pretty normal for all of us.

"I guess the embarrassment comes when I would think of the sexual part. That bothered me. I didn't understand. I still don't really understand those feelings, because I'm not gay. But today I know that I don't need to understand them. I don't have those feelings, and that's okay. And Tina doesn't have feelings for men. It doesn't really matter."

Growing Pains

If you are faced with the coming-out experience, P-FLAG's Henderson counsels patience, from both the parents and the child. Gay youth harbor a good deal of anger and resentment toward their mothers and fathers over their parents' inability to parent them as young homosexuals. But they often underestimate the hardships their families must endure as they themselves come to terms with the issue of homosexuality, Henderson says. Having a gay child redefines the family, and in many ways sends parents back to square one.

"All youngsters are testing the waters of independence. And gay kids are no different," says Henderson. "They push the limits of their parents and may expect immediate support and understanding. I think young people have very little understanding of the investment that parents have in their children—and the desires for their children. Very few of the parents feel that being gay is an easy life. Very few of them have models for happy and successful gay lives, and so for them this is often very frightening and devastating. They too are searching for more information, and it may take them a while to come to an understanding."

As with many parents who have grown to accept their gay and lesbian children for who they are, Tom Sauerman has become a staunch activist on their behalf. Sauerman was the first national director of P-FLAG, serving from 1990 to 1992. He now works with the AIDS Task Force of Philadelphia.

"I have two sons. One of them is straight, one is gay. And one of them has more rights than the other," he says. "I work to change that so they both have equal rights.

"This is the last minority that you can still discriminate against. If my child were in a wheelchair or were black or Hispanic or whatever, there would be plenty of protection. This is the last minority to oppress and still get away with it."

Sauerman is a retired pastor with the Evangelical Lutheran Church in America. He makes it clear that he's not a wild-eyed fanatic bent on tearing down the family institution. To the contrary, P-FLAG is trying to preserve families, he says.

"I think that P-FLAG families are in total support of traditional family values," he says. "Those traditional values include love and honesty and mutual support. We strongly resent religious leaders in particular who would deny us those values. In fact, those religious leaders—who claim to have traditional family values—would have us turn on our own children. . . . These are children that we've given birth to and nurtured and loved all their lives."

As a clergyman, Sauerman has no use for pious bigotry. "A number of our people turn to our religious leaders at a time of family crisis and get no help at all. What they get are moral pronouncements."

Sauerman offers a bit of advice to parents who learn that their child is gay or lesbian: "Tell them, 'There's nothing you can say or do that would make me not love you. And if there are secrets that you would ever want to talk to me about, whatever the secret is, I can handle it.'

"Most of us did all the stuff wrong in the beginning. Our son came out at sixteen. We had difficulty with the announcement, but eventually we realized that nothing about him had changed. He was still the same child we had loved all along."

Today's American family still suffers growing pains as it transcends the romanticized and fictionalized version fostered by the decades-old images of *Ozzie and Harriet* and moves toward acceptance of a more diverse definition of "family." America's institutions—from schools to religion to media—continue to maintain stereotypes of a family that no longer exists, which hampers the appreciation of diversity.

"We grow up in a society where everyone is assumed to be a heterosexual," notes youth worker Leo Treadway, a former ministry associate with a gay-positive Lutheran church in St. Paul. He likens the suspicion leveled at a families with gay children to the once-widespread suspicion leveled at white families with adopted children of color.

"I look forward to a day," says Treadway, "when part of the expectation of families is that it is possible that you'll have a gay or lesbian child."

18

Derek II:

Robbed of My Childhood

Derek Johnson was living three lives: On weekdays, he attended high school, biding his time while holding down a C average. After school, instead of playing sports, he worked part-time at a day-care center in St. Paul and volunteered in the cancer ward at the University of Minnesota Hospital, entertaining terminally ill children. On weekends, he stole away to a Sunday-afternoon support group in Minneapolis called Lesbian and Gay Youth Together.

There were no support services for gay students at Derek's school. The Sunday meetings were the only exposure he had to the gay community. And Sundays couldn't come soon enough. As each weekend arrived, he became a human chameleon, changing from a shy and closeted high school student, one of only a few African-Americans in his class, to a wide-eyed gay young man dying for attention.

But Derek had convinced himself to keep his sexual orientation masked. It was a matter of self-preservation. "It was clear to me that being gay was something that people either wouldn't understand, wouldn't accept, or wouldn't like," he says, looking back. Derek was five years younger than the closest of his five siblings, a brother. So by the time he was in his mid-teens, he was the only child still living at home. Consequently, he was always under the watchful eye of his parents, particularly his mother, a rigid disciplinarian.

During the summer before his senior year, Derek's mother became increasingly suspicious of his behavior. He had been pulling away from his family, putting in more hours at work (against his mother's advice), staying out late at night with friends, and shutting himself in his bedroom or in the basement to use the telephone. Young men she'd never met were calling, refusing to leave messages. Questionable pieces of mail were arriving addressed to Derek.

On a day late in August, Derek's mother was preparing the guest room for the arrival of his aunt, who was flying in from Detroit to visit. His mother hounded him to clean his room, but Derek was on his way out. He was going to a party with a group of his friends he knew from work.

Derek returned late in the afternoon. His father was outside, tinkering under the hood of the station wagon. "I said hello, and I could tell right away that something was wrong," Derek remembers. "I asked him how his day was, and he was very quiet." He guessed that his parents had been arguing.

His mother met him at the front door. He could see that she had been crying.

"What's going on?" he said.

"Go look in your room," she answered.

"What?"

"Go look in your room," she repeated, sternly.

His bedroom looked as if it had been ransacked. His dresser drawers had been pulled open wide, clothes in his closet had been torn off their hangers, and his mattress had been overturned.

He began to tremble. The cardboard box in which he had stored his gay newspapers, paperbacks, condoms, and a pornographic videotape was in plain view, removed from the hiding place underneath his bed. His secret was out.

"Are you gay?" demanded his mother. Derek's mind raced for an excuse. Make something up, he thought. Tell her you're working on some sort of research project on homosexuality. But he decided not to lie and told her, yes, he was gay.

"No you're not!" she shouted angrily, and began questioning him about his friends, his feelings, his sex life.

"I saw the videotape," she said to Derek. Inside the cardboard box he had stashed *The Look,* a movie he bought of men having sex.

"Is that what you want other men to do to you?" she asked him. "Is that what you do to other men?"

Derek didn't answer. He was in a fog. He couldn't believe what was happening.

"How do you know you're gay?" his mother continued. "Have you had sex with a woman? Have you been abused by another man? How long have you *known* this?"

Derek tried to explain: He figured out he was gay when he was thirteen, he told her, and had been going to a support group. But his mother wouldn't have it. "No one knows at thirteen," she said.

All the while, his father sat at the kitchen table, listening. He didn't say a word.

"I can't believe my son is a faggot!" his mother blurted out. She fired off a list of conditions for her son to abide by: "First, I want you to destroy that video. I want you to see a doctor and get some information on AIDS. And I want you to go to a psychologist, so he can convince you that you're not *gay.*"

Derek tried to calm her down. He agreed that meeting with a psychologist might be a good idea, but *not* as a "cure" for his homosexuality, he told her.

But his mother would not be placated. "I won't tolerate this under my roof," she vowed, and left for the airport with his father to pick up Derek's aunt.

Derek immediately phoned the leader of his support group, Leo Treadway. He was afraid that his parents were going to throw him out of the house.

"That was my big concern, that I was going to be kicked out. And there was good reason for fearing that," Derek remembers. "I needed some advice."

Treadway was sympathetic but told Derek there was little he could do. He had to try to work through the crisis, talk to his parents, reason with them if he could.

His parents returned with his aunt late in the evening. The inquest had been interrupted, the crisis postponed. "We pretended everything was just fine and dandy," Derek says.

But far from it. He knew that his relationship with his parents would never be the same.

In the aftermath of his "outing," Derek and his parents avoided any mention of his sexual orientation. "Things just died down for a while." He began his senior year in high school, and continued to work at the day-care center and to volunteer at the hospital. On Sundays, he went to the support group in Minneapolis, and on Saturdays, he spent time at a new social club he had discovered, Teen-Age Gays of St. Paul, or TAGS.

A couple of months after the sudden revelation, Derek's mother asked if he had made the appointment with a psychologist. He told her he had been busy. "She didn't push the issue," Derek says.

His parents didn't speak to him much. Any mention of the word *homosexuality* on the TV or radio was met with a collective nervous gulp by Derek and his parents. No one would break the silence. It was almost as if he were living with strangers. "I came home and did what was expected of me, and basically kept to my room most of the time." Family gatherings at Thanksgiving and Christmas eased the tension, but only temporarily. The gulf between Derek and his parents widened. He told his friends that he was sure he had spent his last Christmas living at home.

Weeks passed and, again, Derek's mother asked if he had seen a psychologist. Again, he stood his ground. "This isn't something that's going to change," he insisted. "This isn't a phase."

Derek was sure his mother was monitoring his telephone calls and reading his mail. So he got a post office box and voice-mail service with his own personal phone number. "It was getting to the point where she interrogated anyone that called me," he says. "Everyone was sort of a suspect—of leading me into this corrupt lifestyle, in her eyes."

By late winter, just weeks before his eighteenth birthday, he decided he had had enough of the silent treatment.

"There seemed to be so much anger," he says. "So I called my sister and told her things were getting pretty bad at home." She offered to let Derek sleep on the couch at her apartment in the suburbs. She picked him up the next afternoon. His parents were out. That evening, he called his mother to explain. He was going to live with his sister, he told her.

"No you're not!" she shouted into the phone. "Until you turn eighteen years old, you're gonna live in *this* house, even if it takes me coming over there and bringing you back home. You're gonna stay *here* tonight."

Defying his mother's command, he remained at his sister's. Early the next morning, his sister drove him home to get a fresh change of clothes before school. But he couldn't get in the door. His parents had changed all the locks.

Two weeks later, at his mother's insistence, Derek moved back home. He was hardly welcomed with open arms, he says. "The utter look of disgust on my mother and father's face. . . ." he remembers. "In their eyes I was just being difficult. My frustrations and reasons for leaving—leaving out of *fear*—were not recognized."

Things soon started heating up again between Derek and his mother. She asked once again if had been to a psychologist for help. He ignored her question.

His relationship with his mother again was rapidly sliding downhill. He avoided eating meals with his parents. "It was like walking on eggshells just to keep from having any reason to start a fight," he says.

One evening, Derek realized that his mother was eavesdropping on a telephone conversation he was having with his gay friend Glen. He had been telling Glen how difficult things were at home and how badly he wanted to leave.

"Who's Glen?" she asked him when he had hung up the phone.

"Just a friend of mine," he answered.

"So, you want to move out," she said. "I'm going to do you a big favor." Derek brightened, thinking his mother was going to offer to help him find an apartment. But instead, she told him to move out—"now."

"It was a few days before my eighteenth birthday," Derek recalls. "She told me I had two weeks to get out."

When he made plans to move in with a friend, his mother backed off her demand and told him he could stay. Then, just as suddenly, she told him to get out. Then, again, she relented. "It went back and forth: You can stay; you can go." The mixed messages hit him like a whipsaw. "I was pretty distressed, pretty frustrated with things."

His father, meanwhile, had ignored the issue altogether, refusing to say anything about Derek's gayness or his plans to move. So finally, eighteen years old and exhausted by his mother's hectoring and his father's interminable silence, Derek left home. He skipped school one day after his morning classes and, while his parents were at work, packed all of his clothes, his books, and his cassette tapes in cardboard boxes and got a ride to his friend's apartment.

That night, he took a bus back to his parents' home to tell them face-to-face that he was gone for good. It was the first time through the entire crisis that his father spoke about Derek's plight.

"So this is it?" he said to his son. "I come home one day and you've moved out? Don't you think we deserve more?"

"Well, no, under the circumstances," responded Derek. He was angry. His parents seemed to be blaming him for being gay. They seemed to be holding him accountable for *their* inability to respond.

His parents had few words for him that night. And none were supportive. They were at a standoff. His father tossed a spare house key across the coffee table. Derek put it in his pocket and walked out.

"Mom tells me you're gay." Derek's sister had reached him by phone at his friend's house. He explained to her that his sexual identity had been the source of his problems at home.

"It doesn't matter to me," she said, "but promise me that you're safe."

It was the first time anyone in Derek's family had expressed any semblance of concern for him. "It was the first accepting response I had got," he says.

For six weeks, Derek stayed with his friend in Minneapolis, sleeping on a hideaway bed with a cat named Harvey. He would get up at 5 A.M., bus to St. Paul to go to school, work a few hours at the day-care center and at another part-time job he found, then study when he came home. The schedule was wearisome. Derek wondered how he would continue. Something had to give. Maybe he would have to quit school.

Just weeks before his graduation, Leo Treadway, the support group leader—and Derek's newly designated surrogate father—arranged for Derek to move in with a gay couple, who volunteered as foster parents for homeless gay youth. "Basically, it was a place for me to stay where I didn't have to worry about a job," Derek says. "I could stay as long as I wanted in order to get on my feet." He lived rent-free in a bedroom in the attic, with the freedom to come and go when he pleased.

The foster home was a lifesaver. Despite the estrangement from his parents, Derek suddenly was on the throes of a personal liberation. Out of high school and on his own, it was the first time he could live out of the closet. "It was much easier to meet people my age," he says. He and a group of six or seven young gay teens he'd met in the support group began hanging out, going to movies and dance clubs, or sneaking into a gay bar once in a while.

"The biggest thrill for me was coming home at three in the morning," he remembers. "I was happy with my newfound independence. Things were beginning to turn out okay."

Derek found a full-time job at the Science Museum of Minnesota, working as a "classroom assistant" with the museum's youth programs. For an eighteen-year-old, the pay—$4.25 an hour—was decent enough to get by on.

He rarely went home, and talked to his parents very infrequently, communicating mostly through his sister. He resented their reluctance to learn something—*anything*—about his sexual orientation. They could have easily gotten their hands on books on the subject, he reasoned, or gone to a psychologist themselves, or talked to the leader of his peer support group, or contacted Parents, Families and Friends of Lesbians and Gays. But they didn't. Instead, they shifted the burden of responsibility to him.

"At the time I needed my parents the most, they were very distant and unwilling to help," he says.

When he was in high school, he had been accepted into a college assistance program for minority students. He had had plans of studying to become a children's social worker. But after he moved out, his college plans evaporated. The door of opportunity slammed shut.

"I felt robbed of something," he says. Pushed out of his home, onto the street, and into the workforce before he was out of school forced him to grow up fast. "In some aspects, I felt I was robbed of my childhood."

Through a friend of a friend, Derek was introduced to a thirty-two-year-old man named Howard at a dance club one night. Howard gave Derek his phone number, and the next night they went to see a movie: *Presumed Innocent*. In the theater, Howard put his hand on Derek's knee. "It became clear that something more was happening," he says.

But Derek was sexually naive. All of his encounters had been with young men his age who were as unsophisticated about sex as he was. "This was my first experience with someone who was interested in more than being friends, without saying so," he says.

Howard was a graphic designer with a nicely furnished condominium in the city. He invited Derek over to watch a basketball game and eat pizza. Derek spent the night.

"This was the first man I slept with," he says, and the first time he had intercourse. "It was more curiosity than anything else. I was sort of intrigued."

But after going out with Howard three or four times, Derek became offended by his racist notions about gay black men—that all black men were well endowed and oversexed. "There seems to be this preconceived question, What is it like to be with a black man?" Derek says.

It was a turnoff. "Hearing that, it didn't seem genuine," he says. "My curiosity was satisfied. Whatever the interest was, was gone." He called off the relationship.

But along with a full-time job and a room of his own, the short-lived affair represented one more threshold that Derek had crossed in his passage to adulthood.

19

SIDEBAR:

Lives At Risk

- Harassment and threats
- Truancy and expulsion
- Sexual abuse
- Unintended pregnancy
- Prostitution
- Homelessness
- Drugs and alcohol
- STDs and AIDS
- Suicide

The roster of troubles faced by today's teenagers grows longer by the year as adolescent life becomes ever more complex and unpredictable.

The problems may apply to all adolescents, but the risks are magnified for gay and lesbian youth. Marked for ridicule and rejection long before they disclose their homosexuality, they've been found guilty by association and are sentenced to an adolescence of scorn and shame, alienated from friends and family and disenfranchised from mainstream adolescent culture. As their gay identity develops, stress and troubles arise, which in the worst cases can lead to a host of devastating problems.

Discredited, feared, or simply ignored in their most vulnerable moments—their coming-out process—young gays and lesbians are woefully underserved by schools and social service agencies. Though the risks are becoming more widely recognized, still absent are the means and the willingness to address those risks.

"We feel strongly that there is a tremendous need to address the difficult issues facing gay and lesbian youth," pledged Massachusetts governor William Weld at the 1992 swearing-in ceremony for the Governor's Commission on Gay and Lesbian Youth, the first of its kind in the country. "We must abolish the prejudice and isolation faced by gay and lesbian youth. We need to help them stay at home and stay in school so they can have healthy and productive lives."

Progress has been incremental, as more and more programs and policies for gay and lesbian youth are put in place—from state-sponsored commissions such as the one in Massachusetts to high school support groups to community-based teen centers. But under a constant scrutiny and threat of being undone, advancements are slow. And the risks continue to take an immeasurable toll on gay adolescents.

Harassment

One of the biggest fears of gay or lesbian teens is the threat of harassment—from parents, siblings, classmates, teachers, coaches, even their close friends. Long before they've revealed their homosexuality, they're sometimes looked upon suspiciously as being "different." If they bend the gender roles and fit the stereotypical characteristics assigned to lesbians or gays—if they're girls who appear "butch" or boys who act "queeny"—it isn't long before they hear the epithets: *queer, faggot, dyke, lezzy.*

Advocates say that gay and lesbian adolescents are stepping out of the closet in greater numbers and at a younger age. They're becoming more visible in American society. In some measure, their visibility is a promising sign that they're sure of who they are and confident of being accepted within their community. But it also can effect a backlash, in schools particularly, as lesbians and gays who are fifteen, fourteen, or even younger become defenseless targets of harassment and violence.

"As a young person comes out, unless they really do have the support, they face violence, discrimination, teasing, and harassment from their peers," says Rea Carey, coordinator of the National Advocacy Coalition on Youth and Sexual Orientation. She points to a 1993 report on sexual harassment in the schools by the American Association of University Women. A survey of 1,632 students at 79 secondary public schools across the continental United States found that 4 out of 5 teens said they had experienced some form of sexual harassment during their school lives. Of those who said they were harassed, 17 percent said they had been called *lesbian* or *gay* (or some derivative slur) when they didn't want to be. Of all the students questioned, 86 percent said they would be upset if they were labeled gay or lesbian.[1]

"The biggest fear among young male students—heterosexual, homosexual, bisexual—was *not* that they would be attacked physically . . . but that they would be called a 'faggot,'" Carey said, citing the survey findings. As they come out, without support at school or at home, gay teens have no one to turn to and nowhere to go that's safe.

"Violence is a very real factor," says Virginia Uribe, founder of Project 10. "It's one of the reasons that they hide their homosexuality. They don't want to be verbally abused, which is epidemic in our society, and in some cases they don't want to be beat up and bashed."

Several campus surveys of gay and lesbian college students have documented verbal abuse as well as physical violence. In studies at Yale, Rutgers, Pennsylvania State, and Oberlin, between 3 and 5 percent of the gay and lesbian respondents said they had been punched, hit, kicked, or beaten at some point during their college careers; 16 percent to 26 percent said they had been threatened with physical violence; and 40 percent to 76 percent said they had been verbally harassed.[2]

In a study sponsored by the Seattle Commission for Lesbians and Gays in 1990–91, nearly 3 out of 4 of the 1,291 lesbians and gays who were surveyed reported having been physically or verbally assaulted. Sixty-four percent said they experienced verbal abuse by a stranger, 20 percent by an acquaintance, and 16 percent by a family member. Sixteen percent overall reported being physically attacked.[3]

The National Gay and Lesbian Task Force reported 1,813 anti-gay incidents in 1993 in six select urban areas: Boston, Chicago, Denver, Minneapolis/St. Paul, New York, and San Francisco.[4] Victim service agencies documented cases ranging from harassment to vandalism to assault to bomb threats to kidnapping to murder. Sixty-eight percent of the victims were male, 26 percent were female, and the remainder were of unknown gender.

"Because of under-reporting by victims, it is estimated that these figures reflect only a fraction of the actual number of incidents that occurred. . . ." said the report. A wide variety of incidents were reported to the task force from across the United States, including the following:

- In Tampa, Florida, the home of an HIV-positive lesbian AIDS activist was burned to the ground while she attended a national march for gay rights.

- Supporters of the Oregon Citizens Alliance distributed a flyer in the Salem, Oregon, public library, calling for the execution, castration, and imprisonment of lesbians and gays. The flyer urged readers to demonstrate their "love" for gay men by slashing their throats and letting them bleed to death.

- In a state park near New Hope, Pennsylvania, seventy skinheads and neo-Nazis held a rally called Gay Bash '93.

- A gay man was shot and robbed by two men who admitted stalking "faggots" in Wichita, Kansas. The incident left the man a quadriplegic.

- A man hiding in the backseat of a lesbian's car forced her to drive to a field near Woodhaven, Michigan, where he raped her. During the assault, the man reportedly said, "This should teach you not to be a queer. . . . This is what you need."

- In Tyler, Texas, three men forced a gay man into a car at gunpoint, drove him ten miles away and shot him at least fifteen times, killing him. The three men boasted that they had robbed and assaulted other gay men in the past.

The threat of harassment hounds nearly every gay and lesbian, both adolescent and adult. They live in a state of caution, obliged to check their behavior and censor what they say in public for fear of being ridiculed or harmed.

"There's always the risk when you're coming out that someone is not going to like you, because of just *that,* no matter how well they get to know you," says Jaime Barber, a lesbian teenager from Seattle who worked as an intern with the National Gay and Lesbian Task Force in 1994. "There's always that risk and that danger. There's always a danger that you'll get kicked out of your house by your parents when you come out. There's the danger that when you walk down the street holding your lover's hand that you're going to get beat up.

"I was queer-bashed in Seattle," says Barber. "There were some frat boys that were just out looking for some trouble or something, and I was walking with my girlfriend. And they had a baseball bat. They whacked me a good one and broke two ribs. And they broke her nose. They hit her with the butt of the bat, right square on the bridge of her nose. . . . I managed to get up and fend them off. It was really traumatic. I was fifteen."

Throwaways

When there's nothing else, there's always the streets. Young gays and lesbians know that too well. Found out and forced out by disapproving families, the most desperate ones quit school and run, sometimes resorting to prostitution in order to survive, while putting themselves at great risk to physical harm.

Estimates of the number of teenagers living on the streets or in homeless shelters across the United States range from 500,000 to 1.3 million. And, like most data about homosexual adolescents, the number of homeless teens who are gay or lesbian is exceptionally difficult to gauge because they are largely a silent and hidden population.

A 1989 report on teenage suicide for the U.S. Department of Health and Human Services estimates that 25 percent of young gay males are forced to leave their homes because of conflicts over their sexual identity.[5] In a study presented to the city of Seattle's Commission on Children and Youth in 1988, the Department of Human Resources reported that approximately 40 percent of the city's runaway and homeless youth were gay, lesbian, or bisexual.

"If you scratch beneath the surface of some data, you find a disproportionately large number of gay-lesbian-bi-transgender, 'queer' youth who are runaways, who are throwaways," says Leo Treadway, who co-founded a peer support group for gay teens in the early 1980s. "I think it is just a matter of basic human decency that we try to respond to the plight of these young people."

In a survey of twenty-nine gay and bisexual male teenagers at the Youth and AIDS Projects at the University of Minnesota, half reported running away from home, more than one quarter reported dropping out of high school, and more than half admitted using drugs and alcohol.[6]

Living out of their homes becomes a desperate act of survival. Underage, undereducated, unemployable, and lacking in community or family support, these "throwaway" youth are left with few legitimate options. Many turn to the sale of drugs, prostitution, or other illegal activities to pay for food or a place to stay.

Prostitution

I'm out there
Waiting for anybody
Anyone there
Looking for someone
There I stand
The seductress
For any man
To undress
If it's right

The offer is made
I'm in his sight
Of the many
In the parade
I am picked . . .
—poem by an anonymous gay prostitute

Working the streets usually isn't a chosen occupation. More often than not, young gay prostitutes hustle out of economic need. Many come from dysfunctional families or broken homes and are on the run or kicked out by parents who don't understand or won't tolerate their sexual orientation, says Dr. Robert Deisher, a Seattle pediatrician who did some of the first research on gay youth and male prostitution in the 1960s.

"It is an oversimplification to say that young male prostitutes are just youths with emotional problems who need treatment, or delinquents who can be dealt with exclusively through legal machinery," stated his groundbreaking 1969 study. "They have come to live this life because of social, economic, psychological and physical factors. . . . Undoubtedly, the repulsion people express for the behavior of these young people has an effect on them and often keeps them out of agencies such as medical clinics, where they might otherwise be helped."[7]

The assessment still holds true today. For gay youth, "survival sex" often is a dire byproduct of family trauma. Disowned by their parents and equipped with few employment skills, they gain a sense of control of their lives, as well as a source of instant income, through prostitution.

"These kids come from all socioeconomic backgrounds, but what seems like a common denominator is that they come from pretty dysfunctional family backgrounds," says psychologist Eli Coleman, who has studied male prostitution. "They're searching for something. Some of them, because they're out of their homes, are merely searching for economic security. It's really about survival. And they have learned that this is a means of survival."

A survey of 131 gay and bisexual African-American and Hispanic teens in New York City showed that nearly one quarter bartered sex for drugs or money, placing themselves at high risk for HIV infection.[8] A demographic study based on interviews and observations of forty-seven male prostitutes in Seattle showed the average age to be sixteen, and the average age at first prostitution to be fourteen. Seventy percent of the prostitutes identified themselves as either gay or bisexual. The education levels of their parents were rarely beyond high school; 83 percent reported that their parents were divorced or separated. And at the time of the survey, 74 percent of the respondents were not in school.[9]

The incidence of childhood physical and sexual abuse is high among male prostitutes, says Coleman. In essence, street hustlers are repeating the victimization process of their past, setting themselves up for being hurt and taken advantage of. "That's all that they know," he says.

According to a survey of male prostitutes in San Francisco, nearly one out of three reported that sex was a motivation for "tricking."[10] "A portion of them are exploring their sexual identity this way," Coleman says. Without a support system at home or at school, and without other legitimate ways to meet other young gays, prostitution becomes "the only avenue available" to find out about sex. "For some, it's a real power and glamour trip that boosts their very low self-esteem and gives them a false sense of security in a short-term way," he adds.

Of course, not all young gay men with an abusive background or from a dysfunctional family turn to prostitution. But the risk is clearly present, particularly among gay youth who walk on society's periphery. "With more and more support groups available," Coleman notes, "we might see less and less of this."

Suicide

Perhaps the most publicized and most controversial risk linked with adolescent homosexuality is suicide. Each year, about two thousand adolescents kill themselves in the United States. Within the past decade, a handful of studies have suggested that the number of gay and lesbian teenagers who take their own lives is disproportionately high.

• In 1989, researcher Stephen Schneider of the Suicide Prevention Center in Los Angeles found that 20 percent of 108 self-identified gay men ages sixteen to twenty-four have attempted suicide. "Nearly all of the attempters were aware of their homosexual feelings, but had not yet established a 'positive gay identity' at the time of their first suicide attempt,"[11] stated the report.

• A study in Seattle and Minneapolis in 1991 by Drs. Gary Remafedi, James Farrow, and Robert Deisher found that 30 percent of 137 gay and bisexual young men ages fourteen to twenty-one reported having attempted suicide at least once.[12] Nearly half of all attempters described multiple attempts.

• The most attention-grabbing study was prepared by the U.S. Department of Health and Human Services Task Force on Youth Suicide. Completed in 1986, the study was released three years later, delayed by the Bush administration under pressure by conservatives in Congress. The report placed suicide as the leading cause of death among gay and lesbian youth, estimating that as many as 30 percent of the completed youth suicides were by young gays.

"Gay and lesbian youth belong to two groups at high risk of suicide: youth and homosexuals,"[13] stated Paul Gibson, a licensed clinical social worker in San Francisco and author of the report. "A majority of suicide attempts by homosexuals occur during youth, and gay youth are two to three times more likely to attempt suicide than other young people. They may comprise up to 30 percent of completed youth suicides annually."

Critics of the task-force report say the research was lax and the conclusions were politically motivated. Dr. David Shaffer, a psychiatrist at Columbia University in New York, took the report to task in a

June 1993 article in *The New Yorker* magazine. "The paper was never subjected to the rigorous peer review that is required for publication in a scientific journal, and contained no new research findings."[14]

Moreover, critics argue that the samples in most suicide studies are negatively biased; that is, the gay and lesbian subjects were troubled youth recruited at drop-in shelters or outreach programs and therefore predisposed to a higher risk of suicide to begin with.

"It's a big controversy," says psychologist Mary Jane Rotheram-Borus of the University of California at Los Angeles, "because some people's political agenda is to make kids look at risk for suicide, and other people's political agenda is not. And so it's hard to sort out how to interpret the data."

There are problems with *all* data that involve gay and lesbian adolescents as samples, says Rotheram-Borus. Because most of them are in hiding, the only available samples are gay and lesbian teens who are confident enough to be self-identified as homosexual or who are seeking help.

Beyond the controversy surrounding the number of gay and lesbian suicides and attempts lies another area of contention: the reason why gays and lesbians would kill themselves. Psychiatrists, including Shaffer, claim that suicidal teens suffer from mental health problems, including depression.

But Dr. Gary Remafedi, editor of the book *Death by Denial: Studies of Suicide in Gay and Lesbian Teenagers,* argues that depression is not necessarily a predictor for suicide among gay and lesbian teens. Rather, social factors such as stigmatization and stress could play a part in their suicidal tendency.

"In the studies that we did, despite very high rates of suicide attempts, there were not unusually high rates of depression or hopelessness," he says. "So, maybe the suicide attempts of gay kids are unrelated to depression and more related to social factors, being stigmatized by society and wanting to escape the stigma and degradation.

"To say that kids kill themselves for social reasons is currently heresy," he adds. "And that's what a large part of this controversy is about."

Despite the quarrel over data and scientific methodology, the tragic stories of gay and lesbian teens who have tried or succeeded in ending their lives are impossible to disregard.

"What the exact figure is, who knows?" says John Gonsiorek of the American Psychological Association. "And it's almost irrelevant. There are enough impressions from clinicians to suggest that clearly there is a subgroup where there is high risk. And figuring out who those people are and what interventions they need early on is an important issue, whether it is 30 percent or 20 percent or 10 percent or whatever."

In the summer of 1994, a panel of specialists was convened by the Centers for Disease Control and Prevention, the National Institute of Mental Health, and the American Association of Suicidology to discuss the subject of suicide and sexual orientation. It was the first such conference organized by the federal government to examine the issue.

HIV/AIDS

In 1992, a congressional report warned that HIV, the virus that causes AIDS, was "spreading unchecked among the nation's adolescents, regardless of where they live or their economic status."[15] According to the U.S. House of Representative's Select Committee on Children, Youth and Families, AIDS was the sixth leading cause of death among fifteen- to twenty-four-year-olds. Thousands of teens and young adolescents in communities small and large across the country are infected with HIV, stated the report, while millions live in danger of contracting the virus.

Hailed by activists as a bellwether report, the four-hundred-page analysis recommended an expansion of AIDS-education programs, particularly within the schools, a recommendation also endorsed by the Federal Centers for Disease Control and Prevention. "Most [important] for the teens, parents and schools remain essential sources of support," concluded the congressional committee. "We must reinforce their ability and confidence to respond to the epidemic."

But the report also acknowledged that putting such programs into place requires overcoming long-fixed political and social barriers, not the least of which is prejudice against gay youth.

HIV is epidemic within the homosexual population. And because homosexuality continues to be socially stigmatized, the majority of gay youth are hesitant to identify their sexual orientation, and thus remain hidden and inaccessible to most prevention strategies. The rejection and harassment that are leveled at gay youth routinely occur in the very places that AIDS education could be most effective and wide-ranging—at home and at school, where the potential exists to reach hundreds of thousands of gay youth. Dropouts and runaways are doubly hard to contact. And at home, parents who are unaware or unaccepting of their child's homosexual identity might also be unable or unwilling to reinforce safe-sex messages.

Quantifying HIV infection rates among gay teens is a tough task; studying a group that is largely invisible is indeed a challenge for researchers. Still, experts and advocates place gay and bisexual young men high on the list of groups that are at risk for HIV infection, because of what they know about their behavior patterns.

"There appears to be a subgroup of gay kids that have a pattern of well-entrenched behavior—multiple partners, substance abuse in sexual situations, non-use of condoms, non-communication with partners about safe sex," says Dr. Remafedi, director of the Youth and AIDS Projects, which was cited within the congressional report as a model intervention program. "These people need intensive help when they're young in changing these patterns." A study released in 1994 by the project found that, of 239 gay and bisexual males ages thirteen to twenty-one, nearly 2 out of 3 were at "extreme risk" for HIV exposure, based on histories of practicing unprotected anal intercourse and/or using intravenous drugs. One third of the teens reported having had unprotected anal sex with at least one of their last three partners in the previous year.[16]

The reasons for this pattern of behavior are partly social. "Young gay people often have no means to explore their sexuality other than through sexual behavior," Remafedi says. "Up until the relatively recent past, we haven't had good support services and opportunities for young people to meet other young people. So often they've landed in high-risk sexual situations as a means of exploring who they are."

The opportunity for exposure, of course, increases greatly when safe sex is not practiced, something that is hardly automatic among gay teens despite the hazards. Unlike their heterosexual counterparts, gay youth usually are operating without a "social script" on how to act in a sexual relationship. The sexual experience itself takes precedence over HIV prevention.

One of the more widely held misunderstandings about safe-sex practices is that partners in a monogamous relationship are safe from HIV infection. Not using condoms is a calculated risk measured by the status of a relationship, and people in steady relationships are more likely to have unprotected sex, a dangerous practice, say experts.

"In order to get HIV, one usually needs to have *repeated* exposures," Remafedi says. "So the most dangerous situation is to be having unprotected intercourse on a regular basis with someone you perceive to be HIV-negative. Nowadays, for both straight kids and gay kids, most of HIV transmission is occurring in the context of relationships that are ongoing."

The biggest barrier against HIV prevention is "true love," says Rotheram-Borus. "When they love each other, which they usually decide within a week or two, they throw the condoms out. That's very dangerous. The relationship is very likely to be short-lived, on average about two and a half months, even though they believe it's going to be forever. Second of all, the partner is very likely to be infected and not know it."

Gay youth ordinarily are more knowledgeable about safe sex and more likely to protect themselves than their straight peers, notes Rotheram-Borus. Yet gay teens often are reluctant to get tested for HIV. Or if they are tested, they're reluctant to go back for the results, afraid of the findings.

Paradoxically, among some teens, testing negative for HIV sustains a belief that they're invincible and causes them to become careless about practicing safe sex. "In a way, the testing kind of works against them," she says. "I've had kids say to me directly, 'Look, I've had a lot of unprotected sex and I'm still negative. If God wanted to get me, he would've gotten me.' So the testing becomes rewarding for them: They were able to have unprotected sex and still not get infected."

Some teens turn fatalistic. Young and gay, they believe it's only a matter of time before they get infected. Their attitude becomes, Why be bothered with safe sex? And their credo becomes, Die young; stay pretty.

While even less is known about HIV and young lesbians, they too are at risk. "I think that's an unrecognized problem," says Rotheram-Borus. "Among our sample, 75 percent of the gay girls had had sex with boys, on average, eighteen months before having sex with other girls." By contrast, 48 percent of the gay boys had sex with girls.[17] "But these boys were far less likely to use condoms with girls than they were with their male partners."

HIV-prevention programs have shown marked results in reducing the risk of HIV transmission among young gay and bisexual male adolescents. Yet such programs are few. Within the nation's communities and schools remains an ignorance and fear of HIV transmission, and of teenage sexuality in general, an ignorance and fear that have fostered a deadly silence.

"Every day that we ignore the epidemic," concluded the congressional report, "HIV gains ground and threatens the loss of another generation."

20

Michele II:

We Have to Kill Ourselves

Michele Boyer spent her summer vacation arguing with her parents. She ached for their understanding, and resented the fact that for the first time in her life they were incapable of providing it.

Michele had ended her freshman year at Augsburg College in Minneapolis with the inchoate belief that she might be a lesbian. Weeks before returning to her small hometown of Menominee, Michigan, for summer break, she had visited her first gay bar and had "come out" for the first time, to a lesbian classmate. After years of sidestepping the issue, Michele confronted her sexual identity head-on in a tense two days. The experience was an emotional wake-up call and left her thirsting for much more—more information, more resources, more contact with other women who were just like she was.

"I had opened this huge book about myself," she says, looking back. "And I had just started reading page one before I left school for Menominee."

Returning to the Upper Peninsula of Michigan was a backsliding move for Michele, emotionally and intellectually. She felt stagnant, as if she had walked into a void. She missed the shiny bright-light sensations of the Twin Cities and the red-bricked contemplative milieu of her small liberal-arts college. On campus, she had fallen in with two stimulating classmates—a political-science major and a theater major—women Michele's age who lived on the same floor of her dorm. The trio would hold late-night gab sessions, solving all the problems of the world at a local coffeehouse called the Café Global.

For the first time in her life, Michele was forming strong personal opinions about the great issues of the day.

But Menominee was so *retro*. It was if she were living a totally separate existence there. She worked as a lifeguard at a Lake Michigan beach just blocks from her home and hung out with her old high school friends, most of whom hadn't strayed very far from home after they graduated. Above it all, nagging at her subconscious was this *complication,* this unsolved riddle about her sexual orientation. She couldn't figure it out. Who can I talk to *here?* she brooded. God, I can't wait to get back to Minneapolis. This town is so dumb.

Her mood swung from despair to denial. Externalizing her self-hatred, she was resentful toward gays and lesbians. When she should have observed an empathy and identification toward people who were similar to herself, she instead felt anger and hostility. "I felt that's how people would think of me if they knew I was gay," she says. "I was just angry at a lot of things."

Michele's parents were clueless about her predicament. Mainstream Lutherans and Republicans, their perceptions of gays reflected a misunderstanding of homosexuality rather than an intolerance. Michele's father didn't seem to give homosexuality much thought, one way or another. It was a non-issue. Michele's mother was active in the community theater as a singer and actor, and occasionally collaborated with two men who were gay. "They must have had overly dominant mothers," she once theorized, surmising that they lived "tragic" lives. As for lesbians, the word was never brought up.

In her frustration, Michele came down hard on her unwitting parents. She would castigate them for their conservative values and challenge their opinions on political issues ranging from welfare to the environment to nuclear weapons. "I was kind of forcing things on them, testing the waters," she says. "I was setting a foundation, like I was telling them, Well, be prepared, because I'm gonna be coming out soon."

Michele was also at odds with her religious principles. The Lutheran paradigm she was raised on didn't make room for homosexuals. While it never was stated in her church that homosexuality was forbidden, it was implied that it was unacceptable. "I was a spiritual person, even as a little kid," she says. "I liked going to church. But the impression I got was that homosexuality was negative."

Intellectually, Michele could allow for the possibility that she was a lesbian, but according to her religious tenets, it was wrong. She couldn't settle the discord, and wondered again and again if there was any way out.

I'm going to have to change, because it's just not right, she thought. I'll ask God to help me change.

Midway through the summer, Michele borrowed her parents' van and drove to Minneapolis to attend a friend's wedding. The wedding was a happy reunion for Michele, a renewal of the companionships she had made during her first year at college. Most of her basketball team-mates were there, including a player named Robin. Robin also was a lesbian, and also very closeted. Two months earlier, in an impulsive act of confession, Robin and Michele told each other that they had been to a St. Paul bar called the Castle, known to be patronized by lesbians. With their mutual admissions grew a close bond of trust.

Following the wedding reception, Michele, Robin, and other guests returned to the suburban home of the bride's parents, where they were staying. The night was hot and humid. Michele and Robin were restless and a little drunk. They couldn't sleep, so they decided to take a midnight walk. Under the July moon, swatting mosquitoes as they sat on a log in the woods, they talked at length about their sexuality—their fears, curiosities, and conclusions about being homo-sexual. For three hours, they traded secrets. How long have you known you were a lesbian? Would your parents kick you out if they knew? Would you be banished from your church? From college?

In those pre-dawn hours, a covenant was formed, a sisterhood. For the first time in their lives, Michele and Robin each had a loyal confi-dante with whom to share their most precious intimacies. They talked about other lesbians they had heard about, other women they were at-tracted to. Michele spoke of her affection for a girl in high school.

Robin told about her first lover, a woman she had been living with for nearly two years, who abruptly walked out on her, leaving behind a note that said she could no longer deal with the secrecy and shame.

The discussion between Michele and Robin was a communion of like souls. It was the ultimate reality check. Here they were, two of a kind, living with the same *peculiarity,* the same *condition,* working through something as all-important as their sexual identities, with no guide or references other than their common beliefs and experiences. One of them would make a statement and the other would echo in absolute agreement.

"If God created us, this must be right, wouldn't you think?" Michele would say.

"It *must* be okay," Robin would confirm.

"We were born this way, right?"

"Yeah. It's just who were *are.*"

"I mean, if this *were* a choice, then why would we choose to be part of a minority that's been put through so much abuse?"

The encounter buoyed Michele's spirits, and for the remainder of the summer she was able to put her insecurities at bay. Her resentment softened; her denial waned. She returned to college in the fall with high expectations, excited to be back in the company of her newfound friends, eager to start another basketball season, ready to dive into a fresh set of courses. She changed her major from mathematics to sociology, a discipline that she believed would be more compatible to the social and political issues that she had developed an interest in. But while her self-confidence soared, she was still leery about identifying herself as a lesbian, even to her roommates.

Michele moved into a small two-bedroom apartment off campus with three other women. Michele knew that one of the women, Dena, was gay. Michele, Dena, and another friend had gone to the lesbian bar, the Castle, together, so Michele knew that Dena suspected Michele was gay too.

"She put a mirror up to me," says Michele. "That really brought it close to home. Here's this living, breathing lesbian in my apartment. And I had to deal with it."

But the close-quarters living arrangement made her very self-conscious. She was enamored with Dena, yet couldn't act on her feelings. She didn't know what to do. Her midnight heart-to-heart with Robin over the summer had clarified her thoughts about homosexuality. But she had no manual or blueprint to follow on how to *be* a homosexual.

"I was really starting to get obsessed by it all," Michele says. She became preoccupied with Dena, and with her own lesbianism. But she had no outlet. There wasn't a student group at Augsburg for gay and lesbian youth. She was reluctant to go to the gay bars, afraid of being seen by someone she knew. She knew nothing of the support groups, bookstores, and newspapers for gays and lesbians around the Twin Cities and was too timid to seek out resources on her own.

Michele's grades began to slip. Her enthusiasm for basketball slumped. She was consumed by her attraction to Dena and determined to follow her inclinations, wherever they might lead.

On Halloween night, Michele and her roommates went to a college bar to party. Michele and Dena fashioned costumes for the occasion. They both salvaged baggy pants and dress shirts from a charity store, and bought masks of old men's craggy faces.

The women ordered pitchers of beer in a corner booth as the jukebox played. "Dena, I need to talk to you," Michele suddenly blurted out above the din, and led Dena outside. They slipped off their rubber masks and sat down on the porch steps of a house next door, secluded by shrubs.

"Dena," Michele started. "The reason I wanted you to come outside was because my friends told me you were gay. And there's something I need to tell you: I am too." She leaned over and gave Dena a long kiss on the lips. Dena was startled, but she answered the kiss.

As they embraced, they heard the voices of their roommates, calling for them in the night. It was closing time, and the women were ready to leave the bar. Flushed, Michele and Dena quickly pulled their masks over their faces and rejoined their roommates, their identities again concealed.

▲ ▼ ▲

Michele went to classes the next day, flustered and unsure what to do next. Dena was the first woman she had ever kissed in a romantic way, and she had liked it. She thought about dating Dena. But how could they possibly get involved? They lived together in a tiny apartment. Their roommates eventually would find out, and how would they react?

The attraction between Michele and Dena grew, pulling them closer together. They couldn't resist. They would sneak kisses on the couch when their roommates were gone. Or they would fabricate reasons for leaving the apartment and drive somewhere to make out in Michele's car. Once, they slept together, in Dena's bed. Sex never went beyond fondling. Michele was uncomfortable with anything more, and would stop Dena if she tried to go further. "I was ashamed, so it wasn't very pleasurable," Michele says.

After two or three weeks of the secret liaisons, Michele knew she couldn't continue. The trepidation was too great. She was ravaged by guilt and shame for having to hide her affection for Dena and still not completely sure of what she was feeling. She seesawed back and forth between certitude and denial. She enjoyed the intimacy, but felt herself tense up sometimes when Dena touched her or kissed her. On some days she regretted having waited so long to acknowledge her homosexuality. And on other days she doubted she was a lesbian at all. She wished she could just wake up one morning and be *straight*. She wanted to change, but knew it wasn't possible. "I was stuck," she says.

Michele was a basket case, mentally and physically. Her appetite withered. She couldn't study. She couldn't sleep. Dark circles creased the skin under her eyes. Like the inexplicable alienation that had struck before, early in her junior high school years, a deep depression ensnared her. Desperately wanting to talk to somebody, she decided to explain everything to her roommate Julie.

Julie had been one of Michele's closest friends and allies since their first year in college. They both lived on the seventh floor in Urness dormitory as freshman students. Julie was the daughter of Minnesota's Democratic congressman, Martin Sabo, a graduate and favorite son of Augsburg College. Her liberal, progressive politics rubbed off on Michele, who once had counted herself as a Republican. More significantly, Julie was Michele's lifeline. They were the same age, and shared the same absurd sense of humor and outlook on life. But in the year that she had known Julie, Michele could not bring herself to talk about her sexual orientation.

On a rainy evening, with her life suddenly a knot of hopeless contradictions, Michele believed the time had finally come. Michele offered to drive Julie to a Target store to do some shopping. As she parked the car, Michele told Julie she had something important to say.

"I don't think I can tell you," said Michele, struggling to find the right words.

"Well, what is it?" Julie coaxed. "Just say it."

"I . . . I think that I'm a lesbian," Michele stammered.

"Oh," said Julie, unfazed by the announcement. "Well that's okay."

Michele was euphoric. Julie was the first heterosexual she had ever come out to. And she was okay with it. *Why didn't I tell her sooner?* Michele asked herself. *She didn't* care. *Maybe now I can start telling other people. . . .*

But relief was short. Days later, the guilt and shame began hounding her again, as relentless as ever. She avoided Dena, making sure she was out of the apartment when Dena came home from work. She couldn't cope with the stress.

"My memory started going. I couldn't run plays on the basketball team. I couldn't sleep, couldn't think, couldn't *brush my teeth.* I couldn't figure anything out. I was lost." She finally told Dena that she couldn't continue their relationship, that she couldn't handle the guilt. "I just could not emotionally accept it. Just could *not.*"

Helplessly unable to lose the profound gloom, she plodded along, her body exhausted, her mind numb, her senses muted. "I felt like the walking dead, like a zombie," she says. "I would look in the mirror and not recognize the face looking back. I had no spirit. I had no feelings about anything."

Michele didn't sleep at all for three straight days. Finally, in the middle of the night, two weeks before Thanksgiving, she awakened her roommate. She needed help.

"Julie, I don't know what's going on, but I can't sleep," Michele said. "I need to get to a hospital."

Michele was admitted into St. Mary's Hospital and given a dose of Valium. Later in the day, she was transferred to the psychiatric unit on the seventh floor. Psych unit? she thought. I don't need a psych unit. But her diagnosis indicated otherwise. According to her doctor, she was demonstrating classic symptoms of clinical depression.

Sitting in bed in a hospital gown early the next morning, Michele called her parents. She told them she had checked herself into a hospital and asked them to come to Minneapolis as soon as possible. "There's something I need to tell you and I don't want to talk about it over the phone," she said to her mother, and hung up.

Michele's parents packed a suitcase and left immediately for Minneapolis, a five-hour drive. Along the way, they puzzled over their daughter's phone call. "What on earth would she need to tell us that would make her so nervous and so upset?" Colleen Boyer wondered aloud to her husband. "With all her athletic ability and her love of sports, I don't see Michele getting into drugs. And she can't be pregnant. Michele's hardly ever dated." She considered her daughter's sexuality. Since Michele was a child, Colleen intuitively had suspected that her daughter might be a lesbian. She had never voiced her suspicions, but it had crossed her mind. Colleen was familiar with homosexuals; she had become a close friend of two gay men through the community theater.

"Well, you know there's something we haven't mentioned," Colleen said to her husband, Joe. "I wonder if Michele thinks she's gay."

"Do you think so?" said Joe Boyer.

"It could be possible. . . . How would you feel?"

"Well," he said, pondering the thought that his only daughter could be a homosexual. Michele was his favorite child; they had always had a close relationship. "She's Michele, and I love her with all my heart."

They arrived in the city and went straight to the hospital. After a tearful bedside greeting, Michele asked to speak to her mother alone. She had composed a coming-out letter, detailing in a precise order just how she came to know she was a lesbian. Putting pen to paper would be easier than speaking the words, Michele decided.

She handed the letter to her mother. "I want you to read this." Her mother nodded as she read.

"Well, I hope you're a bisexual so that someday you can have kids," Colleen Boyer said, trying to smile. She hugged her daughter, and assured her she would do everything she could to help.

"Don't tell Dad yet," Michele pleaded. She was worried that her father would be disappointed by the news, and didn't want to hurt him. But no sooner had Colleen Boyer stepped out of the room than in walked Joe Boyer. He lifted Michele's hand into his.

"Your mom told me what you just told her," he said, a trace of discomfort on his face. "But I want you to know that I still love you."

The conversation was short. The test was over. There were no tears, no anger, no shock. Michele's parents were supportive, as uncritical as they could be. Michele relaxed, realizing that her fears of condemnation were unfounded. She had cleared an enormous hurdle.

Joe and Colleen stayed at a motel until Michele was stabilized. Before they returned home, Michele gave them a book to read: *Now That You Know: What Every Parent Should Know About Homosexuality.*

After nearly two weeks in the hospital, Michele returned to classes. Anti-depressants had been prescribed and psychotherapy was scheduled. But she was still fatigued. Her mind had been freed of some of the pent-up stress, thanks in part to the disclosure to her parents that she was a lesbian. But her body had yet to recover. Something still was seriously wrong.

She couldn't pull herself out of bed in the morning, couldn't face sitting in class or suiting up for basketball practice. She just couldn't function, and couldn't explain why. She was losing control. Things were spiraling downward. She told her friends that she was thinking of bailing out of school for a while, that she had been suffering chest pains and needed some rest. She drove back to Michigan for the Thanksgiving holiday, despondent, defeated, and utterly convinced that she would never be well again. She arrived home with a bone-chilling cry for help: "Mom, we have to kill ourselves because I can't live with this and I know you won't be able to bear seeing me die."

For weeks in the dead of winter, Michele holed up in her bedroom, sleeping ten to twelve hours a day. When she was awake, she watched television, seldom bothering to dress in anything more than a bathrobe. She left the cocoon of her home only for occasional walks with her mother.

Michele's parents decided to hospitalize her in Green Bay, Wisconsin, the city closest to their home. A psychiatrist prescribed anti-depressant drugs, but still, her emotions flatlined. Her mind, meanwhile, worked overtime to sort things out. She struggled to make sense of her puzzle. Being a homosexual, she reasoned, was incompatible with her values and self-image, but she was resigned to the belief that she would never return to her former self. She could live with being gay, but she feared she would never shake the despondency.

"I thought I would always be that way," she says. "I was desperate. I had no hope. I had no faith that I would ever heal."

After six weeks in the hospital, she returned home. The medication had been ineffective. In her hollow state of despair, her world turned lifeless, spiritless. Her memory dimmed. Her self-motivation bottomed out. Her taste for food and her sense of smell disappeared. "Colors even started to fade," she recalls. "Everything was washed out and grayed. I was completely blank. I would get up in the morning and have no feelings about anything."

Near the end of winter, after negligible results from psychotherapy and several progressions of anti-depressants, her psychiatrist suggested electroconvulsive therapy. It was a last resort, and a gamble. "Everyone was gambling," says Michele's mother. "I was gambling, the doctor was gambling, my husband was just completely lost. It was just like, Do *whatever.*"

Michele agreed to go ahead with the treatment. She was shown a videotape to prepare her for the procedure. Doctors assured her that, despite beliefs to the contrary, there would be no pain or long-term memory loss. Days later, Michele again was admitted to St. Joseph's Hospital in Green Bay. Early in the following morning, she was taken by wheelchair to a treatment room and laid out on a padded physician's table. Two electrodes were glued to her head, one to her right temple, the second to the center of her forehead. She was injected with a general anesthesia and muscle relaxant through an IV line. While she slept, a single, rapid bolt of electricity was sent through her body.

The entire procedure took thirty minutes. "When I woke up, I had the worst headache I ever had," Michele remembers. "But the depression was gone. It had lifted."

Her mother called her hospital room a short time later, eager to hear the results. "Mom, I think it worked," Michele cried. "I've broken through."

Electroconvulsive therapy was repeated several times again that week. Each time, Michele woke up with a trace of nausea and a pounding headache, like she had a bad hangover. But each time the depression had melted away a bit more. Her energy came rushing back, like a river surging over a dam. Familiar tastes and smells flooded her senses. Colors burst into sight. "It was like a fresh spring day," she says. She roamed the hospital grounds for hours at a time in a sensory feast.

Michele was released from the hospital and sent home the day before Easter Sunday. It was a rebirth for her, a spiritual awakening. "It was like a four-month ah-*ha,*" she says. Her depression, while painfully exposing a dark side of her personality, had acted as a catalyst for radical change. She was suddenly more mindful of the little things, of life's simple moments, and less concerned with the seemingly insurmountable problems that had plagued her months earlier.

Michele returned to Augsburg College in May, filled with a child-like sense of discovery and awe. She moved back into her old apartment and made arrangements with her professors to resume classes during the summer. A month later, Michele moved into a huge two-story house on campus—called Lambda House—with twelve other women for the summer. She decided not to tell her friends and roommates about the electroconvulsive therapy, afraid that they would misinterpret the treatment as a "cure" to her homosexuality. She was also apprehensive about people passing judgment on her decision to undergo "shock treatment," considered by many to be barbaric, anti-holistic, and "politically incorrect." Though she didn't advocate the therapy as a cure-all for depression, it seemed to have worked for her.

Michele returned to Minneapolis with a changed perspective on her sexual orientation as well. "The shame was gone, the guilt was gone, the confusion was gone," she says. She began to live an openly lesbian life. She made a point of reading the gay press faithfully and hanging out at Ladies Night, a St. Paul gay bar. Unabashedly, she came out to friends, roommates, classmates, coaches, and teachers, and looked up an openly gay Lutheran pastor at a gay-positive church in St. Paul.

As the fall semester began, Michele was determined to do her part to make the coming-out process easier for other young gays and lesbians like herself.

21

CODA:

A Child's Death

Arlene and Lloyd Erickson discovered that their son Michael was gay in 1965, just months after he graduated from high school. At the time, there were no support services at all for gay and lesbian youth, no teen centers or computer bulletin boards, no gay proms or pride parades, no campus support groups or crisis helplines—no safety net of any sort.

Ten years after his parents found out he was gay—and after concealing his sexual identity from nearly everyone else he knew—Michael Erickson hit bottom. Depressed, alcoholic, and alone, he committed suicide at age twenty-seven. In a brief note to his mother and father, scribbled on the corner of a sheet of notebook paper, he apologized for what he was about to do, and said he could no longer cope with the shame and the secrecy.

"The trauma he went through was as if he had died of cancer," says his mother.

Arlene and Lloyd Erickson raised six kids in their country home near the small town of Valley City, North Dakota. Michael was the second oldest, one of three boys. When he was finishing his senior year of high school, his family moved to Fargo, North Dakota, where his father took a job as an engineer for a television station.

Michael was well liked in school all through his teens. His parents never detected any problems in his personal life. "He seemed to do well in high school," says Lloyd Erickson. "He was active in various organizations. Debate was one of the big things, and drama. He had a lot of friends there, both male and female, so you would never suspect anything was amiss, with all his associations and his dealings."

"He was popular, very popular," echoes Arlene. "He was an excellent student. He was a good mixer."

Never were there any indications that his sexual identity had become a liability among his peers. "We're so aware today," Arlene points out. "But I wonder if back then there was an awareness of gay students or homosexuality at all in the community. It wasn't like it is now."

Michael decided after graduation that he was not going to go to college in the fall. His decision disappointed his parents. "We didn't know why at the time," says Arlene. But shortly after, his parents found a letter torn in pieces that Michael had written to a doctor in Philadelphia, asking about homosexuality. They were stunned.

"Homosexuality was an issue that I knew absolutely nothing about," Arlene says, "other than I hoped my sons were *not*. But as soon as we learned that Michael was gay, these things came popping out at us all over. It was a traumatic time in our lives."

From the outset, the Ericksons tried to be understanding of Michael's uniqueness. "I would have to say the acceptance of who he was came quite early on," Arlene says, "but learning to live with it took time. Mike was quite open with us. We still went through all the wonderings of *why*, you know. We as parents had to constantly reaffirm ourselves and each other that we were good parents."

Michael was candid about his homosexual feelings and attractions. "I asked him when he first realized he was something different, and he said at age nine," Lloyd says.

"Nine," Arlene repeats, mournfully. "And so you just have to think that from then on, when you start to question . . . His desires weren't along the same lines as his older brother's. You know, the interest in girls wasn't there. This was all revealed to us after we had learned. We weren't aware of any of this. You just aren't aware of that struggle.

"It's an everyday struggle," she continues. "It's get up and go to work and face that world, face what the church is saying. And he was raised a Christian, and so in the final analysis, when they say you're a worse sinner than anybody else, how do you face up to all of that? The struggle is just *there*."

The Ericksons looked to their doctor for answers, but he was unempathetic. They made an appointment with a psychiatrist, at Michael's suggestion. "We went with him one initial time and we didn't get a very good reaction from this man," Lloyd says. "He sat across the desk there like a stone and knew absolutely nothing about it at all."

They sought help from the pastors at their Lutheran church, and again were frustrated by the lack of understanding. "I can't even term it negative, because it was almost non-responsive," Arlene says. "At that time I don't think they had ever been confronted with a mother coming to seek advice. They didn't know what to do with me. They didn't know how to deal with this. So that was kind of a dead end. And that was quite devastating for me, because that's where I look for my guidance, through my church. So we had ten years of absolute silence. We talked to no one. We didn't share with any of the aunts or uncles or grandparents or siblings."

Michael, meanwhile, had moved into his own apartment shortly after the family moved to Fargo. He had taken a job after high school as a night auditor for the city. That year was a turning point. He immersed himself in his work and soon saved enough money to buy an older house, remodel it, and rent it out. He bought another house and did the same, and then an apartment building, and then a home for himself in Moorhead, Minnesota, across the state line. "He was really into a lot of that stuff, investing and making a go," says Lloyd. "He was kind of a workaholic in a way."

He eventually enrolled in college and graduated from Moorhead State University, with honors. But while he appeared to be a successful, happy young man, inside he was struggling, say his parents.

"It was the old adage: He was crying on the inside, laughing on the outside," Arlene says. "And that was obvious. He was kind of our family clown. He was musical and he would come bounding up the steps and he would play the piano and he would roughhouse with his sisters. But I think there was depression there.

"I know there was a romance involved in this, too," she adds. "I met the young man several times. But he was married. I don't know a whole lot about that, but I know this affected Michael." Occasionally, their son would introduce them to male friends, whom Arlene and Lloyd assumed to be gay. But he never went out publicly with them.

"I don't think he told anybody," Lloyd says.

"Other than his close friends, his gay friends," agrees Arlene.

Michael had started drinking heavily in his early twenties. "I think the alcohol had more to do with it than we realized," Lloyd says. "The alcoholism, that had to be a big part of his life the last while."

One freezing January morning, the Ericksons received the tragic news. "January 14, 1975—I know it as well as his birthday," Arlene tearfully recalls.

"He called in sick that morning, believe it or not," says Lloyd. "And did all the preparation. He plugged some of the cracks in the door in the garage."

"This was not going to be a false attempt," Arlene says.

"One friend who was staying at his house came home around noon, I think, and heard the car out in the garage," remembers Lloyd. "So he immediately went out there and found what was going on. I'm sure he called for help right away."

Michael closed himself in his garage and started the engine of his car. He died of asphyxiation due to carbon monoxide poisoning. In his suicide note, he asked his parents to forgive him.

"He gave us some financial statements and things to take care of, made some more indications that he was sorry, but that he could no longer cope. Those were his final words. And then it was 'Love, Mike.' *Cope*—that word said volumes. . . . It was all a big charade, really. I mean, he was trying to fit into a heterosexual lifestyle and denying who he really was.

"It was after he had died, when we were at the funeral home, and I was thinking, How can this end here?—only then did we start to realize that we had to open up. We had to try and bring some understanding to what it meant to be gay and what we knew as parents."

Yet it took two years before the Ericksons could tell anyone of

Michael's secret. "We were going through a lot of turmoil," Arlene says. "Not only had Michael died—he died a suicide death, he was gay. There were so many things to deal with. You wondered how you kept your sanity. There was a lot going on in our lives. It was very very difficult. Words just cannot express what it was like. This loss of this young man. . . ."

An announcement in their church bulletin alerted them to a meeting on gay issues that was being held at another Lutheran church in Fargo. The pastor had been arranging open discussions with gays and their families.

"We had to talk to *some*one," Arlene says, "and he was a very supportive pastor, a very loving, caring man. We put our whole trust in him and we just went with it. He then later moved over to Lutheran Social Services, and so then we were asked to speak on college campuses."

Through word of mouth, parents and young gays and lesbians soon were referred to the Ericksons. Lloyd and Arlene would receive phone calls from people, afraid and bewildered, pleading for advice. Some asked if they could come to the Ericksons' home to talk. "We got a lot of one-on-one like that, a lot of telephone conversations," Arlene says. "They kind of like the anonymity of the phone. A lot of them we met in person. A lot of them came to our home."

"That was the very beginning of *our* P-FLAG," Lloyd notes. "P-FLAG is a national organization, but this meeting in our home was probably a forerunner of P-FLAG," formed long before the national parents' group was even organized.

"It wasn't even known as a group of a parents and families," adds Arlene. "But what we ended up with was young gay people. You know, they hear you are an 'out' set of parents, and they would come over, and that was fine. And from time to time there would be different community leaders, too, who were understanding that would come. And this went on like this for years before anything got organized."

In time, the Ericksons were telling Michael's story to college groups and church groups throughout the region.

"We don't consider ourselves to be public speakers here. All we did was go out and tell our story of our journey," says Arlene. "It got to the point where it was almost out of our hands, because people keep calling and they'd say, 'Will you? Will you?' And it was not our intention when we started out to really be that public. It was like the choice was taken from us. You know, you always felt compelled."

Eventually, they included their children in their presentations and began giving interviews to local media. And in recent years, they have become officers in the local chapter of P-FLAG.

"Going public, as painful as it was, just now in these later years have I really allowed myself to realize we have made a difference," Arlene says.

Today, the Ericksons have cut back on the number of public appearances. Lloyd is in his mid-seventies, while Arlene is nearing seventy. Looking back, they speculate about Michael's future had he lived.

"Michael would have been an activist had there been others out there," Arlene says assuredly. "I think he would have been an advocate for understanding and acceptance."

"He was held back by the tremendous hate out there," Lloyd says. "You see what some of these religious groups are doing, and it's enough to do you in. How are these poor people supposed to respond?"

22

INTERLUDE:

Voices of Danger

Beyond the studies and the statistics are the human casualties, the gay and lesbian youth who have fallen victim to the isolation and abuse. Mistreated or disregarded by families, ignored or underserved by schools and social services, they struggle day to day to survive.

Their sexual orientation may not always be at the root of their problems, yet rarely can it be separated out. The scorn and alienation that they face throughout adolescence can only add to their burden.

These are the tragedies, stories that reflect the grimmest consequences of growing up gay.

MARCUS   Marcus's mother suspected he was gay when he was sixteen. More than a mother's intuition, some telltale signs had appeared: He was getting a lot of phone calls from men and very few from women. He was hanging out with other young men who she thought looked gay. And now and then he wore eye makeup.

She discovered a letter to Marcus that mentioned a gay love affair. But for months she put it out of her mind, until a friend told her she saw her son hanging around a gay bar.

Recalls Marcus: "She just came out and asked, 'Marcus, are you gay? Are you gay? Are you gay?' And I just kept saying, 'No. No. No.' "

Telling his family would have meant big trouble—shouting matches with his mother, lectures from his grandmother, and embarrassment for his younger sister. He feared that he might get booted out of his home. So he chose to conceal it. He dodged his mother's questions, not really lying, but not telling the full truth either.

"She asked me whether I'm gay," Marcus says, "which I'm not. I'm bisexual. So I told her no."

Gradually, though, he dropped the denials and tried to explain his sexual orientation. Almost reflexively, his mother disapproved. She had been raised in a strict religious family in which homosexuality was not tolerated, never even mentioned. She remembers seeing a gay-rights rally in Chicago once when she was a teenager and her mother telling her to cover her eyes as a parade of gays and lesbians passed by.

Marcus was the first gay or bi his mother had ever known. She blamed herself for his "problem." She thought God was punishing her. For what, she didn't know. "I would ask myself, What did I do? What didn't I do?" she says.

She insisted that her son abandon the "crazy" notion that he wasn't a heterosexual and tried everything to get him to change. She prayed. She fasted for twenty-one days. She even held an exorcism.

She had done it before to discipline her son, to rid him of "demons"—after he took an interest in becoming a Jehovah's Witness, after he went to the *Rocky Horror Picture Show*, after he began wearing a crystal around his neck and talking about witchcraft. And then again after he showed leanings toward homosexuality.

But Marcus didn't change. Instead, he slowly divorced himself from his family.

Marcus grew up in a broken home. His father and mother never married, and split up before Marcus was born. His mother moved her family around a lot when he was a boy—from Minnesota to Iowa to Colorado and then back to Minnesota when he was fifteen. He had been a good student all through school and was allowed to skip ninth grade. For part of his freshman and sophomore years, he was "home schooled" by his mother, grandmother, and uncle. His mother had dreams of him becoming an engineer someday because he was good at math.

Marcus was placed in a public school for tenth grade. The next year, his family moved across town and he was transferred into another high school. The next year, he transferred again. It was the third high school he'd gone to in as many years. There was a peer support group for gay and lesbian students, but Marcus felt isolated, out of place, partly because he was the only African-American student in the group.

"I'm not really into support groups and counseling and all that other junk," he says.

Marcus still was in the closet at home. For a while, he found support in a community-based peer group that met just blocks from his home. But that got old fast. Again, he didn't fit.

When he was a senior in high school, Marcus ran away from home with a friend. When he returned, he was in and out of school. He had missed too much of his senior year to graduate. But as a black bisexual male, he felt estranged and unsupported. School seemed pointless. So he dropped out.

He regrets the decision. "I wish I could go back," he says. "I wouldn't have messed up my high school career." He feels cheated out of the high school experience. "I really wish I could go back. But I'm not going to. . . . It's a matter of stubbornness. And pride."

Marcus lives one day at time, separated from the few friends he left behind at school, alienated from a family who won't accept him, disenfranchised from black peers he never got along with.

"There is a stereotype of what a black person should be like," Marcus says. "He should fit that gang-member stereotype. . . . And if he deviates from that stereotype, he's trying to be white. My mother told me she'd rather I was a gang member than hang out with the people I was hanging with."

Marcus moved in with a friend in a tiny studio apartment in the inner city. It wasn't very large, barely big enough to cook a meal other than a pan of noodles heated on a hot plate. But it was home, a place Marcus could store his clothes, listen to music, or just gaze out the window at the Minneapolis skyline. Though he lived only five blocks from his mother's home, he relished the freedom to come and go as he wanted, when he wanted and with whom he wanted.

Marcus found a part-time job doing telephone surveys after quitting high school. He made just enough money to pay rent and party, spending his days at work and nights hanging around the video arcades and gay bars along Hennepin Avenue. He had plans to pick up his General Educational Development (GED) certificate and enroll at a technical college to study nursing. Or journalism. Or drama. Or cosmetology. The plans changed with his mood.

But he quit his job after two months. He didn't get along with his boss, he says. His roommate helped him get hired as a server at a restaurant. But he was fired after missing a few days of work. With rent overdue, his roommate asked him to move out. So, with no job in sight, he decided to move back with his mother and sister in his grandmother's house. He'd have a room of his own.

On the day that he had packed his clothes to move, his grandmother changed her mind. She told his mother that Marcus couldn't live with them. She didn't want the added burden. And she didn't approve of his sexual orientation.

"Mostly, it's the gay issue," says Marcus. His mother was on his case about his sexual orientation, too. "She says I'm not bisexual, that the demon inside me is."

Suddenly, his plans for a GED and returning to school were dim and distant. A month later, he was struggling just to feed himself, staying with friends, sleeping on a futon on the living room floor of a Minneapolis apartment, one step away from homelessness.

NANCY Nancy hit the road wearing a T-shirt, a pair of shorts, loafers, and no socks, on an odyssey straight out of *Thelma & Louise*.

The seventeen-year-old honors student was running away from her Milwaukee home—specifically, from her father. He had turned abusive since he found out she was gay. "He hit me a couple of times," she says. So she took his car keys and took off for Madison to find her girlfriend.

Nancy had met Diane at camp the summer before. They had been "accused" of being lesbians by their camp counselors. "They said we were standing too close together," says Nancy.

Nancy came out to her parents midway through high school. But she says she's known she was gay since she was a child.

"Actually, I've probably known since I was little. I've always looked at girls and thought they were pretty. I think I was probably bisexual since I was born."

Nancy had thoughts of suicide when she was coming to terms with her homosexuality. "But now I don't have any suicidal thoughts at all. I have a lot of things to look forward to. At least, I hope I do."

Nancy hid out in Madison for a few days, then called her mother from a shelter for runaways. Her mother was crying. She threatened to have Diane arrested for statutory rape or kidnapping unless Nancy returned home. Nancy told her she had been having nightmares about her father's violence. She couldn't go back.

But her mother said an officer from the Milwaukee County department of social services would come to the shelter and return her to Milwaukee by force if necessary. So Nancy drove back to Milwaukee, afraid she would be arrested for stealing her father's car. She planned to apply for legal emancipation, hoping to have Diane appointed as her guardian.

Two days after she arrived home, Nancy's uncle "kidnapped" her, she says, driving her to his Wisconsin cabin. Like some cult deprogrammer, he offered to give her some money and set her up with a place to live if she went straight.

Nancy told him it was impossible, she couldn't change. Her uncle drove her to his home near Chicago. But before her parents could retrieve her, a friend picked her up and hurried her back to Madison.

Nancy and Diane moved their clothes into a friend's co-op. The police were looking for them. There was a bench warrant out for Nancy's arrest. She was a runaway.

JEREMY Jeremy guesses he has been tested for HIV twenty times. "That's a lot," admits the twenty-two-year-old, contritely.

Jeremy has spent much of his young adulthood as a prostitute. For him, AIDS is an occupational hazard.

Every two or three months he has blood drawn at a local clinic. Each time he has tested negative. So far.

He had been lax a few times lately in practicing safe sex. He was drunk once or twice and didn't think about using a condom, he says. Another time, he just didn't have one with him. So he decided it was time to get tested again.

Weeks later, Jeremy breaks through the swinging door of an AIDS clinic. He has come to hear the results from a doctor.

"Negative," he whispers, excitedly. He's flush with relief.

Jeremy promises the doctor he will be safe and wear a condom whenever he has sex. "Wherever I go, they go," he vows. He keeps them everywhere, now—tucked into his fanny pack, his jean jacket, the glove compartment of his car, as common as pennies.

"Last year, within six months, I slept with over two hundred people," he says. "That's bad. And that doesn't include the people I just made out with."

Hustling is quick money—rent money, gas money, food money, drug money. "It's tax-free," Jeremy says. "You could make three hundred dollars a day, if you work at it."

Jeremy has hustled since he was nineteen, off and on, charging anywhere between $20 and $120 for all kinds of sex. "The first time I did it was because I had no money. I had to get back home. The second time I did it I needed money to pay for rent. The third time I did it I'd just had an accident and I needed to fix my car."

His routine is simple. He stands at a parking lot near a park and waits for someone to drive by and stop. Day or night, it doesn't matter. There are just as many customers during the lunch hour as there are after midnight.

His "johns" are men of all ages and from all walks of life—downtown bureaucrats, uptown doctors, lawyers, police, judges, farmers—usually men in heterosexual relationships, some of them with wives and children and living double lives.

His colleagues on the street are young, many of them teenagers. "The majority of them do it because they've been kicked out of their parents' house or they lost a job," Jeremy says. They're on welfare or Social Security, maybe living in subsidized housing or on the street, he says. Working the park becomes a means of survival.

Some end up with a "sugar daddy," an older man who bankrolls a younger man's living expenses in exchange for sex. "That's what we all wished for. It was like the movie *Pretty Woman*. That was the one thing we wanted so bad, that kind of fairy tale. We knew it wouldn't ever happen, but maybe, maybe it just might."

Hustling becomes an addiction, a habit hard to break. "I crave it sometimes, I crave the park. . . . I kind of enjoy that kind of danger. It's like driving a car really, really fast and hoping to God you don't get caught by a cop or crash and die.

"It's life in the fast lane. It's exciting. But it's dangerous, it's really really dangerous, the danger of AIDS, any sexually transmitted disease, getting beat up, getting raped, getting kidnapped, getting locked up, getting killed."

Jeremy says he owes many of his troubles to a lack of tolerance of his "differences" as a child and as a teenager.

"I knew something was different about me when I was a little kid," he says. "I got along better with the girls than the guys." But his parents grounded him and "slapped me around" for his effeminate behavior. "They found out I was giving my sister tips on how to be feminine," he laughs.

As he reached adolescence, he became increasingly depressed, and spent the bulk of his teenage years in various treatment programs. There were no support groups in school for gay teens and no one to talk to about his emerging sexual identity.

"I just hated life. At twelve, I tried to kill myself. I tried to hang myself." He remembers the attempt vividly. "I'm up in the tree. It's about suppertime. I tie the rope and then I slip out of the tree. I hung for a minute and then the rope up above slipped and I fell."

He attempted suicide and mutilated himself more than twenty times between the ages of twelve and eighteen, sometimes cutting himself and putting salt in his wounds. "It's better to chop up on yourself and feel the physical aspect of pain than to feel the emotional pain, because the physical pain is easier to deal with."

Jeremy has run into trouble with the law several times. He was convicted of check forgery and sentenced to eighty days in jail. With the permission of the court, he enrolled in a technical college, going to school during the week while doing time at the county jail on weekends.

But his life began to slip. Soon after being released from jail, he began hustling again, and wrote hundreds of dollars in bad checks to get money for rent and drugs—pot and uppers.

Jeremy intentionally overdosed on sleeping pills and alcohol one night while home alone in his apartment. He survived the suicide attempt and checked into a twelve-step treatment program. All of his future plans had washed away. "I'm just concentrating on day by day."

But weeks later, he was arrested for writing bad checks. Convicted for theft by check, he was sentenced to eleven months in the state reform school.

RANDY When Randy was sixteen, he was raped. He says he knew the man who raped him, and gave the police his name and a description. But his assailant told police that he and Randy were dating, so he was never prosecuted.

After the attack, Randy got tested for the AIDS virus. He made an appointment at a clinic and took the day off from school. As he walked into the clinic, he tried to look nonchalant. But his casual appearance belied his state of mind. "Here's where I start to get nervous," he said as he read a handout about the blood test.

His first name is called by a smiling nurse, who takes him to an examining room. People in the lobby read magazines or glance at pictures on the walls, trying to mask their worst worry. A radio is tuned in to an easy-listening station. It's like any other doctor's office, except for the ominous red paper covering the window in the door and a small sign that reads: HIV TESTING—BY APPOINTMENT ONLY.

Randy is in and out of the doctor's office in ten minutes. "He asked me a few questions—like, Was I gay? Bi? Did I have sex within the last year? I told him I have, but safe sex, except when I was raped. . . . Oh, and he gave me a nice little gift." He holds up a package of condoms.

Three weeks later, Randy returns to the clinic. He's told that the results are negative. He's giddy with relief.

"Woo-hoooo!" he shouts in the hallway. "I've gotta slow my heart down or I'll have a heart attack."

KEVIN   Kevin had been drinking all day long, mixing burgundy wine with rum and Cokes. Late in the evening, he hopped a bus to Minneapolis and promptly passed out in the front seat. The next thing he remembers, he was being yanked off the bus by police officers with the Metropolitan Transit Commission.

According to a police report, Kevin was acting "wild and disruptive" and forced the bus driver to stop abruptly, nearly causing an accident. Police were called, and an officer boarded the bus to wake him up. "I shook him a little harder and stated, 'Sir, I'm a police officer, you will have to get off this bus,' " stated the report. "At this point, the subject started to get up in a violent, fighting manner." Drunk and disorderly, he was hauled off to a squad car.

Kevin, nineteen at the time, tells a different story: "There were three of them and they were all grabbing me, saying, 'Shut up, queer,' or something like that," he says. Kevin says one officer smashed his head into the side of the squad car as he was being loaded in. The police report differs, saying the officers noticed a small but bloody head wound before they placed him in the car. "We at first had thought the red might be dye, which would have been consistent with his rather extravagant manner of dress," stated one of the officers in the report.

Police claimed that as his wound was being stitched shut at a county hospital, Kevin became uncontrollable. His arms and legs were lashed to a hospital bed.

Kevin says police taunted him and called him "faggot" as they led him to a squad car that would take him to jail. "They were calling me names and laughing and pointing, making fun of me. And I said, 'Yes, I am a faggot. I'm proud of it.' "

In a rage, he spat at one of the officers. The saliva hit him in the face and mouth. Said the police report: "Because this party had just admitted to being a homosexual, [the] officer . . . then reported to the hospital staff to start the process for HIV testing."

Kevin was taken back into the hospital, where a nurse drew blood from both Kevin and the police officer. Kevin was booked at the Hennepin County jail for "obstructing the legal process," or resisting arrest, and "attempting to cause bodily harm," third-degree assault.

Kevin says that when he gave police his address during booking, "One of the cops said, 'Good. Now if I come down with something I know where you live and I can come hunt you down.' "

Kevin was held in jail through the weekend and released. The charges were dropped. He never checked the results of his HIV test.

"Basically, I got fag-bashed by the cops," he says days later, still wearing bloodied blue jeans. "I'm just a skinny little lightweight. They didn't need three cops to restrain me."

The run-in with police was nothing new to Kevin. While living in Michigan, he was arrested as a minor for stealing cigarettes and breaking into a country club.

But his life was a struggle from the start. When he was barely two and living in Illinois, his mother was hit by a car and killed. His father was devastated, and sent his son to live with his grandparents when he was one or two. As a teenager, Kevin went to live with a cousin in Michigan, but ended up in group homes and treatment centers when he became hard to handle. He ran away once to Texas, but returned to Michigan, where he got an apartment with his boyfriend.

Throughout his teenage years, he would run away from home or treatment when things weren't going his way. "That basically has been my escape mechanism—I run.

"I'm a drifter," he says. "I've been drifting ever since I was fifteen." He's been treated for all sorts of ailments, he says—alcoholism, drug abuse, manic depression, bulimia. When he can afford it, he takes Ritalin for attention deficit disorder.

"I've got problems. But I know people who are a lot worse off than me. I'm a survivor."

He drifts back and forth from a small town in Michigan to Minneapolis. His Michigan home can be a dangerous place for him. "There's a lot of homophobia there," he says. "I'm the town faggot."

His flamboyance has made him an easy target for harassment. Eighty percent of his problems in life, he figures, have been due in some degree to his sexual orientation.

"I've been called a faggot ever since I was a little boy, nine or ten. I've been told that I am the gayest person that people have ever met. It's not because I work at it. . . . I am an effeminate gay male. I've been that way all my life. People have been trying to convert me since I was young, and look what it's done. It's had the complete opposite effect on me."

Part III

Community

$\mathbf{A}$*s gay and lesbian teens lurch ahead along the course of coming out, they gradually begin to see that they're not alone in the world after all. Pieces of a gay community and culture become evident—gay newspapers, gay bookstores, Gay Pride parades, gay film festivals. Even in small towns, teenagers manage to make contact—through pen-pal programs, computer bulletin boards, personal ads, telephone date-lines, or simply by word of mouth.*

A gay community serves as a source of information for youth as they continue on their journey of self-discovery. It also provides sanctuary, a place they can turn to for unconditional acceptance and support. They take haven in the community, secured by a sense of belonging and mindful of society's prejudices, sometimes turning their backs on their heterosexual families and friends.

With a new network of friends and support, young gays and lesbians can begin to express their sexual orientation. Conflict and confusion subside. Their wounds of alienation begin to heal, their self-esteem swells, and they start to integrate their sexual identity into all other elements of their lives. Being lesbian or gay becomes another facet of their personalities. They find a place for themselves among their peers and within their communities, gay as well as straight.

23

Derek III:

The Cards We're Dealt

One night on his way home from work, Derek Johnson decided to stop by the apartment of his boyfriend, Jonathon. He was worried about Jonathon's health and about his state of mind.

Standing in the kitchen, Derek saw something that alarmed him. Written in candle wax on top of the microwave oven in large letters were the words *life sucks*. He scanned the small apartment for other warning signs, and on a table beside Jonathon's bed he noticed a bottle of pills.

"Things started to make sense," Derek says, looking back. "As brief as this statement in wax was, I knew it was his suicide note."

Jonathon had been drinking. When Derek asked him about the words in wax, he begged Derek to leave him alone and screamed at him to get out.

"Finally, he broke down and told me he didn't want to live anymore. He was crying." Derek refused to leave, and gave Jonathon an ultimatum: Either let him stay, or he would call the police and have him admitted to a hospital.

Derek stayed the night, watching over his friend as he finally fell asleep. It was his duty, he says. "I had feelings for him and I was concerned for his well-being. I was pretty sure of what he would've tried if I would've left."

Since the day his parents made him move out of his home, just days before his eighteenth birthday, Derek's life had been a blur of change and a well of uncertainty. But he had survived. Aided by friends in the gay community and a gay couple who acted as foster parents, who allowed him to live rent-free in the attic bedroom of their Minneapolis home, Derek had forged an independent life. He was obligated to grow up a little faster than he would have wanted. But he was making it on his own.

"I would've done anything else rather than go home," he says. "It just wasn't an option."

He had been doing all right for himself. In less than a year after graduating from high school, he had a full-time job and a promotion, working as community outreach registrar at the Science Museum of Minnesota, registering school kids for science programs and field trips. He had just moved into a studio apartment near the "gay ghetto" of Minneapolis. And he had a boyfriend.

Derek had met Jonathon at a party. He was older than Derek, a little on the short side, with blond hair and blue eyes. Jonathon was from the suburbs, raised by his divorced mother.

By contrast, Derek was tall and thin, a young African-American who grew up in the city in a large Roman Catholic family. Despite their differences—or maybe because of them—Derek and Jonathon were attracted to each other.

"We started seeing each other on a fairly regular basis," Derek says. "He spent the night at my place or I spent the night at his place. And I could tell right away he was a nice guy, but very moody."

Three months into their relationship, Jonathon told Derek he had decided to renew earlier plans to move to Florida. Derek was disappointed. "Well, how would you feel if I moved to Florida with you?" he suggested. Jonathon was cool to the idea, and told Derek he couldn't make a commitment to a steady relationship. He was gone in a week.

"I was pretty depressed," Derek says. Rubbing salt in the wound, Jonathon before he left had admitted to several infidelities. Derek's self-confidence was shattered, his self-respect crushed. He was awash in self-pity.

"I remember telling myself, Well, I really don't blame him. I thought there had to be something wrong with me," Derek says. "This was the first time that my self-esteem was tested."

Derek became absorbed with his work at the museum and stayed home at night and on weekends. He avoided his family, stopped going to a peer support group, and confined himself to his apartment. To pass the time, he began logging on to a computer bulletin board for gay teenagers.

"It was a different way to meet people," he says. "I had very few options. I just wasn't into the bar scene. There was too much attitude. People didn't give you the time of day. And I didn't dance very well."

Sitting alone at home in front of his computer screen, he appreciated the anonymity of the bulletin board network. "Meeting" other guys this way was safe, unintimidating. "They don't know you, they can't hear your voice, they can't see you," says Derek.

He began to use "the board" to line up dates. Though he was hoping to meet someone he could go out with, the affairs were usually brief and always sexual, an unbroken string of one-night stands, he says. Rarely was there a second date or even a follow-up phone call.

"At this time I hadn't heard the term *recreational sex*," he says. "And each time there was this confusion, this, Oh, here's somebody else who's only interested in going to bed."

One night, out of the blue, Derek got a phone call from Jonathon. He was back in town, just four months after he had moved to Florida, and wanted to know if Derek would make good on a promise to take him back. Jonathon hadn't called or written since he'd been gone. "As far as I was concerned, the relationship was over," Derek says.

Yet Derek agreed to take him in. Jonathon was without a job, and Derek felt obligated to give him a place to stay, at least for a while. In the back of his mind, he was clinging to some thread of hope that their romance would be rekindled.

"We ended up in bed together, and he told me he wanted to try the relationship over again," Derek says. "He moved back and, boom! We were in this marriage." Derek was nineteen.

They decided to rent a two-bedroom loft apartment together. "He had said that he was ready to make a commitment to me, at least he was ready to try." But it was an on-again, off-again romance, doomed to fail. Jonathon started drinking heavily and dating other men behind Derek's back. Sometimes he would stay out all night, shrugging off Derek's questions about his whereabouts. It was becoming clear to Derek that Jonathon wasn't capable of maintaining a relationship, but Derek couldn't let go.

To Derek's dismay, Jonathon told him he was feeling uncomfortable with his homosexuality. Though the two had been lovers for more than a year, Jonathon said he had doubts about himself. "He said he didn't think he was gay, he thought he was straight."

Again, Derek took Jonathon's words to heart, thinking that he was to blame, that his inadequacies had somehow caused Jonathon's sudden doubts. "I remember telling him, 'At the bare minimum, you're bisexual,' " trying get Jonathon to admit to his contradiction. "I thought he was basically denying something, and I was willing to wait it out."

Derek couldn't shake Jonathon loose from the denial. "It was clear that he was depressed. Something was going on. . . . I think at that point I saw that things weren't going to work out."

On the morning after his near-suicide attempt, Jonathon woke up sober and ashamed. He apologized to Derek. "He said he was happy he made it to the morning," remembers Derek. "He basically thanked me for saving his life."

Four days later, Jonathon checked himself into a treatment center. He was placed on medication for clinical depression and began counseling for chemical dependency and his confusion over his sexual identity.

The episode was a painful lesson for Derek as well. "I was finally able to see this had nothing to do with me," Derek says. "This was his problem, not mine." He had reacted to Jonathon's ills while ignoring his own needs. "I told myself I would never get myself in a situation like that again."

It was months before his sense of self-worth was restored. But he became more sure of himself, more comfortable with his own sexual identity. "His denial reinforced in me the awareness that I wasn't heterosexual," Derek says. "It was obvious that, like it or not, we all have to play the cards we're dealt. It does no good to lie to yourself."

The turbulent relationship with Jonathon was only one of several hurdles that Derek faced in his nineteenth year. He seemed to be exploding with personal truths and revelations.

Another issue that he wrestled with was his race. Growing up black and gay was doubly burdensome. "It's a double-edged sword," says Derek. Not only did he feel isolated as a young black man in a predominantly white gay community, but he was estranged from the African-American community because he was gay.

"I don't fit in with the black community," he says. "I've constantly heard that I'm a very white-acting person, that I don't fit in because I'm gay. . . . People think being gay is predominantly a white thing."

Maybe it's the strong ties to traditional Christian ideologies within the black community that accounts for the particularly vehement intolerance toward gays, Derek speculates. Or maybe it's a rigidity about gender roles. Diversity is discouraged. So an expression of uniqueness by gays and lesbians is frowned upon.

"There seems to be less of a tolerance in the black community for gays and lesbians than of any other minority," Derek says. As a result, he has been forced to forfeit a measure of his heritage. Even family members—those siblings and relatives who know he's gay—think of him as a square peg in a round hole, he says.

Conversely, within the gay community, his blackness is also conspicuous. "Nothing overt," he says. "I'm hesitant to use the word *racism,* but there seems to be a lack of understanding, a lack of recognition that there are black people within the gay community, and just kind of a lack of awareness of what it's like to be a member of two minority groups."

When he first attended a support group for gay and lesbian teens, he was the only African-American in the room. "Until they saw me, it hadn't occurred to them that there can be a black gay man."

As a result, it was difficult to find other gay black men to go out with. More than once, Derek heard the slur "snow queen," a derogatory reference to a black gay man who dates white gay men. And when he dated white men, there often was an unspoken presumption that he was a sexual brute, "that black people in general are somehow wild or oversexed."

Earlier in his teens, when he was coming out to himself, his status as a double minority added another level of perplexity to his incipient sense of self. Was he black first, or was he gay first? "At some periods it was, Who do I identify with? Who do I connect with?"

As a young adult, after years of living on his own, Derek came to a mutual understanding with his mother about his sexual orientation. They gradually reached an unspoken truce on the topic of homosexuality. They finally made their peace.

His mother's comfort level on the issue had climbed. She finally was able to accept him for who he was, and even suggested once that what he needed to cure his loneliness was, *not* a girlfriend, but "a significant other." It was a big step for his mother.

"She knew I was gay. And she knew I wasn't going to change," says Derek.

His father, though, remained silent, forever unapproachable. "Never a word about it from my dad, to this day," Derek says. Instead, the extent of conversation between father and son has been idle conversation about Derek's job or his pet cat or the weather.

Derek tries to empathize, tries to speculate what his parents were feeling and thinking when he told them, at age seventeen, that he was gay. In raising Derek, the youngest child of six, his folks had drawn on the failures and pitfalls of his older brothers and sisters as lessons in shaping him, in setting him on the right course, says Derek. But nothing had prepared them for suddenly being confronted with a gay child.

He still has a hard time excusing them for what he sees as their abandonment during a crucial moment of his life. "It really wasn't a very easy time for me, or a happy time," he says. He remembers how desperate he was during those first few weeks of living on his own, holding down a job and finding a place to live while trying to stay in high school. He remembers distinctly one desperate evening, telling a friend through his tears: "I can't handle this anymore," and wondering how he was going to go on.

In retrospect, though, he believes that the experience made him stronger in a way, and maybe readied him for the unpredictable tests of gay adulthood.

"Looking back, I think the anger and the resentment are gone," he says. "And sometimes I wonder, well, maybe this was the best thing for me. I don't know what would've happened if I wasn't forced out. It sort of put a fire under my butt to get my life together."

From the window of his office on the top floor of the Science Museum of Minnesota in downtown St. Paul, Derek has a grand view of the State Capitol. The office is narrow but bright, large enough for a small conference table, a supply cabinet, a photocopy machine, and a desk.

Facing the window, Derek tapped away on the keyboard of his computer. His brown leather jacket was slung over the back of his chair. A Walkman waited on his desktop. A coffee maker dripped his favorite blend from Starbucks. On the corner of a table sat copies of a thick report on lesbian, gay, and bisexual students titled "Breaking the Silence," prepared by a select committee at the University of Minnesota.

If Derek's job is any measure of success, he has thrived. At age twenty-two, he was promoted to become coordinator of diversity affairs at the museum, an administrative job. As supervisor of more than twenty members of a diversity team, he is responsible for devising and setting into place diversity policies at the museum. Among his aims: to advocate for the hiring of more racial, ethnic, and sexual minorities.

"At twenty-two, where I am now, I think I'm doing fairly good for myself," he says modestly. "I wouldn't say I've necessarily found my niche, but I at least found something that's worked for me. I've gained skills in one area and was sort of able to carry them to the next."

But he's dissatisfied with the slow process of making change. "Diversity training is pretty much a thankless job. It's very difficult. Nobody wants to talk about racism or sexism or homophobia or whatever. . . . I know that things just slowly happen over time. But it doesn't have to be. Everyone has to be willing to put their best foot forward and support things when they can, and just sort of be honest about how they're feeling about the whole process."

Derek has come out gradually to his colleagues, either telling coworkers one-on-one or letting the word circulate through the grapevine. "Personally, I don't think I need to wear my sexuality on my sleeve." He has been accepted as gay at his job; as far as he knows, no one ever made an issue of it.

But in his family, he still feels he has been denied. On holidays, when the Johnson family gets together at his parents' home and his sisters and brothers and aunts and uncles pair off with their husbands or wives, boyfriends or girlfriends, teasing and laughing and kissing in the kitchen, Derek is a foreigner among his own kind. Always, he comes alone. And never has anyone asked why.

"I'm kind of mournful about it," he says. "It's not like I feel cheated of some opportunity or anything. It's just . . . unfortunate."

Derek has grown impatient with the silence. He vows that the next time he's in a steady relationship, he will bring his "significant other" home.

"The thought of bringing someone home is a big commitment, a big step," he says. "How my family would respond, I don't know.

"But I would insist upon it."

24

Tara III:

Nothing Wrong with Being Queer

Tara Lumley's cousin had her heart set on going to the March on Washington. She was a closeted lesbian, and insisted that Tara make the trip with her.

Tara, who had just turned twenty, couldn't really afford to go to Washington, D.C. She had just gotten back from Colorado Springs, where her girlfriend, DeAnn, went to college. Spring break was ending, and Tara was due back at college herself. She was in her second year at St. Benedict's, a Catholic school for women, an hour from Minneapolis.

But things hadn't gone very well in Colorado. Tara had found out that DeAnn had been going out with other women, breaking a promise of fidelity that they had made to each other. After going together for a year and a half, DeAnn and Tara officially agreed to slacken the boundaries of their relationship and date other women. So maybe a quick trek to Washington wouldn't be such a bad idea after all, Tara thought.

After they had driven straight through from Minnesota to the East Coast, the march was two days of blissful culture shock that affirmed Tara's belief that being gay was something to be proud of.

Dupont Circle had been absolutely overrun. Everywhere they looked were lesbians and gays, of all ages, from all over. It was a walking, talking dream come true. "It was overwhelming. There were just so many queers," Tara recalls. "I just walked down the street with my jaw open."

All weekend, Tara and her cousin hiked around the Capital City, absorbing the electricity of the crowd. They listened to impassioned teenage manifestos at the Youth Empowerment Speakout, stepped sadly around the panels of the AIDS Quilt on the Mall, watched admiringly as thousands of women filled the streets for the Dyke March.

"We walked and walked and walked," says Tara. "It was my first big thing like that. It was very empowering. Even at that point, I hadn't really seen that many other queers, other than going to a bar. . . . It was just incredible."

The collective power of the march was staggering. "The subways were filled with queers," says Tara. "You could talk to anybody: 'Where are you from? What's it like?'. . . Things like that. If you were walking down the street and you saw a straight couple, *you* were looking at *them*. There were queers everywhere. Pretty much, D.C. was queer that few days. It was like, if we can take this town, we can take *any* town."

But when the wave of wonderment began to wear off and the magnitude of the event sunk in, Tara was struck with a sobering revelation.

"When I saw all of these queer people, it was like, I can't believe we're so oppressed, there's so many of us. But I realized when we're *not* together, we have to be in the closet so much. You lose a lot. . . . It made me think, there's so many people here, but there's so many people who *aren't* here."

And it made her angry to know that many of the marchers would return to the closet after the weekend.

There's nothing wrong with being queer. Why *can't* everybody know? she thought. The hypocrisy was unfair, not just to her, but to the people who knew her, too. Why should her family be made to feel uncomfortable about who she's dating? Why should her sexuality be an open issue to her father and mother and grandmother? Why should lesbians and gays be forced to wear their sexuality on their sleeves when straights aren't?

Tara went home to Minnesota inspired, activated, ready to plunge into the lesbian and gay community. She gave a presentation on the March on Washington to classmates in her college human sexuality class. Beginning that summer, she joined up as a volunteer with the Central Minnesota Lesbian Center, a resource service in St. Cloud. She signed on with a lesbian softball team. And she marched in her second Gay Pride parade in Minneapolis.

College life had become stultifying. There wasn't much of a lesbian community at St. Benedict's, a Catholic school of 2,700 students in St. Joseph, Minnesota. A College Lesbians United group had been formed, but there were only four members, including Tara. The more out she became, the more people shunned her. Women would turn and walk out of her dormitory bathroom if she was taking a shower. And her roommate transferred to another room after walking in on Tara and DeAnn sitting together on the bed.

So, following her sophomore year, Tara decided not to return to St. Ben's and made plans to enroll at Minneapolis Community College. "I just couldn't handle not having a gay community around me. And I needed to be in the city."

In her twentieth summer, Tara drove to the Michigan Womyn's Music Festival with a lesbian friend and DeAnn, who had come home to Minnesota from school in Colorado after a trip to Alaska. "I was still carrying a torch for her," Tara says. She was hoping to rekindle their romance.

If the March on Washington was a call to action for Tara, the Womyn's Festival was a cultural jubilee. The annual celebration, by Tara's description, was a sexually empowering, musically inspiring, spiritually invigorating week-long campout. And a chance to lie topless in the sun without any men around.

"The thought of eight thousand women all running around naked—that pretty much got me interested," says Tara. "With ninety percent of the women there queer, it was so cool."

There was good food, good music, and good company—comedy acts, dramatic performances, poetry readings, pottery classes, drumming ceremonies, personal-growth workshops, a sweat lodge, giant bonfires, and the occasional all-night orgy, she says. Everywhere she went, there were ongoing free-for-all discussions about lesbianism and women's issues—liberating, uninhibited, and "manless."

"It was really something to see all these women running around totally being themselves. I came back with some ideas about who I was. . . . D.C. seemed a lot more political. Michigan was a time for people to be where they wanted to be and who they wanted to be."

The festival was another giant step toward personal empowerment. "Packing up was so sad. It sucked to put a shirt on."

Back in Minnesota, Tara's solidarity with the lesbian community grew more complete. She marched in the streets of Minneapolis with the Lesbian Avengers on Halloween night, and went topless to a fundraising party for the upcoming twenty-fifth anniversary of the Stonewall riots, with a women's symbol, the "Sign of Venus," painted on her chest in her own menstrual blood.

Three weeks before her twenty-first birthday, Tara volunteered to speak at a gay and lesbian youth forum. A panel discussion was scheduled at St. Cloud State University, in recognition of Bisexual, Gay, Lesbian Awareness Day. A local newspaper reporter and photographer were invited.

Tara gave a lengthy version of her life story as a young "queer," telling the student audience about her first attraction to another woman, her high school friend Emily; about the high school softball coach who helped steer her to an understanding of being gay; about the scorn she had experienced at her Catholic college; about her parents' reluctance to talk about her homosexuality; about her integration into the lesbian and gay community.

"I realized this culture existed and I surrounded myself with it," she said. "It gave me security, and I felt like I was part of something for the first time."

The next day, a four-column photograph appeared at the top of the

Local page in the *St. Cloud Times,* along with an article about Tara. "Clearwater woman tells crowd of coming out," read the headline.

"Everybody saw it," Tara recalls. Her father and stepmother, her stepmother's family, her great aunt and great uncle, her grand-mother's best friend—suddenly she was out to them all.

Her father phoned, angry. Tara wasn't home to take the call. But a few days later, she ran into her stepmother, who cornered her about going public.

"So why didn't you tell us about this article?" she asked Tara.

"What article?" she said, playing dumb.

"What do you mean, what article?"

"Oh, you mean the article on me speaking at State? I didn't know it was gonna be in the *paper.*"

"What do you mean? There was a photographer there." Her step-mother was enraged, and told Tara that she had brought nothing but humiliation to her father.

But little by little, with Tara faithfully forcing the issue, her father in his own way began adjusting to the fact that his daughter was a les-bian. Occasionally, Tara would meet him at a bar for a drink. And often she brought a date. He would taunt her, sarcastically telling her: "You're a phase, you're a phase. You haven't found the right guy yet." And she would laugh and give her girlfriend, Lisa, a squeeze.

One night, Tara and Lisa went barhopping with Tara's father, her uncle, and their friends. They met up in an American Legion post in Clearwater, Tara's hometown.

"This band was playing," Tara says. "And I go, 'Lisa, come on, let's dance.' I finally got her out there to dance. We were two-steppin' to this band. And the band loved us . . .

"So then I started talking to my dad. And I was drunk, or I wouldn't have even brought it up. And my dad was drinking. It's the only time he'll say anything. . . . He was talking about how the article came out in the St. Cloud paper, and he was all pissed off. And then he talked to some of his friends, and they said, 'Well, you know, who cares about it?' *They* didn't care. And so then he figured if nobody else cared, *he* shouldn't be upset about it either, and that's just the way it is. He was afraid that everybody was gonna look bad on *him*.

"So then he gets the whole table's attention and he says in this loud voice, 'You know, when I was younger it was a big thrill to go down to Loring Park and harass the queers. And goddamn it if I don't *got* one *now*.' And everybody was laughing. He's like, 'That's what I get.' "

While her father is far from celebrating Tara's lesbianism, he has stopped denying it, Tara says. "He's seems to be doing okay with the whole thing. I mean, it'll never be just the *coolest* thing in his life. . . ."

Her mother, meanwhile, takes it in stride. Their relationship at times is strained, but she kindly welcomes her daughter's girlfriend into her home.

"I think it has been easier for my mom to understand and accept than my dad, because her other daughters, my stepsisters, are so much more gender-typical than I ever was. So I think she's able to see that I was different."

Tara holds no resentment toward her family.

"I guess I could've had parents a lot better about the whole issue," decides Tara. "But I could've had parents a helluva whole lot worse. I'm just one of those people in the middle. My parents wouldn't be caught dead marching at a Gay Pride parade with P-FLAG or anybody. But I know that when I'm ready for a commitment, they'll both be there at the ceremony."

The Festival of Pride Dyke March is a rowdy, bawdy, unauthorized demonstration of lesbian rights. Organized annually by the Lesbian Avengers, it is meant to defy and to shock.

Tara was happy to supply the shock. At 7 P.M. on a Saturday night in July, as a throng of lesbians began to fill the streets along Loring Park in Minneapolis, Tara slipped off her T-shirt and tucked it into the back pocket of her jeans. A minute later, a friend rushed up, hands covered with green paint, and planted a green handprint on each of Tara's breasts. Tara was ready to go. She took a place near the end of the pack.

"Ten percent is not enough! Ten percent is not enough!" chanted the marchers as they clogged the congested Hennepin Avenue. Lesbian Avengers in black capes locked arms at intersections to control the traffic as motorcycle cops watched curiously from the curb. Occasionally, someone would take chalk to pavement and scribble a slogan: DYKES RULE! or DYKE POWER!

The size of the crowd swelled, occupying two city blocks as it looped through a downtown neighborhood. Leading the march was a contingent of motorcyclists, revving their engines to announce their presence. Just behind the Dykes on Bikes, a women's drumming corps rattled and banged as hundreds of women of all sorts—adorned in red lipstick or tattoos, cornrows or shaved heads, in lacy black brassieres or high black boots—monopolized the streets.

Tara was one of just a half-dozen women who shed their shirts. "If I was born this way, I should be able to march down the street this way," she explained defiantly. "In this march, I feel like I have the safety to do so." She recited a line from Kahlil Gibran's *The Prophet:* "Meet the sun and the wind with more of your skin."

Though her attitude about nudity was matter-of-fact, she knew her appearance would be noticed. Topless, wearing green body paint, and sporting a blue mohawk, Tara was turning heads all along the route. Cameras flashed from the sidewalk as she walked by. Men on motorcycles circled alongside. Office workers pointed from second-story windows. Tara lit a cigarette and waved.

"You have nice breasts," a woman shouted from a car, and Tara smiled and gave her a thumbs-up.

The marchers took up another chant: "We're hot, we're wet. And we ain't talking sweat." And from the curb, a group of men held up placards and chanted, "Eeney, meeney, miney, mo! Lesbians are good to know!"

The march was a double-take spectacle for the Saturday-evening dinner and theater crowd. Motorists honked; pedestrians gawked. Patrons waiting in line outside an Italian restaurant cheered as the Dykes filed by. At a taxi stand in front of the Hyatt Hotel, an older woman shook her head in disapproval and mouthed the word *disgusting* at the passing women. She was answered with jeers. "Woo! Woo! Woo! Woo!"

The river of marchers flowed past the Walker Art Museum and emptied into Loring Park, where it had begun. Tara walked hand in hand with Lisa, and stopped to give her a kiss.

"So what's going on?" a friend said, approaching Tara.

"I'm just *nekkid,*" she said.

A police cruiser rolled up and, reluctantly, Tara pulled on her T-shirt.

Tara draws a distinction between "lesbians" and "dykes."

"Dykes to me have buzzed hair and are young, like in their twenties. Lesbians are the more PC, granola-eating type. I think dykes are more radical. Lesbians are into playing softball and drinking beer or are into issues, totally into issues. Lesbians are hanging out mostly with other lesbians and gay men. Dykes are out clubbing it with gays, straights, other dykes, whoever."

Tara has straddled both camps. She has fit the part of tree-hugging, beer-drinking shortstop, and she has lived the life of a "baby dyke," born into Generation X and bent on "dissing" heterosexual customs and convention. After moving into the city at age nineteen, she immersed herself into gay culture as fast as she could, looking to other lesbians for support and unity when her family offered none. At twenty-one, she pondered her place within the community at large. She was impatient with lesbians and gays who isolated themselves in the safe cluster of only the gay community.

"When I moved down to the city, I was definitely looking for more queer culture." But queer culture was not a utopia. She was looking for more of a multicultural balance, contact and friendships with gays, straights, people of color, young and old.

"I see people cutting themselves out of anything that isn't queer culture. They've struggled for so long to find a place to fit, and when they finally find it they're not going to leave. I just don't need it. I need it, but not every minute of my life. I don't need to be with queer people all the time. There's so many parts of life that *aren't* queer. I go to the grocery store, and I don't think about being queer. I suppose it has something to do with self-confidence or self-image or whatever. But for me to go somewhere and not be accepted by people is fine, because I know there are plenty of people who will accept who I am.

"I just want to experience everything I can. To experience one kind of place or one kind of people is, like, too limiting. To me, I'd rather experience a little bit of as much as possible, than to know everything about just *one* thing."

Tara moved in with her girlfriend, Lisa, in the summer of her twenty-first year. She was employed full-time at a woodworking shop, putting in long hours of overtime, trying to pay off a motorcycle she had bought and student loans she had accumulated. She wanted to go back to school.

Tara still has high ambitions to be a teacher. Her dream is to teach social studies to high school students, to teach an American history class that would include the cultures of all minorities, "everything the book leaves out," she says, the history of women, African-Americans, Asian-Americans, Latin Americans, Native Americans—and, of course, "queers."

25

Dan III:

Let's Go Dancing!

Just weeks out of high school, Dan Birkholz finally freed himself from the isolation of his rural home by moving into a one-bedroom apartment in Minneapolis with an older man he'd been dating. It was not the ideal situation, Dan admitted. But it was a rush at independence, something he had craved for too long, living an hour outside of the city with his family. On the day he moved out, as he was loading his clothes and books and cassettes into his friend's car, Dan defiantly spat onto the street outside his family home. "It was a great symbolic gesture," he said. "But it went right over my dad's head."

Dan was reluctant to commit himself to a steady relationship with his roommate, Warren, so the two made a pact: Warren would share his place until Dan was able to get a foothold in the city—find a job, buy a car, enroll in a community college. Dan would sleep on a fold-out futon in the living room. Rent was set at $125 per month, plus half the utility fees.

"Warren's a very nice guy, a big teddy bear," Dan said after moving in. "He knew how uncomfortable I was living at home, and he totally supported me."

Dan had met Warren over a "fantasy" phone line a month or two earlier. "I was eighteen and he was . . . well, he *told* me he was thirty. And I found out shortly thereafter, he was thirty-five. I'd had some one-night flings with older men before, but that's all they'd ever been was flings or whatever. Nothing that was any big deal."

The relationship with Warren *was* a big deal to Dan's parents. They were incensed that he was going out with someone so much older than he was. "They didn't like it; they did not like it at all," Dan said. "They were totally convinced that I was being used for some horrible sexual thing and that he was just some kind of slimeball, you know. My mom started in on this: 'What would you do if I suddenly started dating someone your age?' And my dad did that too. Basically, I just said, 'Well, this is who I'm dating, I don't really care what you think.'"

But when his parents finally met Warren at Dan's high school graduation party, they were won over, Dan said. "My mom thought he was the neatest thing since sliced bread. The face-to-face talk with him, when they got to look at him—they needed something like that. It went pretty smoothly during the course of the party, and he was being really casual about the whole thing."

Dan's freedom didn't last. The pact with Warren was quickly broken, and they began sleeping together. Dan enjoyed his emancipation, but he wasn't ready for the accountability that a sexual relationship demanded. Barely a month after he moved in with Warren, they had a blow-out argument, and Dan suddenly was back home, living with his father and younger brother again, stuck in limbo.

"I was eighteen years old, I didn't have a job, it was a one-bedroom apartment," said Dan, regretfully explaining what went wrong. The age discrepancy was a big factor too, he said. "There are a lot of things that I have more in common with a twenty-year-old, little nuances, little things that happen when we grew up and things that we remember and that kind of thing. It is a very valid argument that the young impressionable youths can be taken under the wing, blah, blah, blah, blah. And I get sick and tired of hearing about it. It's just nice to be around someone. . . . You know, we children of Generation X are constantly struggling. Partly through no fault of our own and partly because that's the little design we've given ourselves. So it's nice to be around someone who's a little more stable."

He saw someone older, like Warren, as a mentor, as a teacher, as someone who could introduce him to the gay community, who could explain by example what it meant to be a gay man. He was impatient with his peers' adolescent naiveté.

"When I come across people my age, it's like they stepped out of the Dark Ages or something," Dan said. "They view things that are different from them as innately threatening and stupid and unnecessary. And I've never been like that. . . . It's generally a question of maturity. I don't think like most people my age. It's a question of getting along better; it's a question of temperament. I've never really gotten along with my peers to begin with. I just simply get along with older people better—and it falls that way romantically."

Things would be way different, he acknowledged, in a world where gay teens could openly meet and date in school, just like their straight peers. "I doubt that I would be dating as many older men as I do. I would much rather date someone my age than someone who is in their forties, just because of the numbers. There's a lot of things that get lost in the translation."

With a portion of a $1,300 inheritance he received after his grandmother's death, Dan bought a plane ticket to Washington, D.C., for the 1993 March on Washington. His parents wanted him to save the money for college. But getting to Washington seemed to be all that mattered to him at the time. His personal march to Washington represented more than a rally for gay rights. It was part of his metamorphosis. He was determined to make a place for himself in the gay community, to exchange his doleful, guilt-ridden adolescence for a vital, proud adulthood.

Dan kept a journal of the three days he spent in the nation's capital, beginning with his flight from Minneapolis to Cleveland, where he caught a connecting flight to Washington:

Friday, April 24—Well I'm on the plane and surviving quite nicely, thanks. OK. OK. There's this really hot guy in the seat in front of me. He looks kind of like a blond and graying Campbell Scott. Nummy. Nice beard, too.

Oh boy. The flight from Cleveland is full. Totally. Happy, happy. Joy, joy. The airport terminal here in Cleveland is a wonderful Queer Fest!

Saturday, April 25—*Oh my God.* . . . That's the understatement of the decade. I absolutely cannot describe in words what I've experienced. I got to the March via the Metro (of course). There were hundreds of people on every train. The energy on the Metro alone was incredible. Everybody talking with everybody else. I got cruised by too many men. I don't even know how many. . . . I saw the Lincoln Memorial. It was big. I saw the bear men. They were hot. They seemed to look through me. (Where's a Cubs hat when I need one?) I ran into some people from the LGYT support group and wandered around with them for a bit, taking pictures of people kissing . . .

Sunday, April 26—Marching was great fun. I needed to vent my frustrations, but I didn't get really mad until I saw some of the counter-protesters' signs: GOD HATES FAGS and then some Bible verse, or YOU'RE GOING TO BURN IN HELL, followed by another verse, and other such hellfire and brimstone messages. Of course, I neglected to get pictures. Oh well. . . . I only saw two groups counter-protesting along the way. Passing by them, we'd chant: "2-4-6-8. Are you sure your kids are straight?" I liked that part.

We got done marching at the Mall. I went to see the Names Quilt. That really got to me. Hard. I only know (for sure) one person with HIV and no one with AIDS or anyone who has died from it. Lucky me.

So I listened to the speakers when I got back to the Mall. They got pretty intense. Not intense, really, as much as I was remembering a time when I lived in [the rural town of] Zimmerman feeling so incredibly alone I didn't know what to do.

So anyway, the march was incredible, and afterward I bopped my very sunburnt self down to Dupont Circle. Again. The place was crowded. How can I put my mood Sunday night? Happy, exhausted, and probably a few more things in between. Dupont was extremely special that night, and I wandered around with

Sebastian and Mike (two guys from the Minnesota youth group). Sebastian dragged us into this leather shop. Boy, was that a trip! They had toys in there for stuff even I hadn't thought about—and I have a very fertile imagination. Some people's kids . . .

Well, I hung around Dupont until 6:30 (my flight left at 10:00) and met some nice people from basically everywhere across the country. That was pretty cool. I took a cab to the airport, caught my layover in Cleveland, and was back home, sunburn and all. My description here can't really capture what I felt and went through . . .

On Easter weekend in his twentieth year, Dan moved into an apartment in Minneapolis, his second attempt at liberation. This time, he was in the heart of the city's gay neighborhood. And this time, he vowed, the move would be for good.

Dan had been working full-time at a fast-food carry-out grill as a food server. He hated the job—selling Coke, cookies, coffee, and baked potatoes to the hustle-by lunch crowd. But the weekly paycheck gave him the opportunity to live on his own.

He shared a three-bedroom apartment on the third floor of a mammoth boardinghouse with two young women and a cat. One of the women was his co-worker. Rent was $190 a month. A personal phone line to his bedroom was extra.

The gray clapboard house, an elegant mansion during better days, was within walking distance of his downtown job and just five short blocks from District 202, a center for gay and lesbian teens. A week before he moved in, his mom and dad helped paint his bedroom walls and loaded him up with supplies. "My parents bought me everything," Dan said. "I was floored. They said, 'What do you need for your apartment?' And then they bought it. And then they said, 'What do you need for food?' And then they bought it." Peanut butter, Ramen noodles, Ragu spaghetti sauce, pretzels, and Coke. Laundry soap, aluminum foil, a trash can, a glow-in-the-dark toothbrush, and a pillow.

The cold war with his parents had thawed. "They're getting over it," he said. "They're getting over their own homophobia. I get along so much better with my dad now. But I don't think he's told anyone that he has a gay son. My mom has, to some of her close friends. And I've told both of them that I trust their judgment enough and that if they feel they need to tell someone then they can. My only exception with that is with my dad's family. If he's going to tell, I would appreciate him telling me first—'Oh, by the way, I'm going to tell Aunt . . . whoever.' It doesn't really bother me anymore. I don't know about my dad's family. I'm closer with them than my mother's family. But I don't really know. I haven't told them anything. They've stopped grilling me about, 'Do you have a girlfriend yet?' so I think they've kind of put it together by now. Usually twenty, twenty-one is when you start bringing your little loved ones over for Christmas or Thanksgiving or Easter or something. And I haven't done that yet. So I think they're kind of putting it together.

"But my mother's told some of her friends. And she only tells people if she knows they're going to be cool about it. Otherwise, they can go climb a tree. They can go somewhere else with their little prejudices. . . . She'll be talking to the people at work and, you know, they'll be talking about their kids, and they'll say, 'Oh, you know my son George is seeing this girl Emily . . .' And my mother isn't comfortable with saying, 'Oh yeah? Well, Dan met this guy over the weekend and I guess he's a really nice person.' I don't really *care* what her co-workers think. So the ball's entirely in her court."

Dan hoped that someday soon he would have something to give his mother reason to boast. He was ready for a steady relationship. "Like a big-time, knock-down, drag-out relationship," he said. "I could do it. I've done the playing-the-field crap and I'm tired of it. I would just like a nice, quiet kind of relationship where we have enough in common to make things interesting and enough differences to make things interesting."

His loneliness was reflected in one of his poems:

I woke up alone again
Some days I wonder if I will
    ever wake up, roll over,
    look deeply into another
    man's eyes and say
"I love you"
And mean it
And he'd mean it back
It's become such a boring thing
    for me, sex
A couple of bangs and it's
Done.
He gets up to go
And I'm back at
Square One
I wake up alone again
Guess some people never learn
Guess I'm one of them.

Dan had hung a Depeche Mode poster on a freshly painted wall in his bedroom. A caricature of himself in a Star Trek uniform leaned against another wall. And on a shelf above his clothes rack was a lava lamp, his prized possession.

"I think this is really nice," he said, settling into the living room couch and surveying his new home. He was satisfied with how things were coming together. "I'll be able to go places, do something. Like dance. Some people jog, I dance. Last night, it was ten o'clock, and I'm like, Okay. Let's go dancing!"

Dan was eager to make new friends, gay and straight. "I think it's just my nature. I think it's always a good idea to know as many different people as possible, as many different social groups as possible." Maybe he would join the Queer Street Patrol, a group of volunteers who patrolled the parks and streets against gay-bashers. Or maybe he would volunteer at the teen center, District 202. At twenty years old, he was a bit old for that crowd, but he could pitch in on Friday nights when they held their dances.

He was thinking about going to college, too. He had heard that he could get his tuition waived if he was a full-time employee at the university. So he began checking the classifieds. "I want to go to school, I really do," he said. "But I'm very good about saying I want to do stuff and not very good at following through with it."

Dan already had found a hangout, a nearby coffeehouse. The Café Zev at one time was a gas station. It still had an operable sliding garage door. Tacky brass chandeliers hung from the corrugated steel ceiling, and erotic paintings hung on the walls. Rummage-sale furnishings, sturdy wooden tables, and a black baby grand piano—bedecked by a wax-encrusted silver candelabra—occupied the cement floor. Just off the downtown Nicollet Mall, the Zev was patronized by an erudite crowd of urban gays and lesbians in their early twenties. Dan enjoyed sitting at a table, watching the crowd and listening to New Age "trance" music, with a plate of pastry and a cup of tea, reading a fantasy-horror novel or writing in his journal, hoping to be noticed by someone "nummy."

A month after he moved, Dan and his co-worker roommate threw a party for their colleagues. It was the first party Dan had ever hosted. Weeks later, he attended his third consecutive Gay Pride parade. This year, the parade route was just blocks from his home.

Dan also began going to weekend "raves"—marathon dances, dusk till dawn, presenting non-stop pre-recorded "techno" rock in huge warehouses on the industrial side of town. Sometimes live bands would come in from Chicago or New York, groups like 4-d or Adam X. Though the raves were non-alcoholic, four dollars would buy a "smart drink," a concoction of mineral water, sugar, Gatorade, and mega-doses of vitamins that jolts the senses into a manic high.

By chance, Dan hooked up with a local theater company, and volunteered to operate the lights in a four-week production of a play based on Alfred Lord Tennyson's poem "The Lady of Shalott." He took the job as a favor to the assistant director, a gay friend. It didn't pay, but it didn't matter; it was "another notch in my belt," Dan said. Maybe something good would come of it, maybe he'd find his way into the city's theater crowd, maybe he'd try out for a role in another production.

Through word of mouth, he discovered near his home a new "18-plus" dance club called the Cage. Periodically, the club would hold "Queer Nite"—drawing young gays and lesbians from the city and suburbs as well. The Cage, Dan explained, was "totally Goth," or Gothic, "a combination of attitude and dress," in his description, that borrowed heavily from Anne Rice novels, the movie *Blade Runner,* and cyberpunk fashions. Once a week, with his high school friend Carol, Dan would dress totally in black—black Doc Martens, black denim jeans, black laced shirt, black lipstick, black eyeliner—and march six blocks to the Cage, "scaring old ladies off the sidewalk" on the way. Standing around and copping attitude at everyone in sight, Dan loved the role, and fancied himself as a variation of Brandon Lee's character in *The Crow.*

Dark images, dark dress, "dark-side techno"—it was the Goth style. "For me, there's also an underlying hope and sensuality to it," he said, "just because that's the kind of person I am." Dan and Carol began working on a Goth "fanzine," writing text and rummaging through the trash bins of a Kinko's copy center for cover art. Named *Drowning,* the four-page fanzine would include prose, poetry, CD reviews, and a pictorial collage of Dan and Carol in full Goth regalia. They planned to distribute it at local record stores.

Dan was beginning to find a fit. Still cynical and oh-so-sarcastic—defense mechanisms that he attributed to a painful adolescence—he could see a world unfolding before him. "I have other activities besides work and sleep," he marveled. He recognized faces at the coffeehouses and the dance clubs, and some of the faces recognized him back. Now and then, he would find a date. One man in particular, a "bear" just a few years older than Dan, would call him fairly often, and the two would get a pizza or catch a movie. "Things are going slow enough," Dan said, as optimistic as he gets, about the young relationship. "It's not meet-passion-sex-love-passion-'bye."

Since he moved to the city, even his appearance had been changing. Black was his color of choice; but occasionally he would lace up a pair of purple high-tops. He had shed the slouched, self-conscious posture that he carried in high school, and seemed to have gained an inch or two in height. He was still awkwardly shy and prone to moods of sullenness. But the moods passed. The shame and sorrow had lifted.

And he wore earrings, in *both* ears, two gold hoops in his left ear and a tiny ruby in his right, a freedom—and a statement—that he had been denied by his mother when he still lived at home.

As if destined to follow a script, Dan's life began to coincide with a poem he had written years ago in high school, a long and agonizing account of his struggle with his parents during his coming-out years. In the final verse, he had managed to summon up a flicker of hope:

I've been dealing with it
Day by day with my parents.
They're still having some difficulties,
But they're trying,
And doing a decent job.
I even have a boyfriend now.
Huh, what do you know?
My life
Can be normal.

26.

SIDEBAR:

Networks of Hope

It's never been easy for gay and lesbian teenagers to find one another. Afraid of being rejected by their friends and family, gay youth mask their sexual identity by mimicking the social scripts of their straight counterparts. A fundamental piece of who they are becomes invisible as they retreat into the closet, with little chance of meeting gay or lesbian companions.

But out of a stubborn objection to the closet has grown a network of social and political activists. A movement has taken flight, launched on the foundations of the gay-liberation movement, guided in part by an older generation of gay and lesbian adults and fueled by the impatience of youth itself. Responding to a call for openness and capitalizing on strides made by the previous generation, more gay and lesbian teens are coming out than ever before. "We're here, we're queer!" is their in-your-face rally cry. "Deal with it!" is their demand.

The vast majority of gay and lesbian youth are isolated as they come of age, driven to secrecy out of a fear of being deserted or ridiculed by their family and friends. Yet those who break the silence refuse to be ignored. And, in a wave of personal empowerment, their coming-out stories become the inspiration for others.

To furnish teens with relief and protection during their course of coming out, gay youth advocates and, more notably, gay youth themselves are building a safety net of resources. From high school peer groups to drop-in teen centers, hubs of support are forming in communities across the country. More than a dozen teen centers have been organized for young gays and lesbians, from Seattle to Denver to

Austin, Texas. Magazines are being put out nationally by and for gay and lesbian youth. Online computer services have linked countless teens to a community of gay youth across the country. Where there once were only single centers for gay adults and youth alike, there are now service agencies and social programs for teens only. Where there once were only the gay bars and parks, there now are gay coffeehouses and proms.

"There are people who still lead lives of quiet desperation," says Leo Treadway, who helped form one of the country's first peer support groups for gay youth in the 1980s. "But inasmuch as you can read the signs, I think you're seeing a shift from just trying to help people crawl out of this pit and get to ground zero—which was sort of my generation—to youth who begin without that deficit and pick up the ball and run with it. There are more islands of hope than when I was young."

Although progress has been tardy in the education system, notice is being taken within the mainstream. "We are seeing that more and more service organizations are recognizing that young gay and lesbian youth are in need of support, and that they do exist," says Rea Carey, of the National Advocacy Coalition on Youth and Sexual Orientation. "That's the first step, the recognition that they exist."

A decade ago, support groups and services for gay youth were novel ideas. Today, their numbers are growing exponentially.

"There's been an explosion of youth groups," says Chris Kryzan, founder of the National Coalition for Gay, Lesbian and Bisexual Youth, a resource clearinghouse and referral service in San Jose, California. More lesbian and gay adults—such as himself—are shaking off the mythic reputation that they are "recruiting" adolescents into a life of homosexuality, Kryzan says. "Certain organizations and individuals—whether it be the L.A. Gay and Lesbian Center or Joe So-and-So down the street—have gotten beyond dealing with their own coming-out process and integration into the world, and they're at a point where they're able to help teens."

And more teens are helping themselves. "I've seen kids fifteen, sixteen come out," he says. "When I was growing up, that was unthinkable. But as people see that you can come out as a gay teen and not be ostracized, they get comfortable, and it empowers them to come out. So we're in this domino effect right now."

Schools, the Frontline

On a Monday morning, an announcement is broadcast over the public address system at South High School in Minneapolis. Like most announcements, it's a reminder of an upcoming meeting or event, but this notice is purposely vague.

"The support group for gay, lesbian, and bisexual students will be meeting this week . . ."

Confidentiality is a sworn requisite. Details of the meeting—the day, the time, the place—are available only from a guidance counselor or school nurse. Most of the students in the support group have not come out to their parents or friends. The weekly meeting is the only time they allow themselves to be openly gay or lesbian.

Led by school nurse Sharon Bishop, meetings are informal and freewheeling. Periodically, guests are invited from the gay and lesbian communities—artists, activists, doctors, ministers, politicians— adult role models of the students. But most of the time, the agendas are unplanned.

School is out at two-thirty, and a half-dozen teenagers fly into the music room on the second floor, landing in a circle of chairs. Loosely organized but tightly knit, the meeting is something between group therapy and a party at the home of a friend whose parents are out of town. The students are like family, brought together by their shared uniqueness. Their look is androgynous—high-top sneakers, backward baseball caps, T-shirts, black jeans—and their temperament is soaked with serious attitude.

"I do *not* look like Alan Alda," protests one girl to a friend as he lifts her off the floor in a bear hug.

Conversation is animated, impulsive, uncensored. The students bad-mouth their parents, rag about their teachers, rattle on about music or TV or movies or religion, whatever shoots into their minds.

They joke about condoms and their sex lives, trying to one-up and out-shock each other with their latest stories of exploration. They're fresh and squirrely, and shoot quick from the lip.

"I'm dyeing my hair on Wednesday," says the Alan Alda lookalike. "Bright red. We'll have a party."

Bishop asks about plans for the coming summer.

"I'm taking belly dancing. And I'm hoping to get a *job*," beams one girl.

"I'm taking some summer classes at the university," brags another. "And we're gonna hang out and harass people, bring some embarrassment to the world."

"I have to go to summer school," groans a boy.

"I'm gonna stay home and *not* run away again," pledges another girl.

"I'm getting tested this week," mentions a sophomore, and he tells the group that he has an appointment at an HIV/AIDS clinic. "I'm not worried about it." He tries to smile.

His announcement is taken in stride, without alarm or condolence. He is neither coddled nor condemned. HIV is a fact of life among gay teens.

It is disclosures such as these that make a peer support group invaluable to gay and lesbian youth. Having a place to talk about AIDS or sex or parents—free of fear or ridicule or humiliation—goes a long way toward fostering healthy adolescent development.

"Before I started going to group, I didn't know any gay people," says Annie, a sixteen-year-old lesbian. "I was suicidal and stuff. In group, it was like, Wow, I'm not alone. It made me happy."

Scenes such as this are replayed daily across the country: in an open-air classroom at Monroe High School in Sepulveda, California; around the kitchen table at the Lambert House teen center in Seattle; at the campus library of Western Connecticut State University in Danbury; in the offices of the Lesbian and Gay Community Service Center on the west side of Cleveland; in the back room of the New Connections youth agency, two blocks from West Virginia's state capitol in Charleston.

The stringent opposition to gay and lesbian programs has not disappeared; homophobia clearly has not abated. To the contrary, the religious right's anti-gay campaigns have been more persistent than ever, going so far as to target school-based support for lesbian and gay students. But in the face of the resistance, support services for gay youth continue to spring to life, from Phoenix to Philadelphia, Lansing to Little Rock. In most places, advancement comes gradually—one step forward and two steps back. Activists in several states have been successful in changing laws and policies to guarantee human rights to gays and lesbians. Massachusetts, for instance, in 1993 passed the Gay and Lesbian Student Rights Bill, legislation that protects sexual minority youth against discrimination, violence, and unfair treatment in the schools.

Yet the closet still looms large. For many gay teens, school is a dangerous and scary place, rife, as is society itself, with homophobia. For every high school that recognizes June as Gay Pride Month, there are hundreds that don't.

Historically, it has been the role of the schools to provide a safe and positive learning experience for students. At the very least, say youth advocates, schools should be a nurturing influence to kids of all diversities and a reliable resource for students with special needs. When families are incapable of providing support, students turn to their school for guidance.

But up until the most recent years, schools have failed gay and lesbian students on all counts. Instead of creating a nourishing environment, the education system through its neglect has sustained an atmosphere of harassment and sometimes violence that has only enhanced the risks that teenagers face when in the midst of reckoning with a homosexual identity.

Up until the most recent generation of high school students, few secondary schools acknowledged gay and lesbian youth, sensitive of the potential for negative public reaction. That ignorance, say gay youth advocates, has contributed in a large measure to the desperate isolation that gay teens suffer.

"It's terrible for the institution of education to be fostering prejudice and discrimination, and that's exactly what happens," says Virginia Uribe, creator of Project 10. "We are supposed to be affirming kids and giving them a good sense of who they are. And yet many gay and lesbian kids are told flat-out that they're sick perverts. They're told that by their teachers, by their counselors, by the administrators. And certainly they hear that from their peers."

Uribe founded Project 10 in 1984 in the Los Angeles Unified School District. One of the oldest and most visible models in the country, Project 10 combines in-school sensitivity training with weekly support groups for gay, lesbian, and bisexual teens at more than half of the district's fifty high schools.

In addition to Project 10, an alternative high school was formed in Los Angeles for at-risk gay and lesbian students. The Eagle Center opened in 1992 in a old house in the city's Wilshire neighborhood, with one teacher and thirteen students, some of them wards of the state or runaways and nearly all of them on the verge of dropping out. In two years, it tripled in size.

"Any kid that's hurting should have attention," says Jeff Horton, a gay Los Angeles school board member and political caretaker of the Eagle Center and Project 10. "I don't limit that to sexual orientation—any group of kids. The added thing with gay and lesbian kids, of course, is they don't even have their families as role models or protectors. Often their families are actively hostile. So the need for school programs or some other outside agency is even sharper."

Just the existence of a support group for young gays and lesbians validates their sexual orientation and begins to wipe away what Uribe calls their "moral tarnish."

"Every student is deserving of a sense of respect and dignity," says Uribe, a science teacher since 1954. "And we have not given that to our gay and lesbian students. . . . No one is asking for special treatment. We are asking for justice."

The Eagle Center's older cousin is New York City's Harvey Milk High School, the first public high school in the country exclusively for gays, lesbians, and bisexuals. There, two full-time teachers work with about thirty to thirty-five students who have dropped through the cracks, academically and socially. Many of the youths have been kicked out or have run away from troubled homes.

Named for the gay San Francisco city supervisor who was assassinated in 1978, the Harvey Milk High School was opened in 1985 by the Hetrick-Martin Institute, a Greenwich Village social service agency for lesbian and gay adolescents. It's now fully accredited and funded by the New York City Board of Education.

Like the Eagle Center, the goal of Harvey Milk High School is to integrate these marginalized students into mainstream high schools when possible. "School is in a sense the most important place for teens," says Joyce Hunter, a co-founder of the school. "And there must be something in place in those schools that says to gay and lesbian kids that they are welcome there." Whether through a multicultural curriculum or peer support programs, gay and lesbian teens should be included in the celebration of diversity in school, she says. "They should do that for *any* minority group."

In San Francisco, the board of education in 1990 created an office of support services for gay and lesbian youth. "This is the only program that's completely integrated within the school district," says Kevin Gogin, the program's full-time director. Gogin runs sensitivity training sessions for faculty, gives presentations about sexual orientation in health classes, and works with staff on curriculum relating to homosexuality. For example, a high school social studies class now includes the history of the modern gay-rights movement.

Additionally, the principal of each of San Francisco's forty middle schools and high schools is required to designate a "gay/lesbian-sensitive adult"—a paid staff member whom gay and lesbian students can call on confidentially if they have concerns. With that person readily available at each school, students have an outlet to express their feelings about their emerging sexual identity. And as a result, says Gogin, more kids are coming out—and at a younger age.

"The young people themselves are demanding it," adds Tom Ammiano, a gay member of the San Francisco Board of Supervisors. "The times have changed that way. It's not a trend. It's a significant social change."

Indeed, it is often the will and the courage of gay and lesbian students themselves that propel the change. At high schools in St. Paul and Minneapolis, for example, it was only after the very vocal demands of a handful of students that gay and lesbian support groups were formed in two high schools. Four years later, the St. Paul board of education endorsed a proposal to install peer support groups in all of the district's high schools.

One of the broadest improvements on the state level has been in Massachusetts. Support groups were started in five schools in 1992. A year later, with the backing of Governor William Weld and an aggressive grassroots campaign by gay, lesbian, and bisexual high school students from around the state, a law was passed, guaranteeing protection to gay and lesbian students. By the end of the 1993–94 school year, support groups—called Gay/Straight Alliances—were expanded to thirty schools statewide.

Run by a faculty adviser, the Alliances meet weekly and are open to gay as well as straight students. "We really are seeing many changes with the new generation," says David LaFontaine, chairman of the Governor's Commission on Gay and Lesbian Youth, the first of its kind in the nation. "They're much more out and more visible. At the same time, we're seeing they're much less inclined toward what I think of as a separatist mentality. Most of them would rather be in an organization that includes their friends who are straight than to feel that it has to be just a gay and lesbian group. I think that's a real advancement.

"Having a group in a high school really can be a lifesaver for many students," he adds. "It gives students a sense of security. It makes them feel that school is a welcoming place. . . . The number of kids have just come out of the woodwork. There really is a groundswell going on."

Think Globally, Act Locally

HIV outreach worker Charlie Tamble is standing before two groups of gay and lesbian teenagers. "Heads or tails?" he asks, innocently enough, poised to flip a coin that will decide which team will go first.

But somebody smells a joke and is quick with a randy remark. "You *always* want tails," a young man baits a friend, and the room fills with laughter.

And so begins another match of AIDS Jeopardy, an amusing approach to the not-so-amusing task of HIV education, presented by a two-man delegation from the University of Minnesota's Youth and AIDS Projects.

It's a Wednesday afternoon at District 202, a come-and-go hangout for gay, lesbian, and bisexual teens in the heart of Minneapolis. School is out for the day, and kids saunter in from Nicollet Avenue. Some flop onto an overstuffed sofa to watch the contest, others drift over to the pool table in the back. A volunteer sits behind a coffee-and-soda bar, fingering chords on an acoustic guitar.

Two teams have been chosen and named: The Virgins will take on Three Bones and a Fish, competing for points in five categories— Facts & Frequencies, HIV 101, Sex Accessories, Transmission, and Potpourri.

Charlie calls out the answers to the missing questions, à la Alex Trebek, as his co-star, Tony, keeps score on a huge sheet of butcher paper.

The Virgins win the coin toss, and choose Sex Accessories for 200.

"Item used to prevent HIV transmission in oral sex among women . . ." reads Tamble.

"What is a dental dam?" blurts out a Virgin, and it's high fives all around their table.

"Potpourri for 500" is their next choice.

"In 1969, an event in New York that sparked the beginning of the gay-liberation movement . . ." says Tamble.

"What is Stonewall?" and the Virgins pull ahead.

"Transmission for 200."

Charlie: "The length of time it takes for HIV to show up in blood . . ."

"How long is six months?" Slowly Three Bones and a Fish make their comeback.

Rarely do the contestants stumble on an answer through the course of the game. Though young, they're remarkably well versed in AIDS prevention, an encouraging sign to Charlie and Tony, who sometimes take their show on the road to school support groups.

After playing to a tie, the dueling teams make their wagers for the final Jeopardy of the day: "The teenage activist who died in 1990 of AIDS who influenced national legislation in AIDS funding . . ."

"Who is Ryan White?" Both teams answer correctly, but Three Bones and a Fish have wagered the greater amount. "You are the winners!" announces Charlie to their cheers. And as he hands out prizes—Pez dispensers, Go-Bot action figures, a purple-haired Barbie doll—the proud champions spontaneously break into the Jeopardy theme music.

A high school support group can provide gay teens a safe space for self-disclosure and consultation, but it's not much of a place to party. By and large, school is a social wasteland for most lesbian and gay students, who are shut off from same-sex partnerships and shut out of traditional dating rituals. Adolescents are presumed to be heterosexual; few allowances are made for anyone who deviates from that norm. As a result, there are no gay student groups, no gay proms, no gay parties in most high schools.

That lack of social activities has prompted youth advocates to build youth centers. Part sanctuary, part social club, a youth center gives lesbian and gay teenagers a chance to cultivate friendships and learn the ropes of same-sex relationships in a non-threatening atmosphere: to make friends, to have crushes, to line up dates, to fall in love—to develop healthy gay and lesbian identities free from judgment or fear.

One such center is District 202. Organized in tandem by adults and teens, District 202 opened its doors in January 1993 in a storefront near downtown Minneapolis. Founded with seed money from a local foundation, it now operates on grants, funding from the gay business community, and private donations.

"We wanted to create a space where teenagers could just be

teenagers, where they could do what teenagers do and not have anyone hassling them for doing what they do," says Elissa Raffa, one of the founders.

Open four days a week, District 202 holds a dance every Friday night, shows videos on Wednesdays, and simply gives teens the breathing room to meet each other. From the start, it has been seen by teenagers as well as adults as an alternative to the socially awkward and potentially exploitative bar scene.

"Here, they can explore their sexuality, they can date people their own age, they can go through a relationship in what's a more average way of getting to know someone, and then they can decide if they want to explore their sexuality with them," says Michael Kaplan, coordinator of the center. "Before this, if someone thought they were gay and they wanted to see what it was like, the only choices were the bars or the parks."

District 202 is for youth twenty-one and under. The only adults allowed in are staff members and volunteer escorts. "When I go to the bar, I have forty-year-old men trying to pick me up because they think I'm a young boy," says a nineteen-year-old lesbian. "And if I *was* a boy, I'd look like a pretty young boy."

"It's a place to be with people who share the same background and identity," says a twenty-one-year-old bisexual woman. "It's almost like having a second family."

In Seattle, the Lambert House gay, lesbian, and bisexual youth center was opened in June 1991, the first community center for gay teens in the country. Based in a roomy two-story Victorian in the center of the city's Capitol Hill gay community, Lambert House divides its mission—and its floor space—into two parts. Former bedrooms upstairs have been converted into offices rented to social service agencies for youth, including a counseling service and a crisis hotline.

Downstairs is for socializing, for hanging out. Teens can watch the traffic go by from the front porch, tune in to MTV in the living room, play a game of Ping-Pong in the dining room, or cook up a pan of macaroni and cheese in the kitchen, which doubles as an informal boardroom of sorts.

"It's like a rec center; it's like a Y," says Arlis Stewart, with American Friends Service Committee, who helped organize Lambert House. But she also views Lambert House as the locus for building coalitions with the city's political, educational, social service, and philanthropic communities. "We are more than direct services for youth," she says. "We're really organizing a community," building a grassroots social and political movement.

The groundwork for Lambert House was laid in 1988, when a Seattle task force issued a critical report on the city's dearth of services for gay teens. The report found that gay and lesbian youth were at a disproportionate risk for homelessness, sexual abuse and exploitation, drug and alcohol abuse, depression and suicide.

Two years after the report was issued, a city commission on gays and lesbians earmarked funds for a host of youth programs. And out of a coalition of adults and teens grew Lambert House.

"It's a safe place for me," says one nineteen-year-old gay man. "It's a place where I can be around people my age and people like me. It's like a home away from home, like having a family you never had."

Across the country, centers such as the Lambert House and District 202—formed specifically for teens—barely number a dozen. Yet some types of services for adolescents—whether counseling, peer-led workshops, crisis lines, or social programs—are offered at most gay and lesbian community centers, from the Drop-In Center at Denver's Gay and Lesbian Community Center to the Lavender Youth Recreation and Information Center in San Francisco to the Sexual Minority Youth Assistance League in Washington, D.C., to the Boston Alliance of Gay and Lesbian Youth to Los Angeles' Gay and Lesbian Adolescent Social Services, an agency that operates a group home for adolescents. The National Coalition for Gay, Lesbian and Bisexual Youth lists 3,500 referrals in its database of support services, everything from counseling groups to HIV-prevention programs to chapters of P-FLAG.

A national toll-free helpline for gay and lesbian youth (1-800-347-TEEN) was started in 1990 by the Indianapolis Youth Group. Staffed by gay and lesbian youth twenty-one and under, the hotline receives as many as two thousand calls each month, ranging from two-minute in-quiries to two-hour suicide threats.

The IYG Center also provides space for support group meetings, training workshops, drug and alcohol treatment programs, and social events. In 1993, it opened a transitional housing program for home-less youth in a five-bedroom house on the city's north side.

In Chicago's Lincoln Park neighborhood, the Horizons social ser-vice agency began drop-in support groups for gay youth in 1979. Dis-cussion groups are now held four times a week, drawing as many as one hundred teens for one sitting.

"Kids need a safe place, a setting where they can talk to other gay and lesbian kids and adult role models," says psychologist Andrew Boxer, who co-authored a book on the Chicago agency titled *Children of Horizons: How Gay and Lesbian Teens Are Leading a New Way Out of the Closet.* "That's a pretty simple thing, but it can make a big difference."

New York's Hetrick-Martin Institute began direct services for gay youth in 1983. Today, the institute provides a myriad of services, from counseling to drop-in care to outreach for homeless youth to the op-eration of the Harvey Milk High School.

"We are getting more involved in policy work," says executive di-rector Frances Kunreuther. "We also started a legal clinic, in conjunc-tion with a legal agency in New York, specifically for gay and lesbian youth who have legal needs."

In 1994, the institute moved into an enormous building in the mid-dle of New York's Greenwich Village, a highly visible site for gay youth. "We've had a real explosion since we've moved," says Kun-reuther. "We've grown from this little one-person thing in 1983 to a staff of forty-eight full- and part-time staff."

While the level of commitment given to gay teens in New York or Chicago certainly will differ from that in, say, rural North Carolina, there are more ways than ever for the new generation of gays and les-bians to reach out to each other, no matter where they live. The Out-reach to Rural Youth Project, for example, grew out of the efforts of one gay man, Scott Thiemann, who, in 1991, began traveling to small rural communities throughout Oregon, eastern Washington, and the

Idaho panhandle, meeting with high school principals, teachers, and counselors along the way. Because of his grassroots work, gay and lesbian youth conferences have been organized and support groups have been formed in some of the schools he has visited—at the high school, for example, in Bend, Oregon, population 18,000.

"My big thing is direct visibility and putting a face on gay, lesbian, and bisexual people," says Thiemann. "It just takes somebody who is willing to take the risk."

Whether face-to-face, through a gay-and-lesbian pen-pal program, or across the phone lines to a computer bulletin board, teens are able to see that their fears and frustrations are mirrored in someone else's life. Knowing that their journeys are not solo, they become heartened.

"When our son came out, there was nothing," says Mitzi Henderson, president of P-FLAG and the mother of a gay son, now in his thirties. "There was no group for us to go to, no place that we could get information. . . . Now there are gay community centers. There are many more books and other resources. There's much more.

"Despite all of the political opposition, I think it's easier today," says Henderson. "I think counselors, school nurses, social service people, are much more aware, much better informed, much more empathetic, much more realistic in their understanding. And that's terrific. We have many more allies than when we started. People are coming forward and saying, We *need* this. So in a sense there's more hope."

Networks

I have not yet come out to my family, and have only told four people. . . . I live in a very conservative part of the state. Owing, I'm sure, to the fact that it is a small town, no one at my high school is openly gay, or at least I have never heard about it. There is a high level of homophobia in the school.

The Internet let me listen in on discussions relevant to identifying with my sexuality, information that I couldn't find elsewhere. I was able to locate some local gay social groups (though I won't contact them until I come out more).

I feel that gay activist groups strongly opposing bigatry (sp?) and homophobia as exhibited by people like Jesse Helms are paving the way for an egalitarian future for homosexuals. I also believe that the Internet is providing new resources to people who were afraid of their homosexuality and is allowing them to explore it before coming out, and is also aiding them in the process of coming out.

—Tim Dee (not my real name)
Somewhere in Northwest Washington
16 years of age

Reshaping the coming-out process for a new generation of lesbian and gay teens is the personal computer. For youth with access to a computer and a modem, an electronic network of interaction and support is available literally at their fingertips, bringing instant entree into a community of gays and lesbians across the country and around the world.

Several of the major commercial online services have forums specifically for gays and lesbians. For example, within CompuServe's Human Sexuality Forum are online message boards, hotlines, question-and-answer sessions, support groups, and live "conference rooms" for gay, lesbian, and bisexual concerns. America Online's Gay and Lesbian Community Forum includes message boards, a resource library, private "chat rooms" for one-on-one discussions, and weekly online conferences. On the Internet—the global crossroads of data banks, "mailing lists," and "newsgroups," or message boards—is a meeting place for a medley of gay interests, from college social groups to the political activist organizations ACT-UP and Queer Nation to the Gay, Lesbian and Bisexual Librarian Network. Added to the global network are local computer bulletin boards, or BBs, in virtually every major city in the nation.

Going online furnishes gay teens with a certain refuge. Usually, they can remain anonymous by identifying themselves only by first names or pseudonyms, "screen names." Freed by the anonymity from embarrassment or ridicule, the young "Internauts" can swap coming-out stories and relate their sexual feelings, argue about religion, and complain about school. Even for those who choose not to join in the electronic communiqués, simply observing the online "postings" and dialogues between other gays and lesbians brings a sense of relief, knowing there are others in their world with similar thoughts and feelings. It breaks the isolation, and provides a welcome measure of commonality.

"There's a sense of community for these teens online," says Kryzan of the National Coalition for Gay, Lesbian and Bisexual Youth, which supplies city-by-city resource guides and support-group "start-up" kits online to youth across the country. "They can go online and be completely anonymous. The first time they say 'I am gay' to them-selves is a very emotional period for them, much less to say it to someone else. Here, they can finally start talking about it with other people and become more comfortable about themselves, without using their name."

They can make the connection in the privacy of their bedroom, their dorm room, even their high school computer lab, without plac-ing themselves in intimidating or risky situations.

"Mom and Dad think they're doing their homework. And in a way they are," says Kryzan. "They would be terrified to go to the library and look under 'homosexuality' and check out a book. Here they have a way that doesn't leave a paper trail in the house. And they can learn things about what it means to be a gay person in America today that they just couldn't in any other way."

Online conversations can be a catalyst for teens who are in the midst of coming out. "It's not really a goal, but it's definitely a positive by-product of online communication," says the "host" of America On-line's Gay and Lesbian Community Forum, who goes by her screen name, QUIRK. "I've received letters from teens who were literally a phone call away from personal agony. They happened upon the GLCF and found a plethora of information and resources that helped them, if not come out, at least find a safe haven to express their thoughts and feelings."

The online conversation between teens ranges from the silly to the sublime. "Often, it's 'I think I'm gay, is anything wrong with me?'—that sort of thing," says Kevin Morgan, a volunteer from Louisiana who coordinates the message boards for America Online's forum. "Other teens give their perspective about what it was like to have the same feelings. Some of them just want to talk to others about stuff like *Star Trek* or *Beverly Hills 90210.* In most cases, they just want to know that they're not the only person who feels the way they do."

Steven Levine, a technical writer with Cray Research Inc., a manufacturer of supercomputers, is a self-professed computer nerd. He is also gay. Occasionally, he'll be approached by gay teenagers on "the Net" who look to him as a role model.

"I feel comfortable on the Net," he says. "I can be very careful about what I write. I can be very careful that there's nothing in there that can be interpreted as a come-on, that can be misconstrued."

When sought out for advice or simple conversation with younger gays, he sends out sort of a boilerplate letter of boosterism, Levine says, assuring teens that, number one, they're not alone, and number two, they're not sick or evil.

Once, through an online dialogue, he observed the rapid transformation of one young man as he soared through the coming-out process. Levine was envious. "It took him like two months to go through what it had taken years for some of us to go through.

"When I was coming out, and this was in 1973 and 1974, I had absolutely no way that I knew about to talk to other gay people. None at all," says Levine. "I could read anything on the gay-liberation movement coming out of New York City. I had suspicions of teachers in high school; I had suspicions of family friends. But there was no way I had of trying to find gay people to talk to. . . . I was bursting for something like that."

There is the potential for exploitation of teenagers online. Several highly publicized arrests have been reported, involving adults who stalked and then sexually assaulted teens after meeting them online.

The Net is hardly immune from abuse—or homophobia. This bit of anti-gay graffiti appeared on an America Online message board: "Silly fagget, Dicks are for Chicks." It was followed by the response, "Why don't you learn how to spell?"

As a precaution against online "bashers" and predators, commercial services require members to adhere to specific terms of service. America Online, for example, prohibits postings that include telephone numbers and street addresses and regularly monitors the message boards. Users of the self-policed Internet also are expected to follow an unwritten protocol or face being denied access to mailing lists and newsgroups. The National Coalition for Gay, Lesbian and Bisexual Youth regularly posts precautionary guidelines for teens, warning them that "appearances can be deceiving" and advising them to be wary of online manipulation.

But for the most part, the new electronic frontier appears to have found an unprecedented niche within the gay and lesbian youth community as an important peer-support service. Indeed, the service could potentially be a lifesaver. One posting, a clear call for help, went out over a gay and lesbian teen message board, with the subject heading "I'm Bleeding!!!!!":

"Hi. I am totally drunk right now and I want to kill myself but I'm too much of a coward to do it. I need to talk to anyone, I keep cutting myself and it is getting real deep now but I don't care cause I can't feel it. Ha, ha, maybe I will bleed to death in my sleep. That would be cool. . . ."

Whether the posting was legitimate or not, responses were "e-mailed" within hours, including these two notes:

"Don't do it! Call the local suicide prevention number and ask for someone to talk to. Things will work out. It is not worth taking your life over."

"I know how you feel right now. I, too, have considered suicide many times to stop the pain inside. I beg of you, please stop hurting yourself in such a way. Please seek help, if not for yourself, then do it for me. Dying is not cool. I've had two friends of mine attempt suicide. One survived, the other did not. The one that survived now loves life more than anything else. The one that didn't does not know the pain and grief he left behind. So please, call a suicide hotline, or e-mail me. Preferably do both. Take care of yourself. . . ."

The next day, the suicidal teen e-mailed this letter of appreciation: "I just wanted to apologize to everyone for last night's topic 'I'm bleeding.' I didn't mean to upset anybody, I just feel like crap sometimes, that's all. My arm has quit bleeding and everything, but I am drunk again. Oh well, what else is new. . . . I also want to thank all of you who wrote me, too. I still really don't understand your concern for me but that's all right, it feels good to feel cared about."

Notes from the Net The following remarks about online gay and lesbian services were received via e-mail:

> I would have committed suicide if it wasn't for the support I got online. I HATED the fact that I'm gay. But through America Online I was able to talk to people that have gone through or are going through the same thing I did. . . . Now, the only friends I have are over the computer. I am rather comfortable with my sexuality and lend my help to anyone else that needs it. There are several files and message boards online and weekly conferences that help you in coming out.
>   —David, age 16
>   Anderson, Indiana

> It sure makes you realize that you're not the only one, and that you don't have to take any of the crap anyone is feeding you that you're immoral, bad, unclean, "a pansy-ass," or anything like that. There's not room in hell for everyone, ya know?
>   —Tony, 22, of Madison, WI

> The Internet was the only place I *could* come out to. I remember that before I came out, I was really frightened that someone I knew would find out my secret. I even thought that that person in the shadows would tell everyone I knew and I'd find myself alone. Nobody I knew hung out in soc.motss [an In-

ternet newsgroup], so I felt like it was a pretty safe place to talk. Through soc.motss, I met someone that has helped me greatly through the past three-and-a-half months. . . . Literally speaking, I was at the end of a dead-end street before I came onto the Net. . . . Without the Net as a starting point, I would not have much of the support I do now.

    —Chuck, San Diego, CA

      Age 18

In all honesty, America Online actually made me come out. At the time I first signed on, I was still going through the "I'm straight but could sleep with women someday" stage. Then day by day I started to hang out in the "women4women" chat room and realized that I was truly sexually attracted to women. I then went through about six months of "Yep, I'm definitely a bisexual," and then after my real experiences started to happen I was off on the "Lavender Road to Oz." Were it not for AOL, it probably would have taken me longer (I can't really say how long, months, or maybe even a year) to realize this about myself. The company in that chat room was very relaxed and comforting. Plus, figuring that I never have to meet these people made me feel open to say anything I had holed up inside. I have thus met some of these people and have made great friends from here.

    —"Vitamin Love"

      New York City

To start off with, I'm 23 now, and I came out to myself when I was 21. Reading the [Internet] newsgroups helped me a great deal in understanding the gay culture, gay issues, and hearing from other gay people. Simply being exposed to a large amount of material, discussions, personal anecdotes, etc. made me feel more comfortable with myself and more informed about the gay culture and relevant issues.

    Second, I met my first real boyfriend on the Net (through a personals posting; he turned out to be a student at the same school I had just graduated from).

Third, I became active on IRC (Internet Relay Chat) on the gay channels, and through this I have met literally dozens of people in my area, made many good friends, and furthered my exposure to and knowledge of gay issues and other people's experiences.

—TD, Los Angeles, CA (age 23)

I find more understanding and acceptance from people I get to know over the Nets and Echomail networks. We can share our problems and count on people who faced the same problem before to help us tackle them. It is not of much help, though, since I'm in such a situation (refer below), but I've definitely become more knowledgeable in general regarding homosexual issues and the rights we should have.

I live in Singapore—where gays are definitely discriminated against. It is sad how a prosperous and aspiring island country like Singapore is STILL rife with discrimination. It is the law. You could get 2–10 years in jail plus fine if you are caught romancing with another guy (I'm a guy) in public and if you are reported having sex with another guy. . . . Depressing fact, but we have to face it. I know there are quite a lot of gay teens over here who face the same problems as me. There's simply nothing we could do. The social atmosphere is just too intolerant. Especially the law.

—Kerry, 18, Singapore

27

Michele III:

Lesbian on Campus

"Ye shall know the truth, and the truth shall make you free."—JOHN 8:32
—Inscription at the entrance to the campus chapel at
Augsburg College, Minneapolis

Throughout her adolescence, Michele Boyer's impressions of gays and lesbians were negative. Her notions of lesbians in particular were dark and doubtful. Based on rumor and snippets of hearsay—and eventually on firsthand accounts from lesbians themselves—she presumed that all lesbians were doomed to lives of tragedy and secrecy and scorn.

The portrayals were consistently grim: When Michele was in junior high school and living in her hometown of Menominee, Michigan, gossip circulated that a lesbian couple played on a city softball team. Her memories, whether real or imagined, are of two overweight, beer-drinking, chain-smoking "lezzies"—improbable role models for the young and athletic Michele, but her first glimpse at homosexuality. *That's what a lesbian is, and I'm not that!* she remembers telling herself.

Joyless, forbidding images continued to distort her view of what it meant to be a lesbian. When Michele was a high school sophomore, students contemptuously labeled an English teacher a lesbian because she always wore pants. As a freshman in college in Minneapolis, Michele ran into a classmate in a gay bar who tearfully recalled how she'd been forced to drop out of school after her roommate began spreading the word that she was gay. And at a college friend's summer wedding, a basketball teammate of Michele's told of waking up one morning to find a goodbye note from her lesbian lover of two years who said she couldn't go on living in shame.

Never were there models of lesbians who were successful, contented, outspoken women. Instead, they were rough and graceless "bull dykes" or pitiable souls who gathered surreptitiously in gay bars for fear of being found out.

Michele had formed such a tarnished perception of homosexuality that when she returned to college after finally coming to terms with her own sexual identity, she vowed to be a positive role model for other young lesbians on campus. After dropping out of school for most of her sophomore year due to a crippling depression, she re-enrolled at Augsburg College at age twenty, healthy and strong and eager to hold herself up as a survivor, to come out proudly and will-fully to her classmates and instructors, teammates and coaches. "After all, I had nothing to lose," she says, looking back. Her spirit had been so thoroughly broken during her months-long battle with clinical depression that there was nowhere to go but out. After conquering her illness through antidepressants and electroconvulsive therapy, she returned to Minneapolis feeling as if she was "back from the dead," she says. The crushing wave of dread and sorrow had ebbed, giving way to a swell of liberation. She was renewed, reborn, and ready to act up. "I'd gotten back the most precious thing—my life."

Staunchly determined to turn a few heads and change a few minds about homosexuality, Michele decided to start with the women's athletic program at college. Once again, she had won the position of starting guard on the basketball team, a group that in the past had been rife with homophobic attitudes. But this season, instead of going along with all the snickers and the wisecracks, she made it known that the homophobic remarks were offensive. Not one to scold or lecture, Michele would take a teammate aside on the court or in the locker room for a little one-on-one sensitivity training. "Hey," she would tell a player or even a coach. "It's real hurtful when you say things like that because, as a lesbian, it's a real put-down."

They got the message. Because they regarded Michele as a friend, her teammates told her they were supportive. "None of my friends or acquaintances—the ones that I took the time to sit down and come out and do the whole process with—none of them had a negative re-action," Michele says. "It was more a curiosity: How long have you known? What's it like? What do you do now?"

With the school's student population at only 1,800, it didn't take long for the news to start circulating beyond the athletic department. "It started this movement in motion of people coming to me," Michele says. "I kind of became the lesbian on campus, so to speak." In classes, at parties, and over lunch, students would corner Michele looking for guidance. "They were looking for someone to talk to, to affirm their own experiences and discriminations that they felt at school," she says. Straight students, too, had questions for her. "The ones who were open to learning approached me, the ones who really wanted to learn. And we would talk. I think the people who were really against it were talking about me behind my back—guys on the hockey team, guys on the football team."

That fall, Michele also joined a women's rugby team called the Amazons, a community-based team that competed around the country. On a road trip to Chicago, when a teammate asked if Michele was gay, she unabashedly acknowledged that she was. Rugby had found a reputation as an especially popular sport among lesbians, yet when she joined, Michele was the only one on the team. The announcement that she was gay was nearly celebrated by her teammates. Finally, the Amazons had an open lesbian player. "I became the lesbian ambassador," Michele laughs.

Step by step, Michele was slowly breaking out of the closet, finally enjoying a life unencumbered by remorse or doubt. "I don't think it was full liberation, partly because of the hostile atmosphere at Augsburg. I was still the new kid on the block," Michele recalls. "Spiritually, I was feeling really free, centered and free. But the coming out part was kind of slow for me."

Michele let the news ripple out gradually. She had little reason to keep her sexual orientation hidden any longer. She had come out to her friends and family with little detriment. Not only had her parents been accepting of her sexual orientation, but they had grown proud of her. Joe and Colleen Boyer had sold their small business in Michigan and retired to the Twin Cities to be closer to their two children after Michele's younger brother decided to enroll at Augsburg College. The Boyers began attending meetings of Parents, Families and Friends of Lesbians and Gays and joined a Lutheran church in St. Paul that had an openly gay ministry associate.

As she came out, Michele began to meet other lesbians on campus, at bars, and through rugby. She started dating. "The first year or so after I came out I was testing the waters," she says. "I had a couple of sexual experiences with women, but it was still a slow process of coming out."

Yet, unlike a brief guilt-ridden relationship with a lesbian roommate the year before, Michele for the first time in her life felt free to explore her sexuality without inhibition. At a bar one night, she met a woman in her early thirties named Martha. "I was just curious enough and had just enough to drink to go home with her, and spent the night," Michele says. "She was very experienced, sexually."

Though they only went out three or four times, Martha was Michele's most intimate sexual partner, and a teacher. Michele tried things she had never done before, including mutual oral sex and genital penetration. She was no longer afraid of her sexual desires. The touch of a woman felt perfectly natural.

Over Memorial Day weekend at the end of her junior year, Michele traveled to Chicago to compete in the national rugby tournaments. During the trip, she met Shawn, who had joined the Amazons as a "pickup" player for the tournaments. Shawn, twenty-three, a year older than Michele, was a part-time political science major at the University of Minnesota. The two women talked for hours on the drive to Chicago and back, and hung out together between games. Shawn's striking beauty and Scandinavian blond hair captivated Michele. She was high-energy, effervescent. And she made Michele laugh.

"It was a love-at-first-sight kind of thing," Michele says. "I was ready and looking for a girlfriend for the first time. I was ready."

Michele had no idea whether Shawn was lesbian, straight, or bisexual, and she couldn't just ask her straight out. But she needed to know. She gave Shawn her phone number and offered to get together for a beer sometime. A day later, Michele's phone rang. "She called and asked me if I wanted to go out with her," Michele says. They went out for lunch.

The next day, Michele asked Shawn if she would like to watch her play in a softball game that evening. And afterward, the two decided to go out for a beer. Michele suggested a gay bar in St. Paul, to test Shawn's reaction.

"There's a bar called Ladies Night. You wanna go there?" asked Michele.

"I've heard of that place. Yeah, let's go there," Shawn said.

A pitcher of beer and pack of cigarettes later, they walked outside to Shawn's car and sat on the hood to talk. The moon was full.

"Finally, I just got enough nerve and leaned over and kissed her on the cheek," remembers Michele. "And she looked at me and then kissed me back. On the lips."

They spent the night together, commencing a two-and-a-half-year love affair, the first long-term relationship for either woman.

"It was wonderful to have her be my girlfriend in my senior year, and to come to basketball games during my last year of college and meet all of my friends," Michele says. "We were interested in a lot of the same things. We would read books together. And almost every weekend we'd go traveling somewhere."

Eventually, they moved into an apartment together. Shawn was welcomed by Michele's parents as an "adopted daughter," says Michele. "Especially my father—he really enjoyed Shawn. She would be out in the garage with Dad working with him on one of his projects while Mom and I would be in the house talking."

An idea had been brewing in the minds of Michele and her friend Lisa for weeks. Wouldn't it be great to have a campus support group for gays and lesbians? They had heard of similar groups at other campuses around the Twin Cities. So why not start something at Augsburg?

Michele and Lisa had come out all across campus. The school year was coming to a close. Michele would be a senior the following year. The time seemed right.

Michele, Lisa, and a third lesbian, Lyda, decided to contact all the gay students they knew at Augsburg. Michele talked to women in the athletic department. Lisa called on her gay friends in the theater department. Lyda tried the English department. A conference room was reserved at the College Center and the first meeting was scheduled.

Eight people showed up—two gay men, five lesbians, and one straight woman, a faculty member who taught a course on human sexuality and volunteered to be an adviser. And from that inaugural meeting in Conference Room G was born BAGLS—Bisexual And Gay/Lesbian Services.

"We felt it was important to have a very visible, formalized, gay-and-lesbian-identified group on campus so freshmen coming into school could see there was support for them," Michele says. "We saw it as a peer counseling program, where, if people had concerns about their sexuality, they could explore those concerns with a counselor or a peer support person."

Lisa and Michele agreed to serve as co-presidents. The eight members promptly appointed themselves the charter committee and got busy drafting a mission statement, to be presented to the Augsburg student council in the fall.

The goal of BAGLS, says Michele, was threefold: To provide gay students with counseling and peer support; to heighten the awareness of gay and lesbian issues among students and faculty; and to push the school administration to include sexual orientation in its anti-discrimination policies.

When classes resumed in the fall, Bisexual And Gay/Lesbian Services prepared to go before the student senate to gain recognition and funding as a bona fide student organization. On a Monday evening in October, at an open student forum before the senate, the BAGLS co-presidents made their pitch. Immediately there was resistance. Oppo-

nents questioned the need for such a group, and condemned BAGLS
as a blatant attempt to promote homosexuality, something that they
said was contrary to the teachings of Jesus Christ. Should a Lutheran
college be in the business of condoning sinful behavior? they asked,
reading passages from the Bible. For two solid hours of stormy debate, Michele and Lisa were put to the test, fielding questions and de-
flecting accusations about their very identities.

"There were a lot of negative things said, hurtful things, untruths,
ignorance," recalls Michele. "Hostility was raising its ugly head. But I
felt a sense of protection, a strong sense of truth and love being on
our side. I felt fueled up to go forward."

BAGLS was not without advocates. Many students and faculty
members spoke in support of the group, defending the rights of gays
and lesbians and lambasting objections based on Christian ideals as
hypocritical, says Michele. "To see people stand up for us and take that
risk was great."

Last to speak before the student senate was Colleen Boyer,
Michele's mother. "You could hear a pin drop," remembers Michele.
Tearfully, Colleen delivered a potent, passionate plea, chastising those
who used Scripture to judge the members of BAGLS, and declaring to
the crowd that her two children were equally loved:

"I love my lesbian daughter as much as my straight son," she told
the crowd. "They're the same in God's eyes. . . . But the eyes of our
compassionate God are looking down tonight, and she does not approve. She does not like what she *sees.*"

The student senate approved BAGLS' charter by a 16-to-3 vote.
But the meeting ignited a firestorm of debate on homosexuality that
brought BAGLS into full view across campus. The pages of the student
newspaper, *The Augsburg Echo,* were flooded with commentaries and
letters to the editor on the subject. "Homosexuality is not supported
by the church nor has it ever been, so how could a Lutheran college
under a Christian charter sponsor such an organization?" wrote one
student. "I feel [BAGLS] will harm the close unity of our school." But
another student asked readers to consider the judgments and discrimination that gays and lesbians face. "Why would these people be so

afraid about 'coming out' to family and friends?" she wrote. "Why would they state that they are not this way by choice? Most importantly, why would they need a support group in the first place?"

The controversy energized Michele. "It just totally inspired me for the rest of the year. For all of us, it seemed to be a sense of calling."

Five months later, BAGLS was back in the news. The group had tried to have the Twin Cities gay and lesbian newspaper, *Equal Time,* circulated on campus. But the president of the college, Charles Anderson, stopped distribution, saying he objected to the paper's content, particularly advertisements for pay-by-the-minute telephone "datelines" and a cartoon called "Dykes to Watch Out For," which he termed "pornographic." "GAY/LESBIAN PAPER BANNED FROM CAMPUS" screamed a banner headline in *The Augsburg Echo.* "Ban of *Equal Time* is censorship, perpetuates homosexuality myths," argued an *Echo* editorial. And suddenly BAGLS was at the forefront of a debate on free speech.

BAGLS organized an alumni letter-writing campaign and prepared to appeal its case to the college's board of regents. The group lobbied the student council for support and formed a legal strategy with help from the Twin Cities Gay and Lesbian Community Action Council.

A month later, President Anderson capitulated, releasing a handwritten statement to Michele and Lisa, BAGLS co-presidents: "The paper will be available," he wrote. "I want to meet with you about the next steps."

The BAGLS episodes empowered Michele, and transformed her from "lesbian on campus" into a full-fledged activist. But looking back, she modestly describes BAGLS' victories as inevitable. "Timing was everything," she says. "We were just the vehicles for what was going to evolve there. We were the means for it to happen."

The formation of BAGLS was one of the most personally gratifying experiences of her life, she says. "When I left college, I felt things coming full circle. Things that we had dreamed of and imagined in our meeting room had happened. That was really rewarding. For my own activism, it had increased from what I had already been doing—

talking about sexuality, being out there in the limelight. I was just able to do that on a bigger scale."

Yet, upon graduation, she was relieved to be able to slip out of the limelight. "I wanted to be anonymous again," she explains. "My sexuality is integral to my being. But sexuality is not a public thing. When you're a spokesperson for a gay, lesbian, and bisexual support group, your sexuality is always a public thing."

Toward the end of BAGLS' first year on campus, the group received a letter from a high school senior living in a small town in South Dakota. His sister was an alum of Augsburg College, he wrote, and received copies of the student paper regularly through the mail. He had been closely following the BAGLS debate from the start, says Michele. "He read about it, and for the first time in his life he realized he was gay, and he could say it to himself. And he realized that there were other gay people out there in the world."

In his letter, the young man said the BAGLS controversy had inspired him to come out to his sister. Says Michele: "For him, BAGLS was a lifesaver."

Michele graduated with honors from Augsburg College with a bachelor of science degree in sociology. After receiving a master's degree in spirituality from an institute in Oakland, California, she went to work for the Minnesota AIDS Project as a case manager. With a lesbian classmate from Augsburg, she began organizing a gay and lesbian alumni association.

In the years after leaving the idyllic house-on-the-corner comfort of Menominee, Michigan, she came to discover something remarkable: Each of four neighboring households at the intersection of 7th Street and 16th Avenue had produced a gay or lesbian child.

Michele returned to Menominee for her ten-year high school reunion, eager to go back to her old hometown. Packed in her suitcase for the trip home was a book, *Now That You Know: What Every Parent Should Know About Homosexuality*—written by two mothers of gay children—a gift to the Menominee Public Library.

28

Troy III:

The Young and the Restless

One o'clock in the morning on a Friday, and the weekend was well under way for Troy Herman, the small-town Iowa boy with big-city fascinations. Happily staggering along the sidewalk, he fell into the backseat of a friend's Saab, more intoxicated by his carousing at a downtown Minneapolis gay bar than by the vodka and beer that he'd drunk earlier in the night. The bar, the Saloon, had closed, and Troy and three gay friends were on their way to "cruise the park."

This joyride was an after-hours ritual, a mating game on wheels that could lead anywhere from idle conversation to traded phone numbers to sex. In the Saab, Troy and his friends cruised along the narrow streets just south of Loring Park, past the Cathedral Church of St. Mark, past the local chapter of the American Red Cross and a row of luxury high-rise apartments, past treatment centers and law offices, scouring the streets and sidewalks for other young men, until they came to the familiar Dandelion Fountain in the park. There, they began the circuit all over again.

The four friends were not alone on their search. Over and over along the route, they passed the same cars, and slowed to almost a halt to check out the passengers. Like in a slow dance, the drivers circled the park, cruising in opposite directions, eyeing each other through windshields as they passed, and sometimes stopping in the street to introduce themselves through open windows.

As the traffic thinned, Troy and friends stopped at "Hump Hill," a steep and secluded stretch of the circuit overlooking the interstate highway. There, an older man, probably in his fifties, sat alone behind

the steering wheel of a pickup truck, watching the traffic and the parade of cruisers. Troy and his young friends immediately identified
him as a "troll," an ever-present fixture near the park—a man looking
to have sex with younger men, and sometimes willing to pay for it.

"I feel sorry for some of these old trolls," said the driver. "I don't
want to be fifty and looking for some young dick."

The four young friends abandoned the circuit for a while and
parked in a cul-de-sac near the fountain. Troy jacked up the volume on
the tape deck and leaped out of the car. Music ricocheted between the
high-rise apartments, and in seconds a half-dozen other cars pulled
up, filled with more gay young men, all burning with teenage hormones. Dressed alike in T-shirts and tight short pants, they flew into
the night to dance under a streetlamp, uncaring of the hour.

"I can't believe this!" Troy shouted, amazed by it all, and ducked his
head into a car's open passenger window to get acquainted with two
men sitting inside. It was an impromptu street party. And though,
characteristically, it was a clandestine celebration, it resembled the
motorized courtship that played out in most other parks during the
summer. On any given night, young teenage girls in shorts and halter
tops would sit eagerly on the fenders of their parked cars, waiting for
passing carloads of high school "hunks" to stop and flirt. While the sexual orientation in the Loring Park ritual was decidedly gay, the purpose was the same—to find romance.

Suddenly, two police cars rolled into the cul-de-sac and a spotlight
was directed at the Saab. "Whoever belongs to this car better move it
out of here or else it's going to get tagged," ordered a police officer
over a loudspeaker. Troy and friends bolted back to the Saab and drove
off. The party was over.

Police patrols had been stepped up the summer before, when a gay
man was shot to death while walking in the park. Though Troy and his
friends were mindful of the killing and the frequent gay bashings reported in the neighborhood, they weren't very worried. There was
safety in numbers, they reasoned. Cruising was harmless fun. The police patrols were just a nuisance.

"Let's try the beach," someone suggested. And they were off to

Bare Ass Beach, a gay cruising spot along the banks of the Mississippi River.

In his first few months of liberation, Troy lived his life in fast-forward. Moving to the Twin Cities from the small town of Charles City, Iowa, had opened a whole new world to him, a whole new set of dreams and expectations. He was awed by the gay scene, a kid in a candy store.

"It was like nothing we could've found in Charles City," Troy says. "Being able to meet other gay people, that was the main thing. That's what the excitement was for me, being in a big city, being in a gay bar—because I spent nineteen years not doing anything."

But the thrill of cruising and all-night parties wore off quickly for Troy. It really wasn't true to his nature, he said. The bar scene was a good place to meet other young gays like him. It was a springboard into the gay community. But it was also loud, smoky, impersonal, and artificial. Troy was more down-to-earth, he said, than the "Saloon queens," the teens who made the Saloon a regular hangout.

"I'm not an attitude person," he insisted, again and again. Instead of industrial rock music and Girbaud pullovers, he was true to his simple, rural roots. He listened to country music radio stations and hunted for bargains at Marshall's and Kmart.

"Cruising the bars, that just isn't for me. That just isn't what I want," he said. "Sure, I like to go out and dance and have a few drinks, but that isn't my whole world. More and more, I just don't like the bars. I go less and less."

Troy was ready for a long-term boyfriend. He wanted some commitment, some stability. "That's the main thing for me—stability. It's what I look for. I'm not into one-night stands."

Rather, he was searching for a relationship not unlike his three sisters'—a steady date, something he was never able to have in high school. Even though he had a boyfriend for the better part of eleventh grade, both of the boys were frightfully closeted, bound to live in secrecy and terrified of being discovered.

"It was really heartbreaking to see my sister Linda get married, because that's what I always wanted. I'd spent too much time alone," says Troy. "I figured if I lived in the city I could have that kind of relationship. . . . I didn't want to have to be closeted."

What would the "perfect man" be? "I don't have a certain look that I go for. Looks do not matter," Troy said. "Personality-wise, I want somebody who is very romantic, as much as I am, who will not be uncomfortable with the closeness I have with my family, who shares my tastes, likes romantic movies. Somebody who is very, very stable, who has their own job. They don't have to have a lot of money, but not somebody who is barely scraping by. Somebody who is standing on his own two feet. . . . And being out, of course, would be a plus."

But his pursuit of a partner was frustratingly bleak. It seemed that no one else his age was ready to settle down.

Though he had gladly moved away from Iowa, Troy still looked back. He made regular monthly visits home, out of a strong sense of obligation and a genuine need to remain in touch with his mother and sisters, nieces and nephews.

On one weekend in the summer, Troy drove home to Iowa with Jordan, a friend since childhood who also was gay. But on their way out of Minneapolis, they stopped at the Mall of America to buy a few gifts for Troy's family—and, not coincidentally, to meet soap opera star Don Diamont. Diamont, who plays the character Brad on the *The Young and the Restless,* was the special attraction at the newly opened mega-mall. And a heartthrob of Troy's.

"Soap operas are my life," laughed Troy, camping it up as he and Jordan took their place in line. It was Troy's third visit to the mall during grand-opening week. He loved the spectacle, and he was into the shopping, big-time, one more advantage of living in the city.

The second-level entrance to Sears was a mob scene on this Saturday afternoon as fans waited patiently for the actor—photo-happy teenage girls with tagalong boyfriends, autograph-hungry housewives from the suburbs with time on their hands and Macy's shopping bags on their arms, curious grandpas and grandmas pushing baby strollers. And Troy and Jordan.

Diamont had stepped out for lunch, soon to return to a table and chair and a stack of pinup-boy portraits. The string of fans grew, stretching through the women's sportswear department, past the sport jackets and crocheted sweaters, past the skirt-and-blouse combinations and imitation leopard-skin vests, all the way down to the lingerie section.

"What's this line for?" asked a shopper as she browsed among the 25-percent-off racks.

"Um, Don Diamont. From *The Young and the Restless*," Troy informed her, clutching his Vivatar.

"Oh. I don't know him." And she walked on.

"Where have you been, in a *cave*?" Troy whispered to himself.

Curious shoppers jammed the aisles. More than two hundred people had clotted around the entrance, and fans were getting impatient. Security guards, fearing an unscheduled visit by the fire marshal, tried desperately to move people into a single line. But nobody budged. Instead, the fans began to chant: "We want Don. We want Don."

Finally, Don Diamont appeared, escorted out from behind a side door. Women screamed, babies cried, the crowd surged, and Don smiled. But his manager was spooked by the unexpected size of the crowd and quickly yanked the actor back through the door and out of sight.

"I saw his arm," said an excitable young woman.

"I saw the back of his head," bragged another.

The crowd was getting unruly. Nervous Sears guards called into their walkie-talkies for reinforcements and set up theater ropes around the staging area to maintain order. Ten minutes later, Don was again ushered out. Women screamed, babies cried, the crowd surged. Don smiled and sat at his table—tall, dark, and Hollywood, a gold chain around his neck and a BOOGIE'S DINER T-shirt from Aspen on his coveted body.

Troy and Jordan elbowed their way toward the front of the line, behind a pack of adoring high school girls, all blond curls and pocket cameras. Along a line of theater ropes, videocams recorded Don mechanically signing his name.

Another ten minutes, and Troy wet his lips, poised with a request for an autograph. And suddenly he was face to face with the star. With a wide smile on his face, Don signed his name and handed an eight-by-ten glossy to Troy as Jordan clicked away on the Vivatar.

Troy glided away, shaking, smitten, triumphant.

"When he gave me the picture, he winked at me!" he gushed to Jordan.

Mission accomplished.

Since he moved to Minneapolis, Troy has worked as a certified nursing assistant at Hopkins Care Center, a 157-bed nursing home. On one afternoon, he was assigned to the east wing of the second floor for his eight-hour shift. As he made his rounds, delivering clean linen and a nightgown to each resident, a white-haired old woman inched down the hallway, holding tight to a railing along the green wall.

"She's one of my favorites," Troy said. "She's a cutie. She told us she used to be a can-can girl. So she'll dance with us."

Troy returned from a fifteen-minute break and changed the clothes of a man who was incontinent. As dinnertime approached, Troy wheeled each of the residents to the dining area and fitted them with terry-cloth bibs. Later, he helped them into the showers, then prepared them for bed.

This was Troy's job, providing the most basic human care for men and women with the names of an older generation—Evelyn, Lester, Hazel, Wilbur, Myra, Eugene, Lottie—some of them suffering from diseases that would claim their lives. He has painful memories of his father's losing battle with diabetes. "And I took care of my grandmother before she passed away," Troy said. "I was fourteen, and she was living with my mother." He would feed her and help her get in and out of bed. She died from cirrhosis of the liver and complications to her circulation system.

"It takes a lot of patience," Troy said of his work. "It's not the most pleasant job. But the emotional reward is what I like the best. A lot of the residents can be real friendly. Some go out of their way to thank you. That's real nice. It makes a difference. You're not just making money."

Troy informed his boss that he was gay a month after he was hired. He didn't see any reason to hide it. He thought, as he had before, that living in a big city would provide greater protections and opportunities for gays. "I had pretty much picked up on people at work who were gay," he said. "So I felt comfortable coming out."

The news swiftly made its way to the care center's administrator, who assured Troy that he would be protected under the company's anti-discrimination and anti-harassment policies.

"It was a very courageous thing that Troy did," said Frank Robinson, the administrator. No one else had come out at the center, but if others did, Robinson assured, they too would be protected.

"It's a company philosophy that if you're *not* doing your job, *that's* when you'll hear from us," he explained. "If you *are* doing the job, I don't care if you're purple. We don't care.

"I would take it very seriously if Troy or anyone else said they were being harassed," Robinson added. "I have a hard time thinking that all employers wouldn't feel that way."

While he has other gripes about his job—the typical complaints of any employee—Troy is appreciative of his company's gay-positive policies. "I feel fortunate," he says. "That's one thing that keeps me working there." He would have a hard time going back in the closet at any job. "I would never do that," he says. "I'm a very open person. I could not handle it. To me, that would be like going back in time to when I grew up. And I don't want to go back there. I would never do that."

When Troy was twenty-one, he moved into a house with two gay roommates, a small bungalow on a quiet, tree-lined street on the conservative side of Minneapolis, a block from a hardware store and an Italian restaurant. The house was comfortable. Hardwood floors and dark-stained woodwork accented the white walls, white sofa, and white chairs. Barbra Streisand film posters and a collection of pewter dishes decorated the dining room. A breakfast nook in the kitchen looked out on a giant lilac bush in the backyard.

Troy's bedroom was spare. A double mattress occupied most of the floor space. A wicker table supported a small TV. Clothes filled plastic trash bags. A framed photograph of one of Troy's sisters and her children rested on a windowsill.

The move was yet another step out of adolescence for Troy and into an independent life as a young gay man. He had found the house through a "roommate wanted" ad in a local gay newspaper. And, by parting ways with his two Iowa friends, Jordan and Barry—his first roommates in the Twin Cities—he had ventured a little deeper into the community.

"I feel that I've grown up a lot emotionally and personally," Troy said one afternoon, reflecting on the past year of his life. "When I moved up here I probably never could have done this. Now I'm more comfortable with people, and with meeting new people."

Troy had been working double shifts to make some extra money for the move into his new place. But on a rare day off, he was content to sit and watch the tube. He woke about noon, showered, skipped the shave, and turned on the TV. Along with his daily fix of soaps and *Charlie's Angels,* Troy kept a vigil eye on the talk shows: *Ricki Lake, Jenny Jones, Leeza, Vicki,* right through to *Geraldo, Donahue,* and *Oprah.* Wednesday was his favorite night for prime-time viewing. On this particular Wednesday evening, the episode of *Beverly Hills 90210* was about a gay fraternity leader who is outed to his frat brothers. Next was *Melrose Place,* a show that also featured a gay character, Matt Fielding. Later, Troy channel-surfed the late-night talk shows, tuning in to Leno and Letterman. But he was mostly a fan of the TV tabloid shows: *Bertice Berry, Rolonda,* and *Montel.*

"So many people on these talk shows remind me exactly of the people I grew up with," Troy said. "They're so Charles City-an!"

Late in the summer, Troy made plans to have his favorite niece stay at his home for a week. Six-year-old Sammy was the daughter of his sister Linda, the youngest girl of the family and Troy's closest sibling. Weeks before Sammy arrived, Troy had made a long list of activities that they would do together when she arrived. He scheduled a week off from work so he could spend all of his time with the girl. He had it all arranged: They would see *The Lion King,* go to the zoo, swim at a couple of city lakes, eat dinner at Circus Pizza restaurant, and have a picnic one weekend afternoon with some of Troy's friends, including one of his new roommates. Before Sammy arrived, he stocked up on plenty of soda pop and snack food, Crayolas and coloring books.

"I've always wanted to have kids," Troy said, smiling at the idea. "And when I thought of having kids, I would always want them to be just like Sammy. She's just the sweetest little child."

When he was growing up in Iowa, he was a happily doting uncle to his sister's four kids, Sammy in particular. "I helped raise her, the teething, the 3 A.M. feedings, changing the diapers, the terrible twos, paying for school supplies. I've been through so many stages, almost every stage of her growing up. And I know it's definitely something I could handle. It's something I look forward to."

Troy was feeling restless. He was tired of his job, tired of living from paycheck to paycheck, waiting for a raise to come through that he'd been promised months ago. He was thinking about moving again, this time far away.

"I was thinking about this last night. I was up until 4 A.M. I just couldn't sleep. I was not tired at all. So I sat outside and smoked cigarettes. And I was just thinking, you know, I really want to move out of Minnesota. I would really like to move out to California. That's something I've always wanted to do, so I figure I'd better get on the ball and do it. It's going to take a lot of money, I realize that. But I could move out there and maybe stay in a motel for a while. No doubt they have roommate ads, just like they do here. That'd be one of the ways I could get settled out there."

Troy had a dream, a dream that he had carried with him since his boyhood, when he played dress-up in the basement with his friend

Jordan. He would move to Los Angeles and study drama and music and somehow find work in the entertainment field. "Going out to L.A. and maybe doing gay theater or whatever, I could kind of get into acting easier. That's what I always wanted to do. I've always wanted to go to L.A. and be in the Hollywood thing. That's something I've wanted to do since I was a kid. And maybe try to get on TV. A lot of people laugh, but . . . I would like to go on *Melrose Place* as the gay character's first steady boyfriend. I don't know. It *would* be tough. But there's actually, like, two shows I've heard of coming out this fall that are going to have major, open gay characters. One's called *Daddy's Girl* with Harvey Fierstein. . . .

"Mom's not too excited about the idea. . . . L.A. is a lot farther from Iowa than Minneapolis. I just couldn't pick up one weekend and drive home. But that's something I've always wanted to do. That definitely is a goal for me."

Maybe by next summer he could save enough money to make the jump. He'd done it before, when he moved away from Charles City. It would be another big adventure. But in the meantime, his dreams of show biz would have to wait. He had a busy weekend planned. A friend that he knew from work was getting married on Saturday. And for Sunday, he had tickets to see Reba McEntire at the state fair.

Two tickets. Troy had a date.

29

SIDEBAR:

A Shining Resiliency

Growing up gay or lesbian can be agonizing to tenderhearted teenagers. The degradation and oppression they face at such a young age can sap them of tremendous potential. The social stigma attached to their sexual orientation can threaten their school careers, their friendships, their family relations, even their physical well-being.

For some, the burden is overwhelming. They become casualties of the closet, withdrawing into secrecy, resigned to years of desperation and defeat. Yet for most gay and lesbian teens who endure the passage of coming out, the tough times are overcome. They push on into adulthood, piece together broken relationships with families, maybe go to college, build careers, pursue love relationships, and enjoy lives of contentment and self-fulfillment.

"I think gay kids have a tremendous strength," says Joyce Hunter, a founding member of the Hetrick-Martin Institute who has worked with gay and lesbian teens for nearly two decades. "When they get the support they need, they do very well, they grow up healthy. . . . I've worked in many different settings, and in spite of hiding their sexual orientation, a lot of these kids manage to develop coping skills and get on with their lives. And that's to their credit. We need to recognize that a lot of our kids are going to have problems, but there's also a lot of kids who just move on, in spite of it all."

And as these kids move on, the trials of adolescence become lessons of survival. They go forth with a durable courage that sustains them as adults as they fend off the hard knocks of a judgmental and homophobic society. Through all the isolation and rejection and despair, they survive with a shining resiliency, an inner strength that steels them for a life of barriers, prejudices, and hatred.

"We know from the experience of children in general that some children face extraordinary negative events in their lives—disasters of losing families, the ravages of war, violence, abuse, and other tragedies," says Dr. Gary Remafedi, assistant professor of pediatrics at the University of Minnesota. "Some children do extremely well and go on to live healthy productive lives. Others don't."

Those who thrive seem to share certain characteristics: They're good at making life adjustments. They're able to seek out help when they need it. And they're successful in finding supportive adults.

"These are some of the predictors of whether a child in a tragic situation will be resilient or not," Remafedi says. "And I think the same factors are probably in play for young gays and lesbians. If they survive adolescence intact, they will bring to the rest of life a great deal of experience and wisdom."

In a way, some lesbian, gay, and bisexual youth—the fortunate ones who find support—have a head start on the road to adulthood. Those who are more likely to recognize their sexual orientation and confront the rejection early on will benefit the most.

"In many cases, gay and lesbian teenagers will become stronger because of the experience," says Virginia Uribe, founder of Project 10. "To look inside yourself and finally say, 'Yes, I am gay,' or, 'I am lesbian,' is such an extraordinarily courageous thing, it can really give a dimension to their lives that they wouldn't have otherwise had."

There are some who will not make it. "And the reasons for that are complex," said Gilbert Herdt, a University of Chicago anthropologist who has studied the struggles that gay youth face. "In any human population there is an enormous variation with respect to the ability of people to bounce back and be resilient." Why some people make it and some don't, nobody knows.

"Because it is not clear, I think the cautious approach would be to say that a society cannot afford to condone prejudice of any kind, because there is going to be fallout and there are going to be casualties.

"The people who don't succumb to depression or suicidal attempts are going to find a variety of ways to cope with their problems," adds Herdt. "The existence of a gay and lesbian social support group in their community is tremendously important in enabling them to make it."

To survive adolescence and heal the wounds that they suffered at such an early age, it is important for young gays and lesbians themselves to recognize that they are not to blame for their despair. It helps to understand that all people who grow up gay or lesbian are victimized by a heterosexist society. Society in general places a low value on homosexuality. As with victims of racism and sexism, victims of heterosexism tend to develop a low self-esteem and a victim mentality, feeling responsible for feeling bad about themselves.

Healing from this cultural victimization involves realizing that social approval for being gay or lesbian is not necessary, says Joe Neisen, program director of the Pride Institute, a chemical-dependency treatment center in Minnesota. Healing comes through reclaiming the personal power that has been negated, beginning in adolescence.

But healing cannot take place until people come out of the closet, he adds. "That doesn't mean that people have to suddenly come out to everybody in the entire world, but it does mean that healing involves continuing the coming-out process. For gay and lesbian teenagers, part of healing is about being able to come out and find some sort of support.

"Too frequently, gay and lesbian people think they're out and think there's not another step in coming out," says Neisen. "But there's always going to be another step."

People certainly should take steps to protect their sexual identity in situations where it may not be safe to come out. But a side effect of any type of victimization can be lingering shame. "And the more willing they are to address that," he says, "the more opportunities there are for growth and healing."

In a heterosexist world, healing is ongoing, just as coming out is a lifetime process. But the process need not be dispiriting. As lesbians and gays move on in life, passing from victim to survivor to thriving human being, their journey takes them to a point where their sexual identity is an enriching and celebrated part of who they are. And through a passage of pride, they become healthy, vibrant, whole-hearted individuals.

"All gays and lesbians are abused, growing up in a heterosexist society," Neisen says. "But I think people do remarkably well, because we see many gay and lesbian people who have coped, adapted, adjusted, and are living very fulfilling, happy, content, productive lives."

A Cultural Identity

Times are changing for all gays and lesbians. The twenty-five-year-old gay-rights movement has given rise to a higher presence and acceptance of gays and lesbians, resulting in more role models and cultural reference points for gay and lesbian youth than ever before.

In every corner of the country, gays and lesbians are being personified in the media. Some examples: Dozens of popular movies included positive portrayals of gay men and lesbians—most notably *Philadelphia, Longtime Companion,* and *The Wedding Banquet.* On TV's *Northern Exposure,* two gay men held a commitment ceremony in the fictitious Cicely, Alaska, named after the lesbian founder of the town. There is the gay fraternity president who was "outed" on *Beverly Hills 90210.* Gay character Matt Fielding became a regular on *Melrose Place.* A lesbian kissed a woman lawyer on *L.A. Law.* A lesbian kissed Roseanne. Martin Mull plays a gay man on *Roseanne.* Daytime soap *One Life to Live* and the prime time *My So-Called Life* included gay teenage characters. And the Book-of-the-Month Club offered a special set of books by homosexual authors James Baldwin, Rita Mae Brown, and Edmund White.

The comic strip "For Better or Worse" featured the coming-out story of a gay teen. Meanwhile, "Doonesbury" disc jockey Mark Slackmeyer announced to his friends and mother that he was gay. From actors Harvey Fierstein and Amanda Bearse to comedians Sandra Bernhard and Kate Clinton to pop stars k. d. lang and Elton John to athletes Martina Navratilova and Greg Louganis—pop culture is becoming abundant with gay and lesbian icons.

"Given the fact that all gay and lesbian adults at some point were gay and lesbian adolescents, I think you can look at the diversity of our community and see the kinds of adults gay and lesbian adolescents grow up to be," points out lesbian psychotherapist Beth Zemsky. "You have TV characters, more pop and rock stars coming out. From well-known performers to government officials to attorneys to loving parents of their own children—these are the kind of people that gay and lesbian adolescents grow up to be.

"When I do workshops, I ask people what their early messages were about homosexuality," says Zemsky. "And invariably, one of their early messages was silence, complete silence. That's not the case anymore. There's not as much silence. They're going to be hearing something. They know that gays and lesbians and bisexuals exist. I think that makes a difference."

In the best situations, the high visibility of gays and lesbians fosters a climate of approval, which in turn encourages other gays and lesbians to come out. Through a domino effect, each coming-out story provides the motivation for the next. And, in places where support has been cultivated, a groundswell is rising of young lesbians and gays willing to come out.

"There's no question that people are coming out of the closet at a younger and younger age with each passing year," says David LaFontaine, chairman of the Massachusetts Governor's Commission on Gay and Lesbian Youth. "People who come out when they're in high school develop a much better self-image than people who spend years hiding in the closet."

Not only are they coming out younger, but they're wasting no time demanding acceptance of who they are. "We are seeing a new generation of gay-rights activists who are very proud of who they are and much more willing to advocate for changing society," says LaFontaine. They seize upon the information and support if it is available, and demand recognition and attention if it is lacking. Given even the slightest measure of relief—a school support group or gay-positive counselor—they realize they don't have to be alone anymore.

"Their youthful idealism clicks in and they simply are unwilling to accept the kind of world that my generation settled for," says Leo Treadway, a gay man who has worked with gay youth since the early 1980s. "They don't want to just fit in, be assimilated, or be tolerated. They want to be able to be who they are."

Even the fact that they tend to refer to themselves as "queer" suggests a difference in self-perception. "There has been an evolution of terminology," adds Treadway, "from *homosexual* to *homophile* to *gay* to *gay and lesbian* to *gay-lesbian-bi-transgender* to *queer*—all of which says something different about how people perceive themselves and how they relate to the world.

"My generation simply wanted to fit in and just be left alone," he says. "Youth that I interact with today want to be as openly gay-lesbian-bi-transgender, as *queer-identified* as possible. And that is a piece of who they are and how they interact with the world."

With the high-energy idealism so characteristic of youth will spring a world more aware and more respectful of its "queer" citizens.

"I hope that some of these kids will grow up and become *our* advocates," says lesbian educator Uribe.

"That's my hope."

30

Amy III:

"'Bye, Mommy!"

The more time Amy Grahn spent with her lesbian friends, the more she began to adopt what she regarded as telltale signs of lesbianism. Though the signs were small and sometimes clichéd, they nonetheless were important tokens of her lesbian identification:

She learned in-line dancing and the country two-step, a craze among lesbians and gays.

She joined a women's rugby team, a rough-and-tumble sport popular with lesbians.

She talked dreamily about buying a motorcycle someday and riding with the local Dykes on Bikes chapter in the annual Gay Pride parade.

She got a tattoo on her right biceps, a black cat with green eyes. The tattoo was an expression of individuality to Amy, and "way cool." To her father, it was foolhardy. "That'll look real good with an evening gown," he kidded.

Indeed, finding a place in the gay and lesbian community was pure joy for Amy, who for years had been denied access to the very people she identified with the most. For her parents, however, an appreciation of lesbian culture was a much longer process.

For Jim and Sue Grahn, having a lesbian daughter meant abandoning certain expectations, letting go of values and customs and stereotypes that had framed their definition of family since the very beginning of their lives. Notions of "family life" had to be reevaluated; views on sexuality itself had to be rethought. In order to come to terms with their daughter's homosexuality, Jim and Sue were compelled to resist the conventions and drop the presumptions that had long been imbedded in their perceptions of gender roles and sexual identity. How, for instance, would they react when they saw their daughter kiss another woman for the first time? And what advice would they give if Amy came to them asking about sex?

This "new family order" would be a colossal adjustment. But since learning that Amy was a lesbian, Jim and Sue had vowed to "come out" with her. They were determined to provide her with as much encouragement and support as they could to make her adolescence a healthy one.

On a Saturday afternoon, Amy was locked in serious negotiations with her father about curfew and the use of his car. It was a routine haggle. Amy lived with her family about a half hour from Minneapolis in the suburb of Shorewood, and unless she could get the keys to her father's Oldsmobile, she would be trapped at home for the entire weekend.

Her day was slipping away, and she was restless. She had plans to spend Saturday night at the home of a lesbian couple she knew and to hang out in Minneapolis on Sunday. But her father was driving a hard bargain. He was lecturing her, droning on and on about caution, responsibility, honor, trust. . . .

"I just want to meet some WOMEN," Amy interrupted, impatiently.

Jim winced and handed over the keys, resigned. It never was this hard to lay down the law with his son, Chris, he thought. There was never any gray area. If Chris had ever asked to spend a night with a couple of girls, it would have been out of the question. Automatic. A no-brainer. House rules were clear and simple: Fill up the gas tank. Be home by midnight. Don't get anyone pregnant.

Likewise, Amy never would have been allowed to stay at the home of two men—and for the very same reason that Chris wouldn't have been permitted to sleep at the home of two women: Men, being the sexual aggressors, typically initiated sex, according to the Grahns' conventional rules of human sexuality. And establishing boundaries to check teenage sexual behavior was the moral duty of parents—parents of sons as well as daughters.

But things were different with a lesbian daughter, of course. The Grahns' dicta on dating had been turned upside down.

"With Chris, whenever he said, 'I'm going into the Cities and spend the weekend with friends,' it was just the guys," said Jim. "With Amy, that was real tough to deal with, because you didn't know whether they were platonic friends or *girlfriend* friends."

Yet, at the same time, Jim wouldn't have thought twice to hear his son say he was going out to pick up women. In fact, he sometimes would swell with a father's pride to hear of Chris's escapades. "It's always easier to hear a son say, 'I'm gonna go out and cruise and meet some chicks,'" Jim reasoned.

A dichotomy had arisen when it came to establishing guidelines for Amy. An entirely new standard had to be set. And it wasn't easy. By their old way of thinking, and by their old set of presumptions, Amy was certainly "safer" sleeping overnight at the home of a woman than at the home of a man. Women, by cultural customs, generally were sexually passive and typically did not initiate sexual behavior. But did that apply to lesbians as well? Probably not. And if not, why were they permitting her to spend the night with two lesbians?

"When Amy first started having same-sex friends over, it didn't really click with us," Jim said. "But finally, after a while, we made sure the bedroom doors were open when her friends were over, that sort of thing. . . . In her case, I look at her as the aggressor. Sometimes I don't know if she doesn't have the hormonal drive of an eighteen-year-old guy."

With Amy, all rules went out the window. Every step was uncharted territory. "It probably would've been easier raising a straight daughter," admitted Jim. "But we didn't have a whole lot of friends who were raising lesbian daughters."

Earlier in the day, a boy who knew Amy in high school had phoned out of the blue and asked her out. She was repulsed, and proudly told him she was a lesbian and had a girlfriend.

"Well," he suggested, without skipping a beat, "why don't all three of us go out?" Teenage ménage à trois?

"He's a *pervert*," Amy squealed as she slammed down the telephone. "All he wants is sex. And he's not getting it from *me*."

But the thought of Amy dating a boy—and someday marrying a man—was still a dream of Amy's parents. Realistically, they knew it wouldn't happen. She was what she was. They knew it and accepted it. They had worked it out, thought it through. But in their hearts, they wished for "The Wedding March" and dreamed of grandchildren. That traditional family wedding—so sentimentalized in the Hollywood movie *Father of the Bride* that it brought Jim and Sue to the verge of tears when they saw it—would never come true for Amy.

The Grahns unselfishly advised their daughter not to worry about pleasing them. They were convinced that she didn't choose to be a lesbian, they told her. Yet, they wondered, if she *could* choose, would she pick homosexuality or heterosexuality? It was a question that Amy couldn't answer.

"As a parent," said Jim, "I think I'll always hold out a hope that she'll meet a guy and turn 'normal.' I don't hold out a lot of hope, but. . . ."

It was an unreasonable hope. Jim and Sue both knew that. "Who says that if she were a heterosexual she would ever get married anyway?" Sue pondered. "Lesbians get married too, you know, and even have children," she rationalized. "But even if she would do that, it could never be the same."

The traditions were hard to put aside. Said Sue: "I told Amy that I would never give up hope—never, ever—that she will be heterosexual. It will always be there in the back of my mind."

Late on a weekend afternoon, a couple of the Grahns' friends unexpectedly stopped by their home to wish Sue a happy birthday. Jill and Fritz, parents of teenagers themselves, had known the Grahns since their kids were young. They brought along a bottle of Leibfraumilch. Jim lined up wineglasses and dished out chocolate angel-food cake with whipped cream as Sue thankfully opened a birthday card. Thinking that it was the right moment to share the news about Amy, Sue wasted no time getting to the point. After chatting about kids and school and the like, Sue dropped the bombshell.

"I have something I want to tell you two: Amy is a lesbian," she said, point-blank, without apology or embarrassment. She went on to explain that Amy's psychiatric treatment and transfer to a special high school a year earlier had been due largely to the depression that she had suffered as she grappled with her homosexual identity.

The couple was speechless. Fritz nodded and said nothing. Jill's mouth fell open, and she abruptly shifted the conversation to Sue's plans for her birthday celebration. Minutes later, though, after a birthday toast, Sue again steered the conversation back to Amy. Forced to react, Fritz and Jill were at a loss for words, but tried to be gracious and understanding.

"Sue, I never would've guessed," said Jill.

"In these days, anything is possible," said Fritz. "You've just got to go with the flow."

Jim poured more wine. And from the living room, Amy's younger sister, Alison, eavesdropped. Waiting for a break in the conversation, she suddenly was compelled to account for her own sexual identity: "*I'm* not gay," she sang out.

As a step in their own coming-out process, Sue and Jim Grahn decided to tell the congregation at their church that Amy was gay. As word began to slowly seep out to family, friends, and neighbors, they thought it would be best to personally inform their priest and, eventually, the whole parish. With the strict stance on homosexuality taken by the Roman Catholic Church, they knew there would be discomforting questions and probably misunderstanding. They didn't want to alienate anyone or cause embarrassment to their daughter.

Amy and her sister, Alison, were altar girls at St. Victoria Catholic Church, a parish the Grahn family had belonged to for twelve years. On the Sunday of Alison's confirmation, Jim and Sue approached the pastor, the Rev. Elstan Coghill, a conservative man in his seventies whom they had known for years. The Grahns suggested that a married couple from the local P-FLAG chapter speak before the church council. They were the parents of a gay son, and the father also was an ordained deacon in the Catholic church. The Grahns hoped he would speak to the entire congregation at a Sunday mass, inviting parishioners to discuss the topic of homosexuality.

Fr. Coghill told the Grahns that he was obligated to clear the idea with the archdiocese of St. Paul and Minneapolis. But when he did, he got a cool response to the Grahns' proposal. The subject matter would not be appropriate for younger children in the congregation, he told them. Why not hold a presentation on the subject after church instead, he suggested, and invite the P-FLAG parents to speak to the confirmation class? But it wasn't exactly what the Grahns had in mind. Relegating the discussion to such few people seemed to be sweeping the issue under the rug. Why should they be forced to compromise?

The priest told the Grahns he expected his congregation to be supportive as they learned that Amy was a homosexual. "We feel compassion for them [homosexuals] because of the fact that they are discriminated against," he said. "They're given a hard time and sometimes they're subjected to violence. It is an awful burden. I would hope my people would understand that."

Yet, to Fr. Coghill, and the catechism of the Catholic Church, there was a sharp distinction between a person being gay and living a gay "lifestyle." While the Church is empathetic to the plight of homosexuals, it does not condone homosexual behavior. "The lifestyle would not be tolerated or sanctioned," said Fr. Coghill. "A person might have that kind of orientation and live a clean, decent life"—in other words, a life of celibacy. "I would suggest that there are a goodly number that do, and we just don't hear about them. . . . Many live unmarried and sexually inactive. It can be a noble kind of life," comparable, he said, to the chaste lives led by priests and nuns.

Fr. Coghill compared homosexuality to a physical handicap, such as a birth defect—a clubfoot, for example. "Everybody in the course of their lifetime is afflicted with some kind of cross to bear, and that may be theirs."

This hard-line position by the Church upset the Grahns. Yet they didn't want to make waves. Better to let the word slowly eke out and deal with parishioners individually, they thought.

Not to be discouraged, they approached the local school district next. Amy had transferred out of her public high school and into an alternative school, driven out by an overpowering isolation. After seeing how alienating Amy's school experience had been, her parents felt duty-bound to pave the way for other teens. They were determined to push for changes that would benefit future generations of gay and lesbian students.

Sue met with Amy's former high school principal, asking that a peer support group be formed for gay and lesbian students and suggesting that sex-education classes be broadened to include more information on homosexuality. The principal seemed receptive, recalls Sue, but school officials at a higher level balked. The school superintendent told Sue that he could not endorse such a program. The community wasn't ready for such a thing, he told her, and moreover, he personally would not approve a program that condones homosexuality.

His personal beliefs were irrelevant, Sue told him, angrily. "A man in your position needs to look at all children in all spectrums of life," she said. "Every child needs an opportunity."

Again, the Grahns' plans to do the right thing were given short shrift. Homosexuality was just too hot an issue for public officials to handle, they decided. Apparently, they had pushed too hard too fast.

Despite the disappointments, life at the Grahn home had normalized following the years of unhappiness that Amy had endured. Her family was coming to grips with her sexual orientation and could speak honestly about it.

"My family used to be pretty dysfunctional," Amy said to a friend one day. "Now we're so open it's sickening."

In that spirit of openness, Amy decided it was time to take her mother to some of the gay bars that had become her hangouts. Sue was happy to be invited. Though a bit apprehensive, she agreed to spend a night barhopping with Amy and a few of her friends.

They started at the Town House, a St. Paul bar that featured country music and in-line dancing every night. "When we left to go," says Sue, "I had mixed feelings—excitement and apprehension of not knowing what to expect. But when we walked in, it was like any other bar. I found it quite nice. People were milling around, talking, dancing. It wasn't what I expected. . . . There was such a warmth in the place."

They stayed for nearly two hours. "Naturally, Amy ran into a ton of friends," Sue says. "I thought, I bet they think it's weird that she brought her mom in here. But a friend of Amy's had done the same thing. I was so glad that there was a place to go that was nice and clean, where people were kind. It's mostly a place where she can be safe to be herself."

Next, they went to the Saloon, a Minneapolis dance club frequented mostly by gay men. With its non-stop booming industrial music, flashing strobe lights, and dance cage above the dance floor, the Saloon made her a little uneasy. Sue remembered a night years before, when she was much younger and out on a date. Walking along Hennepin Avenue, they passed the doorway of the Saloon as group of young men emerged. Sue recalls feeling sorry for the men, and in some ways repulsed by them. "Little did I know that I'd be walking in someday, and with my own kid!"

Her night out with Amy and friends was a small victory for Sue. "I had made it into another part of Amy's world," she says. "It was a good feeling. The love and trust that she was showing by letting me share that part of her life with her, it was a real good feeling, like I did okay, like I had paid the price for all the hell and the sadness that we went through."

Corn dogs and lemonade. Tarot cards and foot massages. Free country-swing lessons and a tribute to Amelia Earhart. Frisbees, iced coffee, motorcycles, folk songs, drag queens, politicians, pink triangles, and lavender *everywhere*.

The Festival of Pride was a party, a rally, a howling, brazen weekend of liberation and solidarity, an opportunity for gays and lesbians to come out to the world in broad daylight, without worry or shame. Women kissed in public and men held hands. Lesbian couples took turns cradling their infants. Health-care volunteers passed out buckets of condoms. Teenagers eyed each other from behind sunglasses.

Arranged like some sort of arts-and-crafts show on the grass of Minneapolis's Loring Park, dozens of information booths introduced celebrants and curious spectators to the local lesbian and gay network, to groups such as ACT-UP, the Youth and AIDS Projects, the Democratic Gay-Lesbian Caucus, the Gay and Lesbian Community Action Council, the Pride Institute, the Gay and Lesbian Business Council, District 202 Youth Center and Delta Lambda Phi, the University of Minnesota's gay fraternity.

The crowd flowed between the booths and a grassy amphitheater nearby, simultaneously laid back and militant.

A slogan on the T-shirt of a woman on a motorcycle: NOBODY KNOWS I'M A LESBIAN.

Another slogan on the T-shirt of a young man: THE FAMILY TREE STOPS HERE.

A bumper sticker on a station wagon: COME OUT, COME OUT, WHEREVER YOU ARE.

At the Youth Booth, two high school girls debated the merits of bisexuality:

"Monosexuality is borrrring."

"Not!"

Under a cloudless sky on this Sunday in June, Amy came to the Festival of Pride with her mother and sister. It was a first-time family event.

Before the festival, the Grahns met up with Amy's newest date, a young woman named Melissa, who came with her mother too. The two mothers had made their introductions earlier on the telephone, sharing stories about the hardships that their daughters had faced. Sitting on a blanket in the park, the moms anxiously eyed the crowd, a little nervous to be surrounded by hundreds of homosexuals, yet proud of their lesbian daughters.

Amy wore a white T-shirt with big black letters across her chest that labeled her a GWF—gay white female. She was bursting with confidence. She had withstood the isolation, the rejection, the depression—the pains of growing up gay. With the help of her friends and family, she had reclaimed her self, rediscovered her adolescence. And, like other lesbian and gay teens, she had survived with a strength that would steel her for a life of barriers, prejudices, and hatred.

It had been a metamorphosis for her family as well. Though their efforts were derailed, Sue and Jim Grahn had pushed hard for reforms in their church and school district. They continued to spread the word among their friends and family. Amy's brother, Chris, awkward at first discussing her sexual identity, told her he would do anything he could to support her, a tremendous confidence boost to Amy. "I've told Amy, 'If you ever want to talk, I'm here,' and she knows that. She knows I'm behind her one hundred percent," said Chris.

Perhaps most deeply moved by Amy's coming out was her younger sister. Empowered by Amy's openness, Alison wrote a term paper on gays and lesbians for a history project at her high school. She poured more than forty hours into the project, working day and night for more than a month. Her work earned her an A-plus.

"I did this project to identify more with Amy and her friends when I'm around them, so I fit in with them even though I'm straight," Alison says. "Out in the suburban schools, nobody talks about issues like this. It kind of seems like a dirty subject with some people. And it shouldn't be. I thought I had to bring it up. You can't just sit around and wait for things to be solved."

As the Gay Pride parade began to form on the street bordering the park, Sue hooked up with the Minnesota chapter of P-FLAG. Positioned directly behind the District 202 youth group and just a backfire away from the Dykes on Bikes motorcycle club, she would march the streets with P-FLAG, openly showing the bystanders, the news media, and the world that she was unashamed of her lesbian child.

The P-FLAGers were greeted as heroes. Among the clergymen and bikers, school board candidates and drag queens, arm in arm in the serpentine crowd were parents and grandparents, brothers and sisters, aunts and uncles of gays and lesbians. Again and again, as the parade looped through the downtown neighborhood and back to the park, the P-FLAG banner brought the curbside spectators to their feet, applauding and cheering.

"P-FLAG! Yeeeaaaa! Thank you! We love you!"

Sue was overwhelmed. She waved exuberantly to the crowd, tears welling in her eyes and a huge smile spread across her face. "It's wonderful!" she exclaimed. As she walked, a headset-rigged reporter from a local radio station appeared and thrust a portable telephone into her face for a live interview. Instantly, she was activated.

"We're glad to be supportive of our gay and lesbian children, because we love them," she said to the reporter. "The only thing that saddens me is that so many people don't have the support of their families."

A few steps ahead, Amy and her sister grabbed the ends of a banner and marched in step together along the boulevard. Amy grinned, knowing that she had earned her moment in the sun. She had come to last year's Pride celebration, but this was her first parade, her first public march, her first outward declaration of her lesbianism.

"It's *cool*," she said, soaking it in, struck speechless by her emotions. Suddenly handing the banner over to a friend, she dropped back to where her mother was marching, gave her a quick hug, and then took her place again alongside her companions.

"'Bye, Mommy!" she shouted over her shoulder as she ran ahead.

31

CODA:

A Son's Liberation

Julian Ulseth is a survivor. The son of Judith Ulseth, a na-
tional officer of P-FLAG, Parents, Families and Friends of Les-
bians and Gays, Julian had an insufferable adolescence that led
him to the brink of suicide—twice. Painfully isolated and be-
sieged daily with threats and slurs at his Minnesota high school,
he dropped out and moved to Northern California, where he en-
rolled in an alternative school run by Quakers. Julian now lives
and works in San Francisco, where being gay is as ordinary as an
ocean breeze. He describes his teenage years with a quiet anger
and regret:

When I was twelve, I made the decision that, when I turned
eighteen, I was gonna run away to San Francisco and never speak to
my family again. This was, of course, before I came out to them, right
in the beginnings of when I was realizing my sexuality. To me, I didn't
even know what San Francisco was. I just knew that I needed to be
here. It was away from all of the things that were dragging me down
that I couldn't deal with. . . . I couldn't control what I was doing anymore. I thought it was best to leave.

School in Minnesota was horrible. I couldn't learn there. I used to
suffer a lot of abuse. In junior high and high school, people used to
pee on me in the shower. All kinds of things. People were slamming
me into lockers in between classes. Constantly I would be standing at
a urinal and somebody would come up and kick me in the small of my
back, you know, kick me into the urinal. . . . I got chased with a base-

ball bat once down the hallway and had to hide in a stall in the bathroom. And all the teachers and counselors could tell me was that it was *my* problem. Some of the teachers, all the way from first grade and up, realized what I was and were uncomfortable with it, and treated me differently or were very irritated with me all the time. . . . There was no way that I was gonna go through that. I couldn't learn anything. I was so distracted all the time.

I used to get punched a lot in the locker room. So I always had this dread of locker rooms, like I couldn't go into them. I'd get panic attacks. And now I swim at the YMCA here. And it's so funny because it's all gay men. . . . Before, I'd always stare at the wall, going above everybody's head, to make sure that you never gave anybody a weird look or looked at them in a way you weren't supposed to. . . .

I was a pretty big mess when I left Minnesota. That was right after my suicide attempt, right in that time frame. I didn't know who I was, who I was supposed to be, how I was supposed to behave. I had no self-esteem at all. I was just looking every day to get through the next hour. I mean, that's how I lived my life. I couldn't ever look past a few days and into the future; I couldn't bear to. I was crazy. I don't remember very much from that time. No therapy. No help. At the time, I didn't realize how bad I was. But now, looking back, I realize how messed up I really was. . . . And that comes from way deep, things that my parents did and abuse that they inflicted on me without knowing. . . .

My parents had problems with my homosexuality. I had two years of both of them dealing with it. They were pretty racked about it and they weren't ready to be out. But I was ready to be out and I needed to be. I couldn't hide anymore. It was just making me feel too ashamed. . . . They asked me to be myself but then asked me what was wrong with me. . . . I wanted to play with Barbie dolls. To me, that was innocent. What's wrong with that? To them, it meant this big thing. I had asked for a doll every Christmas and birthday that I can remember, and no one would ever give me one. I didn't know what I was supposed to be. The only gay role models I had or knew were really effeminate queens. And I didn't know how to be myself. I didn't know what that was.

When I moved out here, for the first time in my life I started to make friends. I never had friends before. I didn't know what friends were. . . . I didn't know freedom before. I guess that's what it is. Freedom is here. And because I've had the taste of it, I couldn't go back. I have real problems with depression and I always have. And that extra oppression would just sink me. I don't think I could keep my head above water there.

So I had no perceptions of what it was going to be like here. I just knew that there were a lot of gay people. But I had no idea that you would see them walking down the street holding hands or just being so open about it. And also, I met plenty of gay people just going to parties and stuff. I never needed to go to gay bars. That was wonderful, and I was just so happy to be here.

A couple weeks ago I was walking down the street here and two straight guys said something to a gay couple that was walking in front of me. I wasn't walking in their group, but I was walking along with them. And the two other guys were pretty effeminate and it was pretty obvious they were gay. And the two straight guys said, "Little girls' night out, boys?" And all of us stopped and turned around and just stood there and looked at them. And they totally cowed down and acted like they hadn't said it. And to me that's like, you know, none of us knew each other, and it was just that little act of defiance right there. Instead of going home and feeling bad about being put down or about being afraid, we could go home feeling empowered because these guys really don't realize where they were at, what city they're in. . . .

Here, there are gay men dancing together, they are kissing, they are making out, they are rubbing their bodies together. There are half-naked boys on risers all the way around the dance floor that are paid by the club to dance. Drag queens can walk down the street. . . . Everywhere I go, there's more than one of us.

I just had a relationship for about three months. And it was interesting because there wasn't a neighborhood that I felt uncomfortable holding his hand in. In Minnesota, there would be maybe one neighborhood that you would feel comfortable holding it, you know. When we ride around on his motorcycle, he has a big prominent pink triangle on the windscreen of the motorcycle and I'd sit on the back of the bike with my arms fully around him. . . . So, to me it's like, Why should I live in Minnesota and be afraid and be a minority when I can live here and not be afraid and be of political power?

I have just as many straight friends as gay friends. It seems more right; it seems like a better balance. Being gay makes you like this odd fourth sex or third sex or however you want to put it. And it just makes life more interesting to have all of this mixed together. . . . I think a lot of gay men in my generation feel the same way that I do, that we don't need to hide in that cluster anymore. . . .

I guess when I moved here—my whole life—I never expected to live past twenty-one, because I didn't want to. I didn't think I could make it. I didn't think I could hold it together for long enough. . . . I was a pretty heavy duty cocaine addict for a couple years. My lover was a heroin addict and a speed freak. I was into those things too. So I got pretty messy for a while. . . .

In the last year I've pretty much stopped drinking and everything. I mean, I'll have a beer occasionally, but I just don't get drunk anymore like I used to. And that seemed to make a difference. I didn't realize how much it worsened my depression to drink all the time. . . .

I've been suicidal nonstop my whole life. I think about it even now, although now it's different because before it was always, *When* am I going to do it? And now it's, I know that I'm *not* going to do it.

So, somehow, I did turn twenty-one, and for the first time in my life I'm looking forward to having a future. I can look at a year from now and kind of make a goal and say, Where do I want to be a year from now? Whereas, before, it was always trying to make the decision, Do I want to *be* here a year from now?

32

INTERLUDE:

Voices of Change

At a conference in Des Moines on gay youth, writer and Quaker activist Katherine Whitlock talked about the ruinous effect of homophobia.

"Homophobia kills," Whitlock said. "If it doesn't kill people right off, it kills the spirit, it kills compassion, it kills hope. . . .

"But hope lies with the youth. We need what they have to offer . . . vision, courage, invincibility, for themselves and for others. They will take steps farther than we could have dreamed possible. They have a sense of human possibility that is greater than our own. The younger generation, their dreams will be wilder and crazier and more wonderful and whole. They can dream bigger than our own dreams can take us. And their dreams will save us."

Already, as they pass into adulthood, young lesbians and gays are laying the groundwork for the next generation of gay youth. They want to be there when the next wave of fifteen- and sixteen-year-olds calls out for support. In projects around the country, they have become leaders in a movement, drawing on their own lessons of youth to pave the way for their replacements.

Listen to their dreams and passions:

CHERYL SCHWARTZ   Outed in high school and alienated in college, Cheryl Schwartz was listening to a panel of gay and lesbian youth one day at a P-FLAG meeting in Denver. "Their stories were not far off from what I'd gone through, and I decided that I wanted to give back and get involved." At age twenty-one, she began leading

Sunday support groups, and at twenty-two, she became the first coordinator of youth services at the Gay and Lesbian Community Center of Colorado.

Seven years later, in 1994, she was appointed acting executive director of the center, with an office on Capitol Hill in Denver.

"Gay youth today really lack positive role models, something that I think is really necessary," Schwartz says. "The broader issue, too, is a feeling out there that there's a lack of empowerment with our youth in general, across the board. All youth are not incredibly empowered in our society. But gay youth are so disenfranchised and so disempowered that they grow into unhealthy adults. And that has a real effect on our community."

It is vitally important to let teenagers themselves lead the way to change, she says. Youth must not be relegated to serve simply as token figureheads or media-hyped poster children in the gay-rights movement. Rather, if promoted into roles of leadership, they will grow into productive assets to the gay and lesbian community, and to society at large.

"We really believe in our youth doing their work," says Schwartz. "They need to be involved. Sometimes it does help to have adults involved with that. There can be a lot learned from working with adults, both for the youth and the adults. But the youth still need to do the work. There's a hope that the empowerment will happen at all levels and the movement will be strong, because it will be produced and carried out by the people that it affects the most. That's a real important piece."

At the center, teens lead support groups, organize workshops, and sit on the board of directors. They're responsible for developing budgets, coordinating fundraising campaigns, and representing the center at national conferences. Gay and lesbian youth have been appointed to the Denver Mayor's Youth Board, and the Colorado Youth Counsel.

"I really do feel like there is a strong movement. It's in its infancy and really needing some structure," Schwartz says. "And I feel like the movement is fairly local at this point and starting to reach the national forum. But I really feel like there is a movement, partially because youth are very out and wanting more for their lives."

And for teens themselves, activism can help heal the wounds of adolescence. "One reason I believe so strongly in youth speaking out for themselves is that doing workshops and speaking and getting involved in the youth movement were some of the most healing experiences of my life," she says. "And I was given a chance in my early twenties to be a leader, and to give back."

JAIME BARBER Jaime Barber, of Seattle, is a civil-rights activist in training. Beginning in June of 1994, at age seventeen, she put in six months as the executive leadership intern for the National Gay and Lesbian Task Force in Washington, D.C., chosen by the task force as "the youth voice" to field phone calls from around the country and to lobby on legislation that would impact young gays, lesbians, and bisexuals. After working with the NGLTF, she signed on as an intern with the Sexual Minority Youth Assistance League, also in Washington, D.C., and then with the Bridges Project in Philadelphia.

When it comes to knowing the concerns of lesbian and gay youth, Barber brings a firsthand sensibility to her work. She was just thirteen when she came out, in her first year of high school. "The reaction was mostly negative," she says. "I got kicked out of my house. I was pretty much the focus of a lot of verbal abuse and a lot of physical taunting and assault. My teachers really didn't stick up for me. They just kind of let things happen and get out of control, and finally ended up sending me to the principal's office because I was a disruption to the class. It was really hard. School was hard. I was the only really out lesbian. There weren't any out gay men that I knew of."

Barber dropped out of school and ran away when she was fourteen. "I was on the street for a year and a half, so I saw a lot. I saw kids get strung out on heroin and ODing in back alleys, and then being thrown into Dumpsters by their friends because they couldn't turn them in or put them in the hospital, because they'd get arrested or shipped back home."

She has no compunction about coming out very young. To the contrary, she believes it was advantageous. "It gave me a lot more time to get comfortable with it, because everything is still so new when you're that young. It tends to be a little easier to adjust to and accept at that young an age. . . . That's a very hard knock upside the head, and I think it was easier for me to deal with it when I was young then if it happened say even now. It would've been hard now."

She acknowledges that for some teens, coming out early in adolescence may be too much of a risk. "Sometimes it's just not safe to come out until you are independent and out of school and out of the house. It just depends on the situation and where the person's at with the acceptance of their sexuality."

After coming out, Barber volunteered her story to students at local junior high schools, high schools, and colleges, through a youth speakers' bureau run by the American Friends Service Committee in Seattle. "And the message really seemed to be getting out there: that this is not tolerable, that you can't call somebody a 'faggot' and expect to get away with it, that we are people too.

"Things are getting better," she decides. "Youth are still not utilized as a very strong group of people by the community, which is so frustrating. We still have no rights and actually don't mean anything until we turn eighteen. But it's getting a little better."

TROIX BETTENCOURT As with a lot of gay and lesbian youth, it was a personal crisis that propelled Troix Bettencourt into political activism.

"I came out to myself around my seventeenth birthday," he says. "I had a girlfriend for three years, and I bought her a diamond ring to kind of justify to myself that I was straight. I was doing everything I was supposed to be doing. But weeks after that, my best friend broke down and told me he was in love with me. And I finally realized I was feeling the same way toward him. But I felt like I was doing something wrong. So I turned to a parish priest, begging him to make me straight, to change me. And he found the Boston Alliance for Gay and Lesbian Youth for me to go to. I became real active there. Eventually, I became the president."

While working for BAGLY, Bettencourt's face appeared in a photograph on the cover of the *Boston Globe*. He had not been out to his parents until that day. "Everybody at my mother's work saw the picture and of course pointed it out to her," he says. "She was pretty hysterical at first. But she didn't know what to say to me. And then all of sudden everything just blew up. She just lost it one day, called the police, and had me kicked out of the house. She knew nothing about what it's like to be gay. She just knew what she was taught to believe. And of course her first reaction was, What did I do wrong raising my son? She turned to a religious group, a fundamentalist Christian group, that told her they could pray and make me straight."

A high school dropout during his junior year, Bettencourt, meanwhile, spent some time living on the streets until a friend of a friend let him live in a spare room in Boston. He eventually received his GED certificate and enrolled in Northeastern University.

In 1993, at age eighteen, Bettencourt was instrumental in the campaign to pass the country's first civil rights legislation for gay and lesbian youth in Massachusetts. Signed into law in December 1993, the legislation extended anti-discrimination protections to gay youth in schools throughout the state. That same year, Bettencourt was appointed to the Massachusetts Governor's Commission for Gay and Lesbian Youth, and spoke at the March on Washington.

Political change should be only one focus of the gay youth movement. "Laws are good if they're enforced," he says. "But many young people don't know their rights to begin with. So I don't know how helpful they can be. When you're in high school and all this is happening, you really don't know what there is out there to fall back on. It's sad, because the people who are supposed to be there to tell you are usually the ones who are making you feel uncomfortable in the first place, like a homophobic counselor or teacher."

Veterans of the 1969 Stonewall riot, the christening of the gay-rights movement, were street kids and hustlers and drag queens, he says, many of whom were living on their own because they had been kicked out of their homes. "If you talk to any of them, they'll tell you that we've come a long way, yet fundamentally we've gone absolutely nowhere. Gay teens are still killing themselves and the reasons why haven't changed. There may be more places to go, but at a point in time when you realize that you're gay and actually seeking out support, nothing's changed."

Institutional changes need to be made, beginning with the schools. "There needs to be some real public education," he says. "It needs to be included in the schools. This is definitely the time when education and visibility need to happen." History classes should teach about gay and lesbian culture. English classes should identify and teach gay and lesbian authors. And sex-education classes should include more lessons on homosexuality.

"It really needs to be known that this is reality for some people."

CHRIS GONZALEZ AND JEFF WERNER   In 1987, Chris Gonzalez was twenty-three and manning the switchboard of a gay and lesbian center in Indianapolis. He noticed that the majority of the calls he got were from youth. At the time, there were few resources for gay and lesbian teens in the area. So the best he could do for them was listen to their stories. With his partner, Gonzalez began holding support groups at his home, drawing five to ten teens at a time.

Thus was born the Indianapolis Youth Group, or IYG, as it is better known. Three years later, Gonzalez started up a toll-free national hotline, staffed by volunteers age twenty-one and under, who took calls from gay and lesbian youth from across the country.

Gonzalez died of AIDS in 1994. But his partner, Jeff Werner, carries on the vision.

In the years since its inception, IYG has grown into a model center nationally, offering safe haven and services for Indiana's gay youth. The hotline now averages close to two thousand calls per month.

"Probably the greatest number of calls are about loneliness," Werner says. "Kids just want to talk to someone. Coming out is probably number two. Number three is issues with families or friends— harassment or being kicked out of the home, fights with parents. Those are probably the big issues."

If there is a national gay youth movement, Werner believes it is best illustrated through the countless stories of individual empowerment. "We go along with the holistic premise that if we make young people feel good about themselves, then everything else is pretty much going to fall into place," he says. "If we uplift them, tell them that they're not bad people, that they have a lot of good things going for them, then that's going to affect a lot of things in their lives. . . . That's where the movement occurs. We're not promoting a movement per se. We're promoting young gay people. And by giving them the tools to feel good about themselves and make good decisions, then they're going to empower themselves to become a movement."

It doesn't take much of an effort to reach out to gay and lesbian youth in need, Werner says. Sometimes just a place to "hang" is enough. "You don't have to start out with a building and a hundred kids running around. It only starts with a couple of people who are committed and one young person. You may just have potato chips and soda at your meeting. And that's really all some young people need. Just a place they can get together and meet other gay folks. And from there all kinds of great things will happen."

Werner came out in 1985 at age twenty, admittedly late in his life by today's standards. "Young people have more of an opportunity to understand homosexuality than I did," he says. "I don't remember seeing anything on TV or reading about anyone who was gay way back in the eighties. . . . It's easier to come out now than it was five years ago, ten years ago. And five years from now, I suspect it will be even easier. It's becoming less stigmatized as more people come out."

There is power in numbers, and as the number of out gay and lesbian teens surges, they're more actively demanding their civil rights. "They're not willing to wait for an okay to be who they are. They just expect people to deal with them."

JENIE HALL Jenie Hall remembers hanging around a leather bar on the streets of Seattle when she first came out, curious about the people inside, but bothered by the fact that there wasn't a place for young lesbians her age to go.

"There'd be a pack of half a dozen to ten young women just standing outside talking," she recalls. "I only went once, and I was not pleased with the situation. I was like, This is disgusting. There's got to be somewhere else where we can go and hang out and just be ourselves, besides standing outside of some bar. It was very clear that this was not acceptable to me and I wanted to see some changes made. It started me thinking . . ."

Hall was sixteen at the time. Six years later, she was hired as director of the Bridges Project, a national resource and referral service for supporters of gay and lesbian youth, sponsored by the American Friends Service Committee at its headquarters in Philadelphia. Created in 1992, the project was born out of the 1989 book *Bridges of Respect: Creating Support for Lesbian and Gay Youth,* published by the AFSC. An overwhelmingly positive response to the book signaled to the Quaker-based committee that people were yearning for information.

Hall has had a hand in the formation of the gay and lesbian youth movement from the start. After a burst of activism during high school, she helped rally support for the creation of the country's first teen center, Seattle's Lambert House, which opened in 1991. Yet, like others her age, she has no pie-in-the-sky illusions about the struggle for the rights of gay youth.

"There's less idealism and more reality checks among lesbian, gay, bisexual, and transgender youth," she observes. "It's not, 'We're going to change the world and save all of humankind.' It's more, 'I want to be included and respected for who I am right *now*. And you may not like that all the time, but I still deserve that.' There's less idealism. And I think that's a positive thing. People have visions, but they aren't necessarily trying to create Oz with that vision."

Yet Hall is buoyed by some of the strides that are being made. "I see a lot of tremendous work happening," says Hall. With and without alliances with adults, teens across the country are leading the push for change in the education system, in religious institutions, in government. The aims are high but not unrealistic, she says. For example, they want protections in schools against the harassment that virtually every open gay and lesbian student faces. They want a greater emphasis on education about HIV prevention for their age group. They want churches that will accept their sexual orientation.

But progress will depend on two tactics: The movement must remain grassroots—organizing in the schools and the communities—and must be led by and for the youth. "If we can make strong commitments to both of those things, the grassroots focus and the youth leadership component, we can make the lesbian and gay youth movement a very lasting and effective movement overall," she says. "But then if we don't, we're going to get bogged down the same way that the national adult gay and lesbian movements have."

Like other young gays and lesbians, Hall voices an impatience with the level of commitment that gay and lesbian adults have made to issues concerning youth.

"I think there definitely are some adults who are stepping up to the plate and saying, 'Yeah, we support you.' They're not necessarily what I would call mainstream lesbians and gays, if there is such a thing. It's the people who are working with youth one-on-one or with the services—who are acting as role models and really coming through. Otherwise, the overall adult community is getting better but is still struggling immensely with these fears of being called pedophiles, and not even wanting to associate with young people or wanting to come in as a savior complex—not seeing young people as whole human beings but as people they need to save or support or be a role model or mentor to. The best role models or mentors that I've ever run into were the ones that treated me with the respect that I deserved as a whole human being rather than as someone that they were going to help. I sometimes wonder if maybe I'm expecting too much from adults, from adults in general, to be asked to be treated with respect, as an equal. But I don't think so."

Gay youth want to be seen as a viable part of the gay-rights movement, not just as the movement's "water boys," says Hall. They want to be included in the decision making and the strategy planning of the movement.

"We need to give youth more credit. We're not talking about the *future* leaders, we're talking about the *present* leaders. If they're not going to be included in the national movement, then maybe they'll just start their own."

MARY TINUCCI   Mary Tinucci wants to normalize the lives of gay and lesbian teenagers, to make their high school experiences as ordinary as possible.

Trained and educated as a school social worker, Tinucci began co-leading a support group for gay students at Central High School in St. Paul. In 1994, at age twenty-eight, she was appointed by the St. Paul school system as the staff leader of Out For Equity, a district-wide support program for the city's gay and lesbian high school students. Endorsed by the St. Paul board of education, the program was directed to create support groups at each of the city's high schools, the first such initiative in the nation.

"In terms of our gay culture and in terms of political activism, I think we're in a new place," she says. Services will always be needed to "pick up the pieces" of troubled adolescents. But beyond providing rehabilitation, Tinucci feels an obligation to find a place for gay teens within the mainstream.

"I hope that someday kids can go to school and hear the words *gay, lesbian, bisexual, transgender* on a daily basis without the negative value judgments attached to them," she says. "Gay kids don't get to talk about their joys in junior and senior high school—falling in love, having a date, meeting a kid. They don't have that freedom to talk about the joys in their lives. That's what I want for kids, for kids to have an average adolescence, with all its ups and downs. . . . That's a long way off. But I think we can sure speed that up a little bit."

Tinucci came out to herself in 1985, when she was nineteen. She was a sophomore in college. She knew of few resources at the time for young lesbians and received virtually no support. Four years later, in a tumultuous four months, she came out to her large Italian-Catholic family. The reaction was overwhelmingly negative. From the very beginning, her course of coming out was private and uncelebrated.

"I kind of grew up in my twenties," Tinucci says. "I did things in my twenties that most straight adolescents are doing when they're fifteen to twenty years old. So that made my twenties a whole different experience, not necessarily better or worse, but different. Now, all of a sudden, we've got kids who are coming out at fourteen, fifteen, seventeen years old. So they're taking care of some of that business, like dating. They're having their first date when they're sixteen instead of when they're twenty-four. That's a whole evolution of our culture that I'm watching before my very eyes."

RICK AGUIRRE   In a tiny rented room at the offices of the gay newspaper the *San Francisco Bay Times,* with a limited budget but a boundless devotion, Rick Aguirre and his staff of volunteers put out *InsideOUT* magazine, giving readers "the inside scoop on being young and out," as its masthead declares.

Aguirre, the publisher, founded the magazine in 1991. He was nineteen at the time, a political-science college dropout who was looking into peer support groups in the Bay area. "I realized that none of them were communicating with each other," he says. "My interest has always been in communication, networking and stuff. So I thought I'd do something on a local level." He started the Bay Area Sexual Minority Youth Network, or BASMYN.

"*InsideOUT* was supposed to be the newsletter for BASMYN," a four-page resource guide for youth around the San Francisco area. "It just kind of grew," Aguirre says. "We started getting letters from people in Vermont and Florida and Texas and from all over the country. I'm not even sure how they heard about us. So I saw a need for it, that nothing existed like it on a larger scale."

Three years later, *InsideOUT* had a national circulation of more than five thousand readers. "For some people it was the only connection that they had," Aguirre says. "And I realized later that this was a great resource, because it was something that was tangible, that they could touch and feel in their hands, and they didn't have to be out of the closet about it. They could get in touch with other young gay and lesbian people and know that they were not alone."

While *InsideOUT* was the first, there are at least eight other newspapers and magazines published specifically for gay and lesbian youth.

"The issues that are covered in mainstream gay press like the *Bay Times* don't really cover the issues that young people face," he says. "Young people have their own issues that really don't have anything to do with an older gay community. This paper provides a voice from the people who it serves.

"The Internet, in a way, is an even better resource, because they can chat with people online and they don't have to have any sexual identity; they don't have to give out their real name or their home address or whatever," he adds. "Nobody really needs to know about it. I don't want people to stay in the closet; I encourage them to come out. But they have to do it at their own pace. This kind of helps them take those baby steps."

Aguirre's coming-out process was forced. At age sixteen, he was thrown out of the house when his father found a letter from a gay pen pal that he had received through Alyson Publications' Letter-Exchange Program. His parents were divorced, and he had been visiting his mother. "When I came home that weekend, all my things were in plastic bags. And my dad said I couldn't live there. I started laughing. I thought he was crazy for invading my privacy." He moved in with his mother, and soon came out to her. "She asked me whether I was gay. And I said I don't know, and she said, 'Well, why not?' And I thought about it for a minute, and I said, 'Yes, I'm gay.' And she said 'Well I'm behind you 110 percent.' "

In the few years that he has been out, the number of open gay role models has vastly multiplied. "When I was growing up, the images that I saw, even here in San Francisco, was basically just around the [Gay Pride] parade times, with the drag queens. I have nothing against drag queens—I think they're super-fabulous. I just didn't identify with that. If that meant being gay, I thought, then I must be something else. So people today are seeing a lot more images.

"I think the youth movement is happening on an individual basis," Aguirre says. "I think the greatest progress is being made by those people who are coming out. There was a guy in Dallas, he was sixteen at the time. He wore an I'M NOT GAY BUT MY BOYFRIEND IS T-shirt to school and was suspended for it. Those people who are out and visible are helping other people come out. . . . There is some organization, but the organized part is a very small part of the actual movement. People are coming out younger. But in a way, it's more frustrating. They have this information, but they still don't have access to resources. There's a lot out there, but they don't necessarily know how to get in touch with those resources. It's like, Okay, I know I'm gay. What's next? Where can I go find other young gay people like myself? A lot of people are still reluctant to come out in schools. We've got a readership of over five thousand and most of our mailing list is from rural towns, more than 50 percent."

On a wall in the small office of *InsideOUT* hangs a large map of the United States. Colored stick pins mark the hometowns of each reader.

"I kind of have this dream," says Aguirre. "There's a couple of places in the middle of the United States where I can put my hand completely flat on the map without touching any pins. I want to get to a point where I can't put my hand *anywhere* on this map without it touching a pin. . . .

"It's just a matter of time before enough people are out of the closet, where people are out enough to get in touch with each other and these little pins can sort of like talk to each other. And from there they can build their own communities."

Epilogue:

History in the Making

In the perfect world, there wouldn't be a closet and gay youth wouldn't have to come out at all. They wouldn't have to hide, disguise their identities, shield their thoughts and feelings from their friends and families.

In a perfect world, gay youth would be appreciated for who they are, without threats and insults and discrimination, in all corners of society—from Sunday school and the Boy Scouts to high school sports and senior proms.

That hasn't happened yet. Recognition of gay youth is conditional. And admittance into the mainstream customs of adolescence remains restricted. So until a day when they're accepted completely, young lesbians and gays continue to make their own circles of support, their own safe havens, their own cultural niche.

For all teenagers, the high school prom is a rite of passage, a symbolic point of departure in their rush toward adulthood. But for gays and lesbians, it's also another unkind reminder of their unwelcomed "difference." Too many gay teens tell stories of prom masquerades, of pairing up with straight dates just to be included in the celebration with their peers.

But in more and more cities across the country, lesbian and gay teens are holding proms of their own. Through gay community centers and teen clubs, they're organizing evenings of ritual and ceremony for students, current and past, who have been shut out of the tradition.

"It's like a proclamation, a chance to express yourself, to be free with your partner. It's a reclaiming of your adolescence," says Terrence Richardson. At eighteen, Terrence helped organize a prom for gay and lesbian teens through the Minneapolis teen center, District 202. With $1,200 in donations and some out-of-pocket cash, Terrence and Hope Artichoker, another young volunteer at District 202, spent three months planning the night. Admission would be free. Only guests twenty-one or under could attend. No alcohol would be served. Dress would be semi-formal. The theme? "Love Like Never Before, '94."

"It's a real big deal," Terrence says. "It's history in the making, something that's been a long time coming. It's like a revolution."

No doubt, a gay prom is a statement, a message to heterosexual society that lesbian and gay teens should be regarded as any other teens. But it's also a good time, with no cares about who might be watching.

"This way, it's a lot safer, it's a lot more fun," says Hope, nineteen. "You don't have to worry about anyone saying anything, and you can be with the one you want to be with. This way, it's like *your* prom. . . . I've never been to a prom."

Three large rainbow flags hang over the doorway to a downtown hotel in Minneapolis, a signal to prom guests that this is the place. More than a hundred free tickets have been handed out. Hors d'oeuvres have been ordered. A disc jockey has been hired. Chaperones have been invited. Hotel security guards have been notified.

It's mid-afternoon, six hours before the start of the dance. Organizers are busily arranging candles and flowers on round tabletops, hanging green-and-black streamers along the ceiling—and worrying about their formal wear.

"Everybody's like, Oh my God, what am I going to wear? It's great," laughs Carol Rogoski, eighteen. She describes her own ensemble: A green velvet top, a short green satin skirt, black heels, nylons, and a choker with a dangling string of pearls. "My grandmother bought the dress," she says. "I told her I was going to a prom," omitting the small detail that it would be a *gay* prom.

Her date will wear a black tuxedo with a green bow tie and cummerbund, to match Carol's dress. "Just being able to do this is, like, unity!" Carol says. "If you compare this to other formals, the same anticipation is there, the same giddiness and excitement."

On one end of the room, a reporter from a local television station tapes an interview with a prom organizer. On the other end, a photographer sets up a strobe and a backdrop for taking portraits. The balloon man arrives and begins assembling an arch of green, black, and white balloons in the doorway.

Standing on the parquet dance floor, Hope and Terrence rehearse the brief ceremony for the crowning of the prom court. There will be two sets of royalty, two kings and two queens.

Later that night, four young women board an elevator to the top of the hotel. Each is decked out in a strapless satin gown, one scarlet, one aquamarine, one sapphire, one black. Two elderly couples share the ride up. "So what school is your prom from?" asks one of the older women, admiring the girls. No one has an answer. Finally, after a long five seconds, one of the girls tries to explain: "It's not a school. It's a special program."

The fourteenth floor is swarming with teenagers—young women in long formal gowns or short skirts, young men in tuxedos or three-piece suits. Women in tuxedos too. One woman is dressed in an oversized blue pin-striped suit, a goatee penciled on her chin. A man is in drag, wearing a black evening dress.

The lights are dim and the music thunders. Colored spotlights pulse as the deejay punches in rap, industrial rock, rhythm and blues. Three sides of the ballroom are glass windows, from ceiling to floor, presenting a glimmering view of the skyline of Minneapolis.

"This is wonderful," says Renee McGaughy, a senior in high school and Carol Rogoski's date. "My school doesn't have proms, but if they did I'd take another woman. I think I'd probably get harassed, but I'd do it anyway. We *should* be able to have a night just like heterosexual people do. I think it's more than just fun. It's showing that there are

gay and lesbian youth out here who love each other and want to celebrate that."

Like any high school dance, young women go to the ladies' room in
packs, whispering urgent gossip to each other behind closed doors,
while young men eye their partners with lustful curiosity on the
dance floor.

At the portrait stand, the photographer adjusts a young man's bow
tie. Two young men in dark tuxes and white gloves, holding white
canes in hand, stand back to back and smile as she captures their
smiles. Two young women pose next, one with freshly dyed blue hair,
the other hiking up her dress to show off a flower tattoo on her leg.
Meanwhile, an AIDS outreach worker circulates, dispensing free condoms and dental dams from an open briefcase that he carries in his
arms.

Mark Lang is a high school junior in St. Paul. "I was going to bring a
guy to my school prom. But . . . two reasons—I couldn't find a date,
and people strongly advised me not to. So I went with a girl."

And then three weeks before the gay prom, he met Matt Kaufman
at the teen center, District 202. Matt, who lives in a small Wisconsin
town an hour from the Twin Cities, agreed to be Mark's date. Both are
sixteen. They each spent $200 on the prom, renting matching white
tuxedos with tails, lavender ties, and cummerbunds.

Mark waited three years before telling his parents he was gay. "For
three long years, I was trying to hide it. I was raised in a very conservative Lutheran church."

Tonight, though, there's no need to hide. And he's ecstatic. "I feel
so happy," Mark says. "Truthfully, this feels like the happiest moment
of my life. I've never had a very happy life and this is kind of overwhelming to me. It's more than I expected. It's high society!"

Mark pulls a pocket camera from his jacket and snaps a picture of
Matt.

"Gay kids today, they don't have a chance to associate with each
other at school," Matt says. "Everybody is so discriminating and judgmental. It's really nice to have a place to go."

He asks Mark if he would like to dance.

Just before midnight, the music suddenly pauses. Terrence has an announcement to make: "Can I have your attention. We're now going to crown the king and the queen, um . . . the king and the king, and the queen and the queen of the first Twin Cities Gay, Lesbian, Bi, and Transgender Prom!"

The guests crowd around the dance floor. Ticket stubs bearing their names have been collected and tossed into Terrence's baseball cap. Hope nervously draws four tickets and reads four names. And, amid squeals and applause, two young lesbians and two young gay men are fitted with paper crowns and scepters.

"This," shouts Terrence, proud to make the introduction, "is your court for 1994! Now, let's finish partying!"

The deejay cranks up the music and the crowd spills onto the dance floor. Someone with a video camera records the moment—for posterity.

Notes

CHAPTER 4—SIDEBAR: The Rude Awakening

1. Nancy Beran, Connie Claybaker, Cory Dillon, and Robert Haverkamp, "Attitudes Toward Minorities: A Comparison of Homosexuals and the General Population," *Journal of Homosexuality,* Vol. 23(3): pp. 65–83, 1992.

2. A. Damien Martin, "Learning to Hide: The Socialization of the Gay Adolescent," *Annals of the American Society for Adolescent Psychiatry,* Vol. 10: pp. 52–65, 1982.

3. The Massachusetts Governor's Commission on Gay and Lesbian Youth, "Making Schools Safe for Gay and Lesbian Youth: Breaking the Silence in Schools and in Families," Education Report, February 25, 1993.

CHAPTER 6—SIDEBAR: The Roots of Homosexuality

1. John Billy, Koray Tanfer, William Grady, and Daniel Klepinger, "The Sexual Behavior of Men in the United States," *Family Planning Perspectives,* Vol. 25: pp. 52–60, March/April 1993.

2. Randall Sell, James Wells, and David Wypig, "The Prevalence of Homosexual Behavior and Attraction in the United States, the United Kingdom and France: Results of National Population-Based Samples" (accepted for publication by *Archives of Sexual Behavior,* 1994).

3. Simon LeVay, *The Sexual Brain* (Cambridge, Mass.: MIT Press, 1993).

4. Randall Sell, James Wells, and David Wypig, op. cit.

5. Dean Hamer, Stella Hu, Victoria Magnuson, Nan Hu, and Angela Pattatucci, "A Link Between DNA Markers on the X Chromosome and Male Sexual Orientation," *Science,* July 16, 1993, Vol. 261: pp. 291–292.

6. Laura Allen and Roger Gorski, "Sexual Orientation and the Size of the Anterior Commissure in the Human Brain," *Proceedings of the National Academy of Sciences,* August 1, 1992, Vol. 89(15): pp. 7199–7202.

7. J. Michael Bailey and Richard Pillard, "A Genetic Study of Male Sexual Orientation," *Archives of General Psychiatry,* December 1991, Vol. 48: pp. 1089–1096.

8. Simon LeVay, "A Difference in Hypothalamic Structure Between Heterosexual and Homosexual Men," *Science,* August 30, 1991, Vol. 253: pp. 1034–1037.

9. Richard Pillard and James Weinrich, "Evidence of Familial Nature of Male Homosexuality," *Archives of General Psychiatry,* August 1986, Vol. 43: pp. 808–812.

10. Richard Green, *The "Sissy Boy Syndrome" and the Development of Homosexuality* (New Haven: Yale University Press, 1987).

CHAPTER 13—SIDEBAR: Coming Out

1. Vivienne Cass, "Homosexual Identity Formation: A Theoretical Model," *Journal of Homosexuality,* Spring 1979, Vol. 4(3): pp. 219–235; Eli Coleman, "Developmental Stages of the Coming Out Process," *Journal of Homosexuality,* Vol. 7: pp. 31–43, 1982; Richard Troiden, "Homosexual Identity Development," *Journal of Adolescent Health Care,* Vol. 9: pp. 105–113, 1988.

2. Gilbert Herdt and Andrew Boxer, *Children of the Horizons: How Gay and Lesbian Teens Are Leading a New Way Out of the Closet* (Boston: Beacon Press, 1993).

CHAPTER 15—SIDEBAR: Identity

1. Gregory Herek and Kevin Berrill, *Hate Crimes, Confronting Violence Against Lesbians and Gay Men* (Newbury Park, Cal.: Sage Publications, 1992).

CHAPTER 19—SIDEBAR: Lives At Risk

1. "Hostile Hallways: The American Association of University Women Survey on Sexual Harassment in American Schools," AAUW Educational Foundation, June 1993.

2. Gregory Herek and Kevin Berrill, *Hate Crimes, Confronting Violence*

Against Lesbians and Gay Men (Newbury Park, Cal.: Sage Publications, 1992).

3. Seattle Commission for Lesbians and Gays, the Seattle Office for Women's Rights, and the Lesbian Resource Center, "A Survey of the Seattle Area Lesbian and Gay Community: Identity and Issues," March 1991.

4. National Gay and Lesbian Task Force Policy Institute, "Anti-Gay/Lesbian Violence, Victimization and Defamation in 1993."

5. Paul Gibson, "Report of the Secretary's Task Force on Youth Suicide," edited by Marcia Feinleib, Vol. 3: *Prevention and Interventions in Youth Suicide* (U.S. Department of Health and Human Services; Public Health Services; Alcohol, Drug Abuse, and Mental Health Administration), 1989.

6. Gary Remafedi, "Adolescent Homosexuality: Psychosocial and Medical Implications," *Pediatrics,* March 1987, Vol. 79: pp. 331–337.

7. Robert Deisher, Victor Eisner, and Stephen Sulzbacher, "The Young Male Prostitute," *Pediatrics,* June 1969, Vol. 43: pp. 936–941.

8. Mary Jane Rotheram-Borus, Margaret Rosario, Heino F. L. Meyer-Bahlburg, Cheryl Koopman, Steven Dopkins, and Mark Davies, "Sexual and Substance Use Acts of Gay and Bisexual Male Adolescents in New York City," *The Journal of Sex Research,* Vol. 31, No. 1 (1994), pp. 47–57.

9. Debra Boyer, "Male Prostitution and Homosexual Identity," *Journal of Homosexuality,* Vol. 17, 1989: pp. 151–184.

10. B. Fisher, D. K. Weisberg, and T. Marotta, "Report on Adolescent Male Prostitution" (San Francisco, Cal.: Urban and Rural Systems Association, 1982).

11. Stephen Schneider, Norman Farberow, and Gabriel Kruks, "Suicidal Behavior in Adolescent and Young Adult Gay Men," *Suicide and Life-Threatening Behavior,* Winter 1989, Vol. 19(4): pp. 381–394.

12. Gary Remafedi, James Farrow, and Robert Deisher, "Risk Factors for Attempted Suicide in Gay and Bisexual Youth," *Pediatrics,* June 1991, Vol. 87(6): pp. 869–875.

13. Paul Gibson, "Report of the Secretary's Task Force on Youth Suicide," edited by Marcia Feinleib, Vol. 3: *Prevention and Interventions in Youth Suicide* (U.S. Department of Health and Human Services; Public Health Services; Alcohol, Drug Abuse, and Mental Health Administration), 1989.

14. David Shaffer, "Political Science," *The New Yorker,* May 3, 1993, p. 116.

15. Select Committee on Children, Youth, and Families, U.S. House of Representatives, "A Decade of Denial: Teens and AIDS in America," December 22, 1992.

16. Gary Remafedi, "Predictors of Unprotected Intercourse Among Gay and Bisexual Youth: Knowledge, Beliefs, and Behavior" (submitted for publication), 1994.

17. Mary Jane Rotheram-Borus, Margaret Rosario, Heino F. L. Meyer-Bahlburg, Cheryl Koopman, Steven Dopkins, and Mark Davies, "Sexual and Substance Use Acts of Gay and Bisexual Male Adolescents in New York City," *The Journal of Sex Research,* Vol. 31, No. 1 (1994), pp. 45–57.

Names and Affiliations of Experts Interviewed

Rick Aguirre—founder, Bay Area Sexual Minority Youth Network; publisher, *InsideOUT* magazine, San Francisco

Tom Ammiano—gay member of San Francisco Board of Supervisors

Michael Bailey—psychologist, Northwestern University, Chicago

Jaime Barber—executive intern, National Gay and Lesbian Task Force, Washington, D.C.

Troix Bettencourt—founder, Boston Alliance for Gay and Lesbian Youth

Andrew Boxer—psychologist, University of Chicago; co-author, *Children of the Horizons: How Gay and Lesbian Teens Are Leading a New Way Out of the Closet*

Rea Carey—coordinator, National Advocacy Coalition on Youth and Sexual Orientation, Washington, D.C.

Eli Coleman—psychologist; director, Program in Human Sexuality, University of Minnesota

Dr. Robert Dreisher—pediatrician; professor emeritus, University of Washington medical school

Kevin Gogin—director, Office of Support Services for Gay and Lesbian Youth, San Francisco Public Schools

John Gonsiorek—past chair of American Psychological Association's Gay and Lesbian Division

Jenie Hall—executive director, The Bridges Project, Philadelphia

Mitzi Henderson—president, P-FLAG: Parents, Families and Friends of Lesbians and Gays

Gilbert Herdt—cultural anthropologist, University of Chicago; co-author, *Children of the Horizons: How Gay and Lesbian Teens Are Leading a New Way Out of the Closet*

Evelyn Hooker—psychologist, retired, Los Angeles

Jeff Horton—gay member of Los Angeles Board of Education

Joyce Hunter—social worker; founding member of Hetrick-Martin Institute for Gay and Lesbian Youth, New York City

Dr. Richard Isay—professor of psychiatry, Cornell Medical College; former chair of the committee of gay and lesbian issues for American Psychiatric Association; author, *Being Homosexual: Gay Men and Their Development*

Michael Kaplan—coordinator, District 202 Teen Center For Gay and Lesbian Youth, Minneapolis

Chris Kryzan—founder, National Coalition for Gay, Lesbian and Bisexual Youth, San Jose

Frances Kunreuther—executive director, Hetrick-Martin Institute, New York City

David LaFontaine—chair, Massachusetts Governor's Commission on Gay and Lesbian Youth, Boston

Joe Neisen—psychologist; program director, Pride Institute, Minneapolis

Dr. Richard Pillard—psychiatrist, Boston University School of Medicine

Elissa Raffa—co-founder, District 202 Teen Center for Gay and Lesbian Youth, Minneapolis

Victor Raymond—national coordinator, BiNet USA, bisexual advocacy group

June Reinisch—director emerita, Kinsey Institute for Sex Research; author, *The Kinsey Institute New Report on Sex*

Dr. Gary Remafedi—pediatrician; executive director, Youth and AIDS Projects, University of Minnesota, Minneapolis

Mary Jane Rotheram-Borus—social psychologist, University of California at Los Angeles

Tom Sauerman—AIDS Task Force of Philadelphia; past president, P-FLAG

Cheryl Schwartz—director, Gay and Lesbian Community Center of Denver, Colorado

Arlis Stewart—coordinator, Lambert House for Gay and Lesbian Teens, Seattle

Scott Thiemann—founder, Outreach to Rural Youth Project, Portland, Oregon

Mary Tinucci—staff leader, Out For Equity, St. Paul Public Schools

Leo Treadway—co-founder, Wingspan Ministry and Lesbian and Gay Youth Together support group, Minneapolis–St. Paul

Virginia Uribe—teacher, founder, Project 10 Program for Gay and Lesbian Students, Los Angeles Unified School District

James Weinrich—psychobiologist, certified sexologist, University of California at San Diego

Jeff Werner—co-founder, Indiana Youth Group, Indianapolis

Katherine Whitlock—author, *Bridges of Respect: Creating Support For Lesbian and Gay Youth*

Beth Zemsky—psychotherapist, coordinator of the Gay, Lesbian, Bisexual Programs Office, University of Minnesota

Index

About the Author

KURT CHANDLER, an award-winning journalist, has written about some of the most provocative social issues of our time—from gay rights to domestic violence to abortion to the AIDS epidemic. He has worked for a number of newspapers, most recently the *Minneapolis Star Tribune*. He lives with his wife and their two children in Minneapolis. This is his first book.